An introduction to studying popular culture

An Introduction to Studying Popular Culture presents a critical assessment of the major ways in which popular culture has been interpreted, and suggests how it may be more usefully studied.

Dominic Strinati uses the examples of cinema and television to show how we can understand popular culture from sociological and historical perspectives. He traces the development of popular Hollywood cinema, addressing key topics such as production, distribution and exhibition, narrative, and genre, with case studies of gangster and horror films, and *film noir*.

Strinati presents a similar account of popular television, but focuses as much on consumption as production. He thus also looks at how the television audience has been studied and evaluated. Returning to the idea of genre, he uses the example of soap opera to show how genre can be used to study popular television. Finally, he assesses whether or not popular television has become a 'postmodern' medium.

Dominic Strinati is a Lecturer in Sociology at the University of Leicester. He is the author of *An Introduction to Theories of Popular Culture* (Routledge 1995) and co-editor (with Stephen Wagg) of *Come on Down?: Popular media culture in post-war Britain* (Routledge 1992).

LONDON AND NEW YORK

An introduction to studying popular culture

■ Dominic Strinati

First published 2000
by Routledge
11 New Fetter Lane
London EC4P 4EE

Simultaneously published in the USA
and Canada
by Routledge
29 West 35th Street, New York,
NY 10001

*Routledge is an imprint of the Taylor &
Francis Group*

© 2000 Dominic Strinati

Typeset in Sabon by Taylor & Francis
Books Ltd

Printed and bound in Great Britain by
St Edmundsbury Press, Bury
St Edmonds, Suffolk

*British Library Cataloguing in
Publication Data*
A catalogue record for this book is
available from the British Library

*Library of Congress Cataloging in
Publication Data*
Strinati, Dominic
An introduction to studying popular
culture/ Dominic Strinati.
    p.cm.
Includes bibliographical references and
index.
1. Mass media–United States. 2. Mass
media–Great Britain. 3.Popular
culture– United States. 4.Popular
culture–Great Britain. I. Title.
P92.U5 S827 2000
302.23'0973–dc21
                          00-024482

ISBN 0–415–15766–8 (hbk)
ISBN 0–415–15767–6 (pbk)

For Jonathan and Adam

Contents

CONTENTS

Acknowledgements

The completion of this book was helped considerably by the period of study leave the University of Leicester granted me, and I wish to acknowledge here the opportunity this provided. This book has developed out of a course I have taught, for a number of years, in the Sociology department at the University of Leicester. Many students have taken this course, and I wish to acknowledge the contribution they have made to the development of both the course and this book. I also wish to thank my colleagues in the Leicester University Sociology department for the help and support they have given me in the writing of this book. There are a number of other people who have made an important contribution to this book. I would like to thank the staff of Routledge, in particular Ruth Graham and Alistair Daniel, for their invaluable work in producing the book. I would also like to thank Brigid Bell for the very helpful and efficient work she has done as copy-editor. Lastly, I would like to offer a special word of thanks to Rebecca Barden for her patience, advice and encouragement. Fortunately for me, she was willing to commission the book, and to allow me to finish it in my own time, while still making sure it was eventually completed. Of course, I am ultimately responsible for what follows.

Introduction

This is a book about popular culture. Its main aim is to consider the study of popular culture, and to achieve this a number of examples will be assessed. It is designed to provide an introduction to studying popular culture. It does not set out to celebrate or denigrate popular culture, nor to evaluate it directly. It is equally not intended to provide a detailed summary of the theories which have been used to explain popular culture (Strinati 1995). Rather, the tentative aim is to begin to show some of the ways popular culture has been, and can be, studied empirically and historically. Needless to say, theoretical concerns are not, and should not be, divorced from this study; their relevance will be apparent at various points throughout this book.

To pursue these aims, this book will look at the examples of popular cinema and television and show how some of their features have been studied. Before we outline these features, a number of qualifications need to be made clear. First, the assumptions of this book are mainly sociological and historical, and it is hoped they will be backed up by the arguments developed below. Second, it is intended to provide a selective overview, rather than an exhaustive survey, of the topics it covers. Since it is an introduction, this will help to bring out the points which need to be stressed, rather than allowing them to be submerged in too much detail. In the end, of course, there is no substitute for such detail. In being selective rather than exhaustive, it thus tries to provide suggestions which can be pursued, instead of delving more deeply into the areas studied. Third, there are some general points which the book makes, and these are set out in the conclusion. However, while the individual chapters contribute to this conclusion, they are also meant to stand on their own as introductory accounts of the specific examples they discuss. This inevitably results in some repetition of points and arguments, but since, to a degree, each chapter can be read separately from the others, this should not be too much of a problem. Finally, the book provides a basic account of the various features considered in it and thus gives a picture as well as an analysis of popular culture. The intention is to describe as well as explain popular culture.

The general aim of this book, then, is to provide an introduction to the study of popular culture. Obviously this is a potentially enormous task, so some selection is inevitable. Therefore, certain examples have been chosen to make the book more manageable and to give the exposition greater clarity and relevance. The examples selected – popular cinema and television – proved to be popular and powerful commercial mass media during the twentieth century and have played a leading and determinant role in the production and consumption of popular culture. Although specific features may well change, their importance looks set to continue well into the twenty-first century. The twentieth century witnessed a transfer of influence from cinema to television; in the earlier parts of the century, popular cinema established itself as a key visual mass medium and its relative decline resulted from the rise to prominence of popular television during the second half of the century. An introduction to certain aspects of these media should therefore give us some understanding of the growth and significance of popular culture, and of what its study entails. In this book we will examine a number of themes and issues that have emerged as popular cinema and television have been studied. We will attempt to assess how popular culture has been studied and consider what this tells us about how it may continue to be studied. The examples selected are therefore analysed with these aims in mind.

The first two chapters look at Hollywood cinema, its formation, its typical practices and its power. Chapter 1 considers its economic and industrial character, the development of, and changes in, its control over the production, distribution and exhibition of films. Chapter 2 adds to this picture by outlining the importance of narrative, ideology and genres for the Hollywood film, and also its role in popular culture. With this general picture of Hollywood popular cinema established, the next three chapters follow it up by analysing three film genres: the gangster film, the horror film and *film noir*. The particular reasons for selecting these genres are put forward in the respective chapters. However, the overall aims of studying popular culture and stressing the power and importance of Hollywood cinema provide equally compelling reasons for the study of such genres. Another major objective in these chapters is to assess the idea of genre as a way of studying popular culture.

In the next four chapters of the book, attention is turned from popular cinema to popular television, though links and comparisons between the two are not forgotten. Chapter 6 examines some of the factors which have influenced the development of popular television. It looks at the ideas and practices of citizenship and consumerism, outlines their varying influence and stresses the contradictions which have emerged between them. It also focuses upon how consumerism is becoming increasingly predominant in the production and consumption of popular television (Murdock 1990, 1994). Although the audience is crucial for understanding popular culture, the chapters on cinema do not consider it that directly or consistently, partly because of a relative lack of evidence (Allen 1990; Izod 1988). In contrast, the television audience has been a long-standing issue, as Chapter 7 shows by focusing upon the research traditions and theories it has attracted and the findings unearthed by some recent research. Chapter 8 follows up the study of film genres with a general consideration of popular television genres. It also selects a specific example, the soap opera, and analyses its production, programme structure and audience, though other examples are referred to where relevant. The final substantive chapter takes account of recent theoretical developments by illustrating and criticising postmodern theory. This discussion refers mainly to popular television, but examples from cinema are also covered. The critique of postmodern theory it advances can also be seen as preparing the ground for the arguments this book has to make about studying popular culture.

In this introduction we have tried to set the stage for the chapters which follow. As noted, the aim is to assess how popular culture has been studied. Apart from the main, substantive chapters, the book also raises some general themes and ideas. The nature of these, however, can be left to the conclusion, when, hopefully, their justification and logic will be evident.

Popular cinema
The Hollywood system

THESE OPENING CHAPTERS examine the economic, cultural and social significance of Hollywood cinema as a type of popular culture. They try to assess some of the characteristic features which have been associated with its development, and the power it exercises. The intention, in presenting an introductory study of Hollywood cinema, is to show how a highly significant popular cultural institution has, and can be, assessed. Hollywood cinema was one of the earliest and most significant developments in the production and consumption of popular culture in the twentieth century. It has since had a general and continuing influence on the popular culture which has come to dominate the modern, industrialised world. It has influenced the ways popular culture is financed, produced, marketed, promoted and consumed. It has played a powerful role in the development of the standard genres into which popular culture has been divided. It has left an almost indelible mark on our understanding of what counts as audience pleasure. It has been centrally involved in the ideologies which have shaped, and been shaped by, these processes. It therefore seems useful to discuss some of the key aspects of contemporary popular culture by looking at Hollywood cinema.

The rise of the Hollywood studio system

We shall start by outlining the rise and fall of the Hollywood studio system. This should convey how Hollywood cinema has been formed by its organisation of the production, distribution and exhibition of films, and how the system it established has developed and changed over time.[1] This outline should provide a basis for the subsequent discussion of narrative, ideology and genre, as well as identifying some of the key features associated with the study of popular cinema.

The film industry is made up of at least three separate activities:

the making or production of films; their distribution to points of exhibition (theatres and cinemas); and their being shown, or exhibited, to a paying audience. Both distribution and exhibition are linked by the promotion of films to the public, and production is clearly associated with technological changes. However, these three processes describe the basics of the industry. The important thing to note about the early film industry is that, for the most part, the production, distribution and exhibition of films were conducted as separate business ventures. The rise of the studio system refers to the economic integration of these three processes. As such, 'oligopoly control through ownership of production, distribution and exhibition represented the full-grown Hollywood studio system' (Gomery 1986: 3). The studio system took thirty years to form, during which time the 'fairly competitive' film industry was turned into 'a tightly held trust'. It reached the peak of its supremacy between the late 1920s and the early 1950s, when Hollywood came to dominate the 'world mass entertainment business' (ibid.: xi, 3, 189). Crucially, as is usually the case, 'it was the profit motive that dictated the nature of film production, distribution and exhibition in the United States during the studio era' (ibid.: xi, 1–2).

The studio system is a narrow definition since the system involved more than merely the use of studios for producing films. It refers to large corporations (eight in all, five 'major', three 'minor') producing profits for each other by acting jointly in controlling not just production but distribution and exhibition as well. 'The fundamental source' of the 'power' of these corporations, in particular the five 'majors', was not provided by 'Hollywood production'. 'Rather, their worldwide distribution networks afforded them enormous cost advantages and their theater chains provided them direct access to the box office' (Gomery 1986: 2). To some extent, the term Hollywood itself was always something of a misnomer. This is partly because the power of the corporations lay not in their production base in Los Angeles and southern California, but in 'the total and necessary corporate cooperation which existed on the levels of distribution and exhibition'. But it was also because real control was exercised from New

York. Indeed, the mystique and fantasy associated with 'the concept' of 'Hollywood' is 'perhaps ... the greatest corporate creation of the studio system' (ibid.: 193–4).

The system was challenged in the late 1940s by declining audiences, the rise of television and anti-trust action aimed at breaking the industry's oligopoly by divesting the majors of their control over exhibition. This period marked the decline of the studio system as it had operated during its heyday. The majors soon adapted to changing conditions with the emergence of the 'package-unit' system. For example, only RKO, among the majors, went out of business; the rest continued, sometimes under different owners (Gomery 1986: xi). Most importantly, even if they lost overt control of exhibition, they retained their power base in distribution.

The emergence of cinema

While it will be necessary to fill in some of the detail as we go along, this is the basic outline of the Hollywood studio system and we need to keep it in mind during the following discussion. The development of the factors referred to here, as well as others, need to be considered when outlining the origins and development of the American film industry.

It has been argued that recognising certain physical and optical properties can help us understand the origins of cinema. There is little doubt, for example, that two 'optical principles' of human perception make cinema as we know it possible. These are 'persistence of vision' and 'the phi phenomenon'. The former refers to how 'the brain retains images cast upon the retina of the eye for approximately one-twentieth to one-fifth of a second beyond their actual removal from the field of vision'. This allows viewers to see the images projected by a reel of film, without noticing the black spaces between the images. The second refers to how we can see the 'blades of a rotating fan as a unitary circular form or the different hues of a spinning color wheel as a single homogeneous color'. This 'creates apparent movement from frame to frame at optimal projection speeds of 12 to 24 fps' for viewers of films (Cook 1990: 1).

These features enable us to watch films and have been necessary for the development of cinema. They are physical pre-requisites for watching films. But while they are basic in this sense, it has not really been claimed that they can account for the emergence of cinema. It is also not clear that this claim could be supported if it were to be put forward. However, Carroll, for example, has tried to relate the 'power of movies' to biological and psychological capacities. He does not directly address the origins of cinema, but his case is relevant to this issue. He argues that the power of films, how they have become 'a worldwide phenomenon', arises from 'pictorial recognition'. This relies upon 'a biological capability that is nurtured in humans as they learn to identify the objects and events in their environment'. As such, it 'is a function of the way stroboscopic or beta phenomena affect the brain's organization of congruous input presented in specifiable sequences to different points on the retina' (1996a: 81). While not wishing to reduce the power of films completely to biological and psychological phenomena (ibid.: 92), he does use this argument to criticise the idea that 'pictures ... are matters of codes and conventions' (ibid.: 81). Instead, 'the power of movies' is determined by the capacity of human perception as described above.

The critical problem here is that we are talking about a fairly permanent biological capacity for pictorial recognition, irrespective of whether it is related to the power of films, or the origins of cinema. Presumably it is not something that can spring into existence quickly. How then can it explain the emergence of cinema in the late nineteenth century, its subsequent world-wide prevalence and the power it has been able to exercise since its invention? This capacity is a pre-requisite, a necessary condition for cinema, but it can hardly qualify as an explanation of the power or origins of cinema and the patterns that marked its subsequent development. The commercial and technological activities of the industrial, capitalist societies within which cinema emerged, as Burch for example suggests, would seem to provide a better basis for explaining the emergence of cinema. To some extent, the very idea of cinema reflects this in that its first appearance is defined by the presentation of a film to a paying audience. The biological capacity to watch films provides no reason to suppose that the cinema would ever have been invented. An understanding of its origins must therefore be related to the societies in which it emerged, though, even in this case, it cannot be assumed that its invention was inevitable.

A useful and contrasting case is put forward by Burch. He argues that the emergence of cinema involved 'the establishment of a mode of representation' which was 'historically and culturally determined', and which has continued to exert its power over cinema ever since (1978: 92, cf. 91). This is a large task and Burch makes some initial and tentative suggestions about the forces which helped condition the emergence of cinema, and some of the features which this cinema took.

He identifies 'three forces or historical and cultural trends which moulded the cinema during its first two decades' (Burch 1978: 93). The first was 'the folk art kept alive by the urban working classes in Europe and the United States at the turn of the century'. This consisted of 'modes of representation and narrative' from such areas as 'melodrama, vaudeville, pantomime (in England), music hall', 'fairground acts', and various kinds of street entertainment. These were linked as 'cause and effect' to cinema, because 'in its early days' it 'addressed itself exclusively to the urban "lower classes"' and 'its practitioners were for the most part "of humble origin"'(ibid.).

However, cinema was emerging within a capitalist society, which meant that the 'second force' to which it was subject was 'the underlying pressures exercised by the specifically bourgeois modes of representation'. These were drawn 'from literature, painting and especially the theatre' (Burch 1978: 93). Burch sees this mode as being defined by such features as 'linearity, haptic screen space and the individualisation of characters'. These were only intermittently present in early cinema, dominated as it was by 'elements' of 'popular origin'. However, this situation was 'gradually reversed between 1908 and 1915' due to 'the economic development of the cinema and the resulting need to attract an audience with more money and leisure at its disposal' (ibid.: 94). Thus, the features of the bourgeois mode became the defining features of the cinema's subsequent, and dominant, institutional mode of representation.

The 'third force' Burch identifies is 'scientistic', which 'figured as an element of dominant ideology', but 'was also linked to genuinely scientific practices'. It refers to the disinterested, scientific approach to technical innovations. For example, 'on a strictly technological level, the first moving pictures came most directly out of experiments by Muybridge, Marey and other researchers whose goal was most certainly not the restitution or representation of movement, but simply its analysis' (1978: 94). For a time, this force worked in association with that exerted by popular representations and against the bourgeois mode, in giving shape and direction to early cinema. However, the commercial potential of cinema eventually facilitated the dominance of the bourgeois, or institutional mode of representation (ibid.: 94–5).

These conditions thus led to a particular type of cinema. This developed out of the pre-institutional mode, or what Burch calls 'primitive cinema'. With this cinema, films lacked 'continuity links, either spatial or temporal', had 'several actions going on at once' and were marked by an 'acentric, non-directive composition' (Burch 1978: 95, 97, 99). It was a collective, non-linear and non-standardised cinema. The institutional mode of representation which replaced early cinema has proved to be very different. It has fostered a linear, narrative and standardised cinema. The institutional mode involves a clearly linear narrative which subordinates time and space to the recounting of a story. It entails a narrative logic in which the scenes or events, which are individualised, build to a clear and unambiguous ending, or what is called narrative closure.[2] This is 'the linearity of the institutional mode' (ibid.: 99, cf. 97–103). This mode began to be established in the early part of the twentieth century. One of its first examples, cited by Burch, was *The Great Train Robbery* (1903) (ibid.: 100).[3] Once firmly established by about 1915 (ibid.: 94), it has been with us ever since.

There are clear comparisons to be made between this argument and that put forward by Bordwell *et al.* (1985). What they both tend to show is how the experiments and lack of standardisation, which characterised early cinema, eventually gave way to the established routines and norms that have governed film making to the present day. The working assumptions and practices which emerged with the institutional mode, or 'classical Hollywood cinema', have continued to be followed as the particular circumstances which gave rise to them have gradually disappeared.

Early popular cinema

The emergence of cinema can therefore be seen as an industrial, technological, narrational and commercial phenomenon. These factors were linked to an emergent public interest in visual spectacle as a type of mass entertainment. This interest had been stimulated by the invention of photography and the popularity of machines at public amusements, such as the kinetoscope, which provided the illusion of moving images. Edison's invention of the kinetoscope in the late 1880s meant that photographs could be arranged into a single piece of film which, when run through a machine, simulated motion. However, the kinetoscope allowed only one member of the paying public to view the moving image at any one time. By contrast, the popular theatre, for example, provided orchestrated displays of visual spectacles, such as violent thunderstorms, which could be viewed by large audiences. The significant date could therefore be said to be 28 December 1895, when the Lumière brothers first showed a film to a paying audience in a Parisian basement café. By the middle of the following year, the first paying audience attended a screening in a New York vaudeville theatre, which used the Lumières' cinématographe.

Films were originally shown as just one among a number of performances and attractions offered by the music hall or fairground, such as dramatic episodes, comedy acts, music, songs and other types of variety entertainment. They were not at first offered as separate types of mass entertainment, such as the staged play in the bourgeois theatre. Nonetheless, cinema expanded very rapidly as a form of mass entertainment. The appeal of these film sequences to larger and larger audiences made music hall proprietors recognise their popularity. It was at the point of exhibition that the possibilities of cinema as mass entertainment first began to be realised. It was also here that commercial profits were first gained on a scale that allowed capital to be accumulated and the industry to expand. This expansion spread outwards from exhibition until it eventually included production and distribution. The first films were part of the music hall or vaudeville package, and often spectacular in the images they projected to the public. Their emphasis on visual spectacle also built upon prior developments in visual culture. The first films showed such things as trains arriving in stations or waves breaking on a shoreline. However, these spectacles began to be governed by narratives, as the screening of films gradually moved from the music hall to theatres specially designed to show films.

The emergence of the linear narrative involves the sequential movement of characters and actions in time and space. This has been linked to technological developments such as editing. Editing allows a film to show, in sequence, different actions that occur at the same time in different locations, or different characters in different situations one after the other. E.S. Porter's ten-minute film *The Great Train Robbery* is commonly regarded as one of the first films to use editing to tell a story (Burch 1978). It recounts, unsurprisingly, a train robbery and the pursuit and successful capture of the robbers by the sheriff's posse. The use of editing enables the film to cut between the robbery and the sheriff being alerted to the crime in progress, and between the robbers and the posse in the chase sequence. The story could have been told without editing, and editing need not be used for narrative purposes. Editing was therefore shaped by the demands of the linear narrative, helping stories to be told in this way and providing an opportunity for them to be more varied and complex. These links between narrative and technological developments thus played their part in developing cinema as a type of popular mass culture.

We should not lose sight of the determinant role of production, however. The early cinema witnessed an increase in the production of 'fictional narratives', but this was not the direct result of increasing public demand. Film exhibitors tried to attract audiences by promoting films according to different categories. These were variety (including comedy), 'trick' films, 'scenics' (which included exotic locales as well as documentaries), 'topicals' (which included major news events, coronations, funerals, wars and even boxing matches) and fictional narratives.[4] In the early years of the century, all of these proved attractive to audiences, and fiction was no more popular than scenics, or topicals. However, the production of films required a regular and steady flow of releases to stimulate demand and meet the need for new films. This 'regular production' was more likely to be provided by fictional narratives than by scenics or topicals. As Allen points out, fictional films could 'be made at a low predictable cost per foot, produced in or near a centralized studio, and released on a regular schedule' (quoted in Bordwell *et al.* 1985: 115, cf. 113–16, 160–1). He therefore argues that 'commercial filmmakers weighted their output toward fictional narratives because of their suitability to mass production', this 'shift' taking 'hold' by 1907–8 (ibid.: 115).

Soon, larger numbers of films, with definite story lines, began to be produced at relatively low costs. Companies such as Edison, Biograph and Vitagraph made films, but at first there was more money to be made from the lease or sale of the projectors and cameras for which they held the patents. Films were thus made to enable this equipment to be sold. The patents held were often infringed as illegal copies were made. In the long term this situation was remedied, but initially companies found it difficult to contain these infringements. The early cameras were not easily moved and production had to be controlled and predictable. This meant that films tended to be shot in studios, particularly in New York, with the help of artificial lighting. Also useful was the efficiency afforded by the nascent division of labour in film making. This was breaking up the work required into activities such as acting, writing, directing, camera operating, editing, scenery design and manufacture, etc.

The business of distributing films from producers to exhibitors was boosted by the expansion of demand. The increasing audience for films meant that theatre owners had to change their programmes more frequently, to provide more opportunities for more people to see films. The larger the audience, the greater the profit that could be made. Therefore, to attract larger audiences, production had to be expanded. As a result, distribution had to become better organised and more efficient. Thus, 'motion picture exchanges' began to emerge. These distributors found it profitable to buy films from producers and then rent them to movie theatres. This enabled theatres to expand in size and number, as more films became available. Cinemas quickly multiplied, especially in big industrial cities, with large working-class populations. Films became longer in length, told stories, and were produced in greater and greater numbers. Even by 1905, the one-reel film lasting about fifteen minutes had been developed, along with an extensive distribution system for film prints.

Cinema was thus becoming a mass public entertainment. Before the First World War, there were established production companies with their own studios, an expanding and efficient distribution system and increasing numbers of cinemas across the country. There was also an early, if eventually aborted, sign of oligopoly control. In 1908, an alliance of patent holders, the Motion Picture Patents Company, was formed. This tried to limit production and the use of equipment to its members by a licensing system. The films they produced were to be distributed only to exchanges dealing with licensed films, and given only to exhibitors using licensed projectors. However, it was undermined by competition between its members (Gomery 1986: 3–4). While this example provides an early sign of the Hollywood studio system, it also shows that, at this time, there was still great scope for smaller independent companies in the film industry.

These developments occurred at the same time as the production of films began to move to Hollywood. There are some fairly familiar reasons why this happened, such as the sunny Californian climate, which provided better light in which to film, fewer disruptions from bad weather and less dependence upon studio production. The architecture and geography of California afforded many varied urban, rural and desert environments for location filming. The closeness of the Mexican border promised a quick escape if the forces of law and order decided to pursue production companies which had infringed patent laws on the use of film equipment. What is perhaps more important is that the labour force in Los Angeles was not as well organised into trade unions as in other places such as San Francisco. This meant labour was easier to deal with and relatively cheap. Local government in Los Angeles used financial inducements and low-priced land (an important condition for film making) to entice the film industry to the city. The ideology of expansion and the conquest of the frontier, which the move to California and Los Angeles represented, was another bonus. Some versions of the American dream, such as the classic 'western', suggest it is achieved by expansion westwards and the conquest of the frontier. The west coast and Los Angeles were therefore places where the American dream could be realised properly (May 1983: chapter 7).

The move to Hollywood coincided with the growing, vertical integration of the film industry. Companies began to gain control over, and integrate, the production, distribution and exhibition of films. For example, Paramount formed the first national distribution company and went on to finance production and build theatres in key locations. This happened as the American industry began to dominate the world market. By the 1920s, 80 per cent of the films shown abroad were made by American companies. These companies controlled a major industry which was also developing financial links with Wall Street. Thus, 'with their studios, national systems of distribution and large chains of important theaters, fewer and fewer companies had come to assume more and more power. In 1925, Paramount, First National, Loew's and Fox were the major entities'. They were later joined by Warner Brothers and RKO whose 'arrival' was 'tied in with the advent of sound' (Balio 1985: 122, cf. 120–6).

The coming of sound

The idea of linking sound with moving images goes back to the origins of cinema itself. It is said that Edison initially became interested in film because he wanted visuals to go with the phonograph he was marketing. However, it was not until the mid-1920s that Warner Brothers and Fox (and to a lesser extent RKO) introduced sound, forcing the other, major studios to compete (Gomery

1985). For example, Warner Brothers wanted to improve its base in exhibition. Therefore, between 1926 and 1927, it distributed a programme of sound films, which went down well with audiences and then presented *The Jazz Singer* to cinema audiences on 6 October 1927. This was the first, major, sound film, though only four segments, consisting of songs, were in sound (ibid.: 240). Its success with audiences effectively meant the end of silent films and the rapid introduction of sound (ibid.).

Sound was an expensive business, which the majors were well positioned to finance, and it led to the 'wholesale conversion' of 'equipment and production procedures' (Bordwell *et al.* 1985: 298). Sound-proofed studios were built and less mobile, sound-proofed cameras were used in production. Cinemas were re-equipped for showing sound films. By 1931 silent films had all but disappeared. Much existing capital had to be scrapped and considerable, new investments had to be made to introduce sound. The scale of finance required tended to favour the largest and most powerful companies which had the capacity to invest and which reaped the greatest profits at the box office. Sound also increased the need for technical experts and research which the studios met by establishing a recording course which provided 'a common set of sound procedures along ... "non-competitive lines"'. This helped to ensure standardisation (ibid.: 299). The move to sound thus favoured the major studios and the vertical integration of the industry. Many of the major studios' smaller independent competitors in production and exhibition were driven out of business, or relinquished their assets to the majors.

Sound also made the telling of stories that much easier and therefore enhanced the narrative power of Hollywood cinema. However, although it is sometimes assumed that sound made a dramatic difference to Hollywood cinema, this is not necessarily the case. We have already noted how Burch argues that the institutional mode was formed in the early part of the twentieth century, and has continued to exert its influence ever since. This suggests that the arrival of sound would not greatly disturb the basic features of this system. Similarly, Bordwell *et al.* show that sound was introduced into the already established 'classical Hollywood cinema', where 'sound technique was on the whole brought into conformity with silent filmmaking norms' (1985: 301). This process was based upon analogies and continuities between image and sound, and ensuring a 'natural' or 'realistic' harmony between the two (ibid.: 301–4). For 'in Hollywood, dialogue constitutes the chief vehicle of narrative action and must be personalized no less than body, face and space' (ibid.: 302). Therefore, sound films exemplified the dependence of the Hollywood system upon the 'coherence of causality, space and time' (ibid.: 304).

The studio system

The introduction of sound thus assisted the 'oligopolistic, vertically-integrated power' exercised by the major corporations in the film industry over production, distribution and exhibition (Gomery 1986: 6; 1985: 251, 229). 'The fundamental point for understanding' this system, Gomery argues, 'is that there were only eight corporations which dominated' these 'three functions'. By 1929 the 'Big Five' or 'so-called majors' were 'Paramount Pictures, Loew's Inc. (parent company of its more famous production subsidiary Metro-Goldwyn-Mayer or MGM), 20th Century Fox, Warner Bros. and Radio-Keith-Orpheum'. These corporations 'fully integrated production, distribution and exhibition'. They each 'owned substantial production facilities in Southern California, a worldwide distribution network and a sizeable theater chain'. Of the 'Little Three' or 'minor' corporations, 'Universal and Columbia concentrated on production and distribution'. The other 'minor', United Artists, 'only handled distribution for independent producers, but for a time, like Universal, was affiliated with a small chain of theaters' (1986: 2 and 6).[5]

This system 'guaranteed its major participants enormous profits, while maintaining effective barriers to keep potential competitors out'. As we have noted, the majors' main source of power and profits 'was not Hollywood production' (Gomery 1986: 2; cf. Maltby 1995: 59, 78–9). These derived from the cost advantages 'afforded them' by 'their worldwide distribution networks' and from the 'direct access to the box office' provided by 'their theater circuits' (Gomery 1986: 2, cf. 8). The former is evident in Hollywood cinema's domination of the world market (ibid.: 11–12). The latter is evident in the enormous box office revenues received by the majors. To achieve this, they did not need to own all or most of the cinemas, merely those which were most profitable. Here the big five made a particular effort to prevent competition and guarantee profits. Thus, 'with approximately 15 per cent of all US theaters (but the majority of first-run) the Big Five could easily gather in 50–75 per cent of the box office revenues' (ibid.: 18, cf. 2, 14, 15–19).

This system also depended upon a detailed and specialised division of labour to produce, distribute and screen films. A hierarchy of decision making and control over activities and resources ran from studio executives to producers, to the specialised labour responsible for particular facets of film making. At the top, decisions would be made about such things as the money to be spent on film production. It would then be up to production executives to make profitable films within the limits imposed (Gomery 1986: 15 and 193). The production of films itself 'was divided into specialized units' of workers, which dealt with such distinct subdivisions of labour as 'finding appropriate stories', script writing, directing, lighting, editing, etc. (ibid.; cf. Bordwell *et al.* 1985).

Hollywood cinema has thus been an industry 'as constrained as any other business by the need to save time and money, to reduce unnecessary excess and risk and to stabilize and regulate the flow of production'. As an industry it recognises 'that to make money, you have to spend money' (Maltby 1995: 59; cf. Gomery 1986). Hence,

> from the 1920s to the 1950s, the studio system was a way of organizing production to suit these economic preconditions, and the stability which it provided produced the familiar style, the immediately recognizable patterns of camera movement, editing, narrative, and genre that identify a Hollywood movie.
> (Maltby 1995: 59; cf. Bordwell *et al.* 1985)

The major corporations which dominated the system, and consequently the industry, standardised film production 'in their quest for profits'. These standardised products, such as feature films, 'embraced now well-known narrative structures' while 'actively' seeking 'to convince potential movie patrons of the differences in their products' (Gomery 1986: 24).

This was the dominant studio system, which held sway in Hollywood between the introduction of sound and the dramatic decrease in the size of the cinema audience that began in the late 1940s. However, the so-called decline of the studio system did not necessarily dilute the power and the profits of the corporations, but rather changed the conditions within which they were acquired.

There are one or two points to note before we consider this decline. After the introduction of sound, the depression of the 1930s demonstrated 'that the industry had expanded far too quickly'. Consequently, 'the Wall Street firms that had financed this expansion recalled their loans and effectively secured control over the major companies'. The film corporations, in any event, had important assets such as their studio lots and cinema chains. However, the change in financial control did not result in any real changes 'in industry policy or behaviour' because 'the American film industry was an industry much like others' (Maltby 1995: 60–1).

The Great Depression of the 1930s led to a 'sharp decrease in revenues' and 'forced exhibitors to differentiate their offerings and seek out new sources of revenue' (Gomery 1986: 20). Among the changes resorted to, one of the most important and durable was the double feature. This became an increasingly prominent aspect of film exhibition during the depression and was 'the dominant US exhibition strategy well into the 1950s' (ibid.). It imposed something of a burden on production because of the demand for more films. This would have been greater if the double feature had involved, as it sometimes did, the screening of two 'A' films. The double feature entailed the development of the 'B' picture, a type of film much cheaper to produce than the 'A' film. It usually had a shorter screening time, and was shown before the 'A' film in the double feature. Each of the major studios made between forty and sixty pictures a year. This total represented only 50 per cent of the films made each year, but 75 per cent of the films made by the major studios were 'A' films. Most of the main attraction 'A' films were shown in the largest and best placed cinemas, and were made by the major studios. It was smaller companies outside the studio system, such as Monogram and Republic, who were responsible for many of the 'B' films produced in Hollywood (ibid.: 2).

By the end of the 1930s, with about 80 million people seeing at least one film a week, the studio system and the major companies were well established. The Second World War obviously disrupted the film industry's operations. However, film production increased again towards the end of the war and 1946 proved to be a peak year for profits. It was, after all, the year which saw the highest ever number of cinema ticket sales in the history of Hollywood.

The decline of the studio system

After 1946, the last clearly successful year for the studio system, audiences and thus profits began to decline dramatically. The early 1950s witnessed the emergence of television as the dominant mass medium and the rise of so-called 'independent film production' or the 'package-unit' system (see below). This is the period which is associated with the decline of the Hollywood studio system and the break-up of the vertically integrated control of the industry by the majors.

To suggest why this happened is complicated, because the fall in cinema attendance began before the rise in the ownership of television sets. Yet television played an important part in the relative decline of cinema as a form of mass entertainment. This apparent enigma is clarified if we take account of the social and historical context in which these changes occurred. The movement of large numbers of Americans from inner cities to the suburbs, after 1945, led to their adoption of a more private and house-bound family life. They favoured more domestic leisure pastimes, such as listening to the radio and watching television, rather than more publicly based pastimes, such as going to the cinema. The growth of suburban living itself started the decline in cinema attendance. Television then greatly intensified this decline, providing a mass medium compatible with the life-style of the emergent, suburban population. By the mid-1950s, television had become the most popular type of mass entertainment, while the cinema was in a state of acute decline (Bordwell *et al.* 1985: 332; Pye and Myles 1979).

The majors tried to hold on to their audience before reaching a compromise with the television industry in the mid- to late 1950s. New techniques and special effects, such as 3-D, cinemascope, Technicolor and the epic film, as well as the traditional formula of more sex and violence, were used to attract people back to the cinema. These experiments were not particularly successful at the time. However, the potentially more graphic depiction of sex and violence did begin to suggest itself as a way of marking off cinema from television, and this became a more obvious strategy in the 1960s. Similarly, the increased use of special effects promised to do the same, and thus presaged the special effects laden 'blockbuster' films of the 1980s and 1990s.

The studio system came under threat from another direction apart from television. This was anti-trust action aimed at divesting the majors of their ownership and control over exhibition, and thereby of their vertically integrated oligopoly. In 1938, an anti-trust case was brought against Paramount by small, independent theatre owners, and it became a test case aimed at curtailing the restrictive practices of the film industry. The action was intended to loosen the hold of the major studios over the industry by divesting them of their substantial financial interests in cinema exhibition. The intervention of the Second World War meant that the case was not heard until 1948, but it was successful and the majors had to give up their theatre chains. The substance of the US Supreme Court's decision was that the majors had an 'illegal monopoly' over 'distribution and first-run exhibition'. It therefore 'ordered the separation of exhibition from production-distribution'. This decision 'effectively undercut the economies of scale that provided the rationale for the system of production' (Maltby 1995: 71). It was another reason for the decline of the studio system and for changes in the corporate power of the majors.

The major companies started to provide studio space and finance for film production rather than making films themselves, and tightened their control over distribution. These changes provided ways for them to influence what was shown on cinema screens.

The decline of the studio system can therefore be associated with, among other things, the rise of suburbia, the emergence of television and anti-trust intervention. One consequence was that the majors could no longer ensure that their films would be seen at the main theatres, though the extent of this problem can be exaggerated. However, this anti-trust action, the fall in cinema attendance, television and more domestic and private life-styles meant the industry had to target specific sections of its potential audience, rather than rely upon the mass market. This led to the search for audiences in more distinct and clearly defined markets, such as the youth or teenage audience, and the 'art house movie'. The former was then associated with the 'drive-in' cinema, though families were also attracted to this venue (Austin 1989: 87–92; Doherty 1988), and this youth market has remained an important target audience for the film industry ever since. The latter involved more intellectual, and sometimes foreign, films, aimed at a more affluent and educated audience (Austin 1989: 80–3). The European 'art' cinema clearly influenced this development, as did the increasing use of explicit sex in films. It was again realised that audiences could potentially be attracted to the cinema by more 'realistic' and 'mature' portrayals of serious themes, including those which were sexually explicit. Audiences may have been able to get some of the things they saw at home, but not on their television screens.

The relationship between cinema and television was not, however, purely and simply competitive. Television needed programmes to screen, and the Hollywood studios began to switch to producing series and eventually films for television. For example, Hollywood companies had extensive experience in producing 'B' feature westerns and were therefore well placed to make western series for television. By the early 1960s, about three-quarters of the Hollywood work force was employed in making programmes for television. The early 1960s also saw, for example, the emergence of the 'made for television movie', the production of feature type films specifically for television. At the same time, the Hollywood majors accommodated and profited from television by selling their films to the networks. For example, RKO, the only company to go out of business as a result of the decline of the studio system (Gomery 1986: xi), withdrew from film production in 1955 and sold its film library to television. Except for RKO, the main corporations continued to operate under different forms of ownership (ibid.). This period thus also witnessed a dramatic increase in corporate mergers, the taking over of film companies by television companies and vice versa. The corporations formed as a result of this process provide an early sign of the global, media conglomerates which dominate cultural production, distribution and consumption today.

The package-unit system

The decline of the studio system did not lead to 'the end of Hollywood' (Maltby 1995: 71). Instead, Hollywood turned to independent production and the 'package-unit' system (Bordwell *et al.* 1985: 332, 368–9). Over time the majors made fewer films and developed their base in distribution. Workers in the film industry ceased to be employed on permanent contracts and had to sell their labour on a freelance basis. Though fewer films were made, they ran for longer than before at prime site cinemas. Maltby notes that 'the majors, concentrating their industrial power in their role as distributors, replaced the studio system of production with one in which they acted primarily as bankers, supplying finance and studio facilities to independent production companies'. Such finance and facilities are provided in return for distribution deals and shares of the profits films make. Therefore, 'production has become increasingly dependent on "packaging", by which a movie's basic "properties" – the script, one or two stars, and perhaps the director – are assembled by a producer or an agent, and sold as a package to a company'. Already, 'by the late 1960s, as much as two thirds of Hollywood's production output was "pre-packaged" in this way' (1995: 72).

'The package-unit' system is described in some detail by Bordwell *et al.* (1985: chapter 26 and 368–71). It involves 'a short-term film-by-film arrangement' and reflects 'the specialized production of a few films by many independents', rather than 'the mass production of many films by a few manufacturing firms'. After 1945, 'the independent trend' based on 'fewer … selectively produced films seemed the best way to make profits'. The self-contained studio disappeared and the package-unit system emerged whereby technology and labour are brought together by producers to realise specific film projects. The producers who decide to make a film organise this process. They secure financing and bring together the required specialised labour with 'the means of production (the narrative "property", the equipment and the physical sites of production'). For this, 'the majors' act 'as financiers and distributors', while the system still relies upon a 'detailed division of labour'. Thus, 'with the industrial shift to independent production, the package-unit system of filmmaking replaced the older studio system' (ibid.: 330–2 and 368–9).

'By the mid 1950s, limited output, independent production, and the package-unit system typified Hollywood' and subsequent film making represents 'a continuation of the package-unit system' (Bordwell *et al.* 1985: 331 and 368). Producers, actors, directors, writers and agents, acting individually or collectively, continue to assemble the packages needed to make films. In this process, 'the current major firms act primarily as financiers and distributors, allowing package units to operate on their own once a deal is set'. The package-unit system may 'give some creative personnel a power to choose projects and working conditions'. However, 'in the Hollywood mode of production', such 'pretexts' as 'spectacle, technological tour de force, and human emotions', 'above all, love', are likely to remain the defining features of film narratives (ibid.: 368 and 370).

The package-unit system is also linked to the blockbuster film, which has, in its turn, partly 'fostered' the 'conglomerate ownership of film production'. Bordwell *et al.* note that 'after the 1940s, when the industry concentrated on fewer, specialized projects, it developed an interest in the film which did spectacularly at the box

21

office' – the blockbuster. The profits made by companies from these films were used to diversify into areas which were more stable and predictable than financing film making. While 'some film firms became parts of conglomerates through mergers with larger corporations', others 'created their own conglomerate organizations through diversification'. For example, 'earnings from blockbusters contributed to various acquisitions, often in the leisure field: hotels and recreation areas, publishing firms, video equipment and cable television, record companies, pinball- and electronic-game machine manufacturers' (1985: 368).

Over time, the profitability of Hollywood cinema has come to depend upon the box office success of a small number of enormously expensive and massively publicised films. By contrast, under the studio system, a larger number of films were made more cheaply. The modern, blockbuster film has emerged from the lavish and spectacular films made in the 1950s, in response to the challenge of television. The blockbuster film is now much more profitable than the individual film was under the studio system, where profits and losses were spread across a larger number of films. While the studio system's most successful films were not as profitable as today's blockbusters, its less successful films were not as obvious as box office failures are now. Also, not all the films made under the studio system needed to be hugely profitable (Maltby 1995: 74).

However, this does not necessarily mean that film making has become more risky for the companies involved. Making films, as we have seen, has become just one of the many business interests of financial conglomerates. 'Film production and distribution companies', Maltby writes, 'have become components in multi-media conglomerates geared to the marketing of a product across a number of interlocking media' (1995: 75). For example, the merchandising of products associated with a particular film – books, T-shirts, toys, games, etc. – can make as much if not more money than the film itself at cinemas and on video release. Under the studio system, costs could be spread across a number of films, whereas now they can be spread across a number of products and activities.

To be as profitable as they need to be, blockbuster films have to reach their prospective audience very quickly and attract consistently large numbers of people to the cinema. Advertising and promotion thus become even more crucial, as does the opening of the film in as many cinemas as possible. The blockbuster has to appeal to a range of different audiences, from families to single people, from young to old, and so on, to make the profits it needs to make. The successful film, of course, does this. In this respect, the success of the film industry again depends upon films which attract a mass audience, as well as those which will appeal more to smaller and more specialised audiences. Indeed, it might be that the need for the blockbuster film is providing fewer opportunities for more serious and specialised films to be produced and distributed.

The successful blockbuster makes enough money to finance further film production, along with the other interests of the conglomerates. The success of a film can, therefore, also be judged by the contribution it makes to developing these other interests. While these films have to reach a mass audience, the markets for films have become more diverse. Successful films can make money not only at the cinema, but also in the video, cable, record, book, toy and computer game markets. Films can thus exploit these markets as they attract consumers to the cinema. Successful films are no longer simply reliant on the cinema audience, a fact that distinguishes the new from the old Hollywood. However, the return of direct cinema ownership by the major companies amounts to an addition of another 'market' to those they already control, rather than a return to the studio system (Maltby 1995: 76–7).

Nowadays, the film industry is still subordinated to the power of Hollywood cinema, which is itself dominated by a small number of very large, globally based, multi-media conglomerates. As we have noted, these financial empires have diversified interests in, and control over, a range of media. The most important include Time Warner, Gulf and Western, Disney and MCA (Universal). These are followed by other major companies, such as Columbia and 20th Century Fox, which are parts of larger financial conglomerates. Also, there are smaller companies which service less lucrative options such as the straight to video market. Despite the changes we have described, the structure of economic power that has controlled the film industry has been able to accommodate them, 're-establishing something not unlike the previous oligopoly' (Maltby 1995: 76–8).

Indeed, there is talk now of a 'big four' among multi-media conglomerates. These are Disney, News Corporation (which includes 20th Century Fox), Time Warner and Viacom. Recently, the latter, whose assets include MTV, Paramount Pictures and the Blockbuster video chain, merged with CBS, the major American television network. This deal, 'the biggest ever in media history', puts Viacom 'above Rupert Murdoch's News Corporation in the league table of media giants'. It creates 'a group broader and bigger, on almost any measure, than Disney, Time Warner and News Corporation' and promises sales 'greater than any of its rivals except Disney'. It also merges production, for example film studios and television programme making, with distribution and exhibition, for example television networks and video chains (*Guardian* 8 September 1999: 2; *Guardian* [Editor] 10 September 1999: 9). This is similar to the vertical integration of production, distribution and exhibition within the Hollywood studio system. But it now occurs on a much larger, financial and geographical scale and involves a larger number of mass media. It is the framework within which much popular culture is produced, distributed and consumed.

Chapter 2

Popular cinema
Hollywood narrative and film genres

The narrative and ideology of the Hollywood film

Hollywood cinema is not just an economic and industrial organisation. It is also supposed to tell stories and to produce dreams and ideology, while being a product of them as well. To clarify these points it is first necessary to define the American dream. We shall need to refer to it at various points in the discussion, and the typical Hollywood film has often been seen to promote and sustain the American dream. When we have done this, we will be able to discuss the Hollywood narrative.

The American dream

To begin a discussion of the narrative and ideology of Hollywood cinema it is, of course, useful to consider the idea of the American dream. Hollywood cinema is not synonymous with the American dream, but it has often been argued that it is made intelligible by its relationship to the American dream.[1] Many Hollywood films are thought to embody the American dream. It has been seen to define the ideas contained in Hollywood film genres, from musicals to gangster films. Hollywood films have been seen to strengthen the hold of this dream over American society and other parts of the world opened up to their influence. This dream forms an ideology commonly associated with Hollywood, the dream that the industry produces and sells to its audiences through its films. It is not the only important ideology, for, as we shall see, it is possible to detect a more general ideology of social order in Hollywood films. However, it would be useful if the meaning of this dream were to be made clear before we go on to discuss Hollywood cinema.

The precise meaning of the American dream has hardly remained constant over time. It is indeed something that is difficult to define precisely. Yet it embodies a distinctive set of ideas, which are clearly identifiable no matter how much they may have been affected by changing historical circumstances (Messner and Rosenfeld 1994: 6–11). Its main proposition is that material wealth and success in life can be achieved by anyone who has the necessary initiative, ambition, ingenuity, perseverance and commitment. The dream itself consists of money, power, fame, happiness, contentment, the 'good life'. The American dream refers to an open and democratic society, which allows individuals to acquire these things and so fulfil their desires. It suggests that the road from rags to riches is open to anyone willing to take it. The only barriers to its attainment lie within people themselves and their lack of the qualities demanded to achieve the dream.

The value attached by the American dream to economic success means that non-economic achievements become less important. The dream stresses the desirability of achieving financial and material rewards, such as high incomes and consumer goods. This leaves little room for achievements and activities which do not conform to the criterion of economic success. Education is valued not because it is an intrinsic and individual achievement in its own right, but simply because it provides the means to achieve the American dream. If it does not do this then it has little value. The same could be said about such things as being a good neighbour or altruism.

The social mobility of the individual is what the American dream recognises as success. It is individuals who, through their efforts, manage to climb the ladder of success. The dream is not about the collective pursuit of success by specific and organised groups, such as trade unions. It is not about material well-being which can be achieved by means other than individual social mobility, such as the collective provision of welfare by governments. The focus is strictly upon the individual and his or her path of social and economic mobility.

The American dream is an inclusive one. In this sense, it is open and democratic. No one is excluded by anything because anyone can achieve the American dream. No extraneous factors such as class, gender, race, ethnicity, or sexuality can stand in the way of the individual's pursuit of economic success. Everyone has an

27

equal chance of reaching the dream. The only barriers individuals will experience will be their lack of the qualities required to achieve the dream, or opposition from enemies of the dream, those who ignore, pervert, or subvert it. Failure is usually a purely individual phenomenon. It is not the fault of the system. The American dream is about success and how to achieve it. It therefore stresses the importance of winning and has little or no time for losers.

The American dream is a universalistic idea since it applies to everyone. Everyone can be a success just as much as anyone can be a failure. The value placed upon winning and individual achievement underlines the importance of competition as against co-operation. It is individuals who can achieve the dream and win out against others. They must therefore compete with each other for the dream. Not everyone, for example, can chair a major company or be a Hollywood film star; individuals have to compete for these measures of success. Everyone is included but not everyone can succeed. Success cannot be arrived at by co-operation between either individuals or organised groups. Competition with others is the norm for the American dream, though a modicum of small-group success, for example for individual families, is possible.

There is, of course, another, pessimistic side to the American dream. It values economic success, individual achievement and social mobility, equality of opportunity, competition and winning. However, it fails to recognise their drawbacks and to consider what happens when large numbers of people fail to succeed. Important non-economic attainments such as education, co-operation and collective provision tend to be devalued, while inequality, deprivation and failure tend to be defined as personal rather than social problems.

The Hollywood narrative

Hollywood's emergence and consolidation as an economic power is associated with the emergence and consolidation of a typical Hollywood narrative. Hollywood is thought to have developed a distinctive way of putting events, characters and objects together to tell stories through its films. This general narrative form, which we shall characterise shortly, is said to have important ideological implications. Also, more specifically, it is argued that the typical Hollywood narrative often contains an ideology of aspiration and conformity consistent with the American dream and the conservation of social order. This claim is therefore also made about Hollywood film genres. We shall now consider some arguments which make these points.

The Hollywood narrative is often seen as being dependent upon a more general and typical narrative, one common to most cultures. The lead in this direction has been provided by Todorov. 'The very nature of narrative ... without which we cannot say there is any narrative at all', means for Todorov *that all narrative is a movement between two equilibriums which are similar but not identical* (1973: 163, original emphasis). What he is saying is that, at a minimum, any narrative begins with a state of equilibrium or order, which is restored after being disrupted by an event which introduces a state of disequilibrium. The narrative tells the story of how this disruption arises, how it is dealt with and how order is restored. However, since the state of disequilibrium has to be dealt with, the restored equilibrium may have changed to accommodate the problems posed by the disruption. According to Todorov, 'the elementary narrative thus includes two types of episodes: those which describe a state of equilibrium or disequilibrium and those which describe the transition from one to the other' (ibid.: 163–4). This gives us a basic narrative which moves from equilibrium to disequilibrium and then back to a possibly altered equilibrium. It is also seen in terms of order, disorder and the restoration of order. However it may be described, it is seen to lie behind the typical narrative of the Hollywood film.

A refined and extended version of this scheme is consistent with attempts to typify the narrative structure of the Hollywood film. For example, Cook (1985: 212–15) sees three main features defining the Hollywood narrative system. The first is the following sequence: equilibrium, disruption and the emergence of a new equilibrium. In this, the initial equilibrium to be found in the film is disrupted by a problem or an enigma, which can often result in conflict, but which is ultimately solved. This allows order to be restored and a new equilibrium to be achieved, which takes account of the problem or enigma that caused the disequilibrium. The Hollywood narrative system means that the typical film follows a linear, cause and effect sequence which ensures the restoration of social order (cf. Newbould 1996; Rowe 1996: 112–16).

This system necessarily has the effect of restoring equilibrium. It is therefore defined as a conservative system because it practically guarantees that the existing social order will prevail. Order or equilibrium has to be the film's conclusion. Therefore, radical alterations of the existing social order are unlikely to be represented. For example, we might see a film in which a pleasant, middle-class, suburb is threatened by a monster or another demonic force. A number of the more heroic inhabitants might then act to destroy the monster and restore order to their neighbourhood. Equilibrium is re-established, but it may be a new one in that some of the protagonists might now know how to deal with monsters, or demonic forces, if they appear again. They may also be forced to recognise that evil does exist. However, evil does not triumph, the monsters do not prevail, the suburb is not destroyed, not all the protagonists die and anarchy and chaos do not reign. If the film ended without any of these conclusions being reached, a new equilibrium would not have been achieved and the social order would have been undermined. Because these things do not happen, the narrative of the Hollywood film is argued to have the conservative function of ensuring social order, at least on the cinema screen.

Cook goes on to suggest that two further features define the Hollywood narrative system. One is realism, by which she means two things. First, 'verisimilitude', which refers to the creation within films of believable worlds with realistic locations, characters and time scales. If the cause and effect structure is to work then it has to be believable. This point does not exclude films which are not realistic, such as science fiction. All that matters is that they are made to appear to be realistic in terms of this criterion. The second thing she means by realism is that the film's narrative stresses the crucial part played by human agents in linking cause with effect and initiating and moving the narrative forward. This structure is animated by the motives and actions of human agents as individuals. The most important agent in this narrative is the hero because it is the hero who ensures the resolution of the problem and the restoration of order.

The last feature she refers to is the high degree of 'closure' associated with the Hollywood narrative system. This point is tied in with the role of human agency. The hero acts to ensure that order is restored even if the equilibrium achieved is a new one. The high degree of 'closure' achieved means that the end of the film is very clear, all the questions asked have been answered and there is little or no ambiguity about what has happened. For high degree of closure, read clear and happy endings. The typical film follows an orderly sequence – a beginning, a middle and an end – that mirrors the sequence of equilibrium, disequilibrium and new equilibrium (or order, conflict and resolution). The restoration of the new equilibrium often arises from a quest and conflict between opposing forces – for example, good and evil, hero and villain – before the requirements of the new order are recognised and put in place (Newbould 1996). The combination of these sequences guarantees that all the loose ends will be tied up and that all the questions initially posed will be answered. It equally prevents any conclusions being reached other than the ones favoured by the film. The protagonists of this narrative are individuals, not groups and they are not usually intended to represent society. Few digressions, be they social, psychological or philosophical, are usually allowed unless they assist in telling the story and moving it forward. This narrative system, a 'chain of events in a cause and effect relationship which revolves around the resolving of a central enigma', dominates the production and consumption of films world-wide (ibid.: 14; cf. 12–16).

The arguments considered so far seem to be comparable to Burch's idea of the institutional mode and the idea of classical Hollywood narration held by Bordwell *et al.* (1985: especially chapters 2, 3, 7 and 30). They point out that the emergence and development of Hollywood cinema have involved the formation and standardisation of practices and techniques which have thereby become the norms and modes which have governed subsequent film production. They do not suggest that once a practice becomes a routine it never changes, but that changes which occur are significantly shaped by the established norms and modes of film making. One of these modes, which the formation of Hollywood cinema has established, is the classical narrative style. This can be basically defined by 'the premise of Hollywood story construction', which is, 'in brief', dependent upon 'causality, consequence, psychological motivations, the drive towards overcoming obstacles and achieving goals' (ibid.: 13 and part 1).

The Hollywood narrative is shaped by psychological causality. This causality is 'character-centered – i.e. personal or psychological' and is 'traceable' to psychologically defined individuals. This means that the Hollywood film will typically involve specific psychological causes of this kind. As such, individual characters serve as the 'prime causal' agents of the narrative and must be identifiable by 'a bundle of qualities, or traits'. Hence, if these 'characters are to become agents of causality, their traits must be affirmed in speech and physical behavior, the observable projections of personality' (Bordwell *et al.* 1985: 13–15). It is 'psychological causality, presented through defined characters acting to achieve announced goals', which 'gives the classical film its characteristic progression' (ibid.: 17). This progression starts from the initial, and initiating, cause of the film and involves 'individual characters endowed with goals' who 'struggle against obstacles' to achieve them (ibid.: 370).

The characters, whose struggles to overcome obstacles and achieve their goals ensure the progression of the narrative from its initial cause, are psychologically defined and usually possess specific and fairly obvious attributes. They can also be defined by the stars who play them since the star system will often identify particular stars with particular character traits. These characters, the protagonists, will be opposed by, and clash with, other characters who will more commonly and freely be stereotypically defined. As a result of the features discussed so far, the typical Hollywood narrative will tend to focus upon personalities and individuals, rather than the structure of social, economic and political conditions. If this social system is considered at all, it will normally be reduced to the goals and problems of individual personalities and not treated as a structure in its own right. Time (the chronology of the action, meetings, chases, etc.) and space (choice of settings, shifts in location of the action) are usually subordinated to the demands of the narrative for ordered, sequential progression and unambiguous, clear-cut conclusions (Bordwell *et al.* 1985.: 370–1, chapters 2, 4, 5).

The consequence of the struggles of psychologically defined characters to reach their goals, by overcoming the obstacles placed in their path, is that the film reaches a clear, definite and transparent conclusion. With this 'narrative closure', the goals of the characters are achieved and the conflicts are resolved in their favour; but this achievement, like the problems confronted, is understood in personal, and not social, terms. It is also often importantly marked by the typical happy ending which finally brings together the male and female leads as a romantic and harmonious couple. We shall have more to say about this in the next section. The Hollywood narrative progresses by posing questions or puzzles relating to the initial cause and answering or resolving them by the end of the film. This 'step-by-step narration' delays arriving at these conclusions until all the obstacles which impede the narrative have been removed, because it is only when this is done that a proper narrative closure can be realised. The logic of this narrative is to 'move towards enlightenment' (Bordwell *et al.* 1985: 376, 374, chapter 3).[2]

The genre or genres that characterise the film will 'operate to shape the story action' (Bordwell *et al.* 1985: 371). This means that the conventions of such genres will characterise the narrative in more precise ways. For example, it would not be difficult to understand the detective story as a variant of what has been said so far about the classical narrative. It places 'a puzzle and solution … firmly at the center of the story'; involves 'investigation, threat and evasion maneuvers' which provide 'most of the film's causal impetus'; and presents psychologically defined characters with clearly defined goals and motives. It reaches a clear-cut conclusion when the detective's investigation, after overcoming various obstacles placed in its path and uncovering the necessary evidence, provides a solution to the puzzle (ibid.: 375–7, cf. 370–1 and chapter 3). The typical Hollywood narrative can therefore also be identified by the genre conventions it can entail.

Narrative and ideology

This narrative style is considered to be important because it describes the mode of storytelling in Hollywood cinema and shows how film production is constrained by such standardisation. It is also important because it is seen to have ideological implications. Some commentators on the typical Hollywood narrative argue it is ideological and, in particular, suggest the Hollywood film fosters a conservative ideology. This ideology is thought to be conservative because it shows how the prevailing social order is restored by the effective resolution of conflicts and the satisfactory settlement of problems and disruptions. The restoration of order in films can thus be related to the maintenance of order in the wider society and the endorsement of the American dream. Order is achieved in films in the way it should be in society. The accepted forms of resolution and social order in films can be equated ideologically with those that are approved of in the world outside. Therefore, the ideology of order in the Hollywood narrative reflects and reinforces the ideology of order in society.

The discussion in the previous section has indicated how this argument might work. Another example is the 'happy ending' associated with the typical Hollywood film. It is an almost foregone conclusion that such a film will often end like this, sometimes even in the most unlikely circumstances. Bordwell *et al.* found in their survey of 100 films that 'ninety-five involved romance in at least one line of action, while eighty-five made that the principal line of action' (1985: 16). The happy ending, therefore, may not only involve the restoration of order, but the coming together of the romantic couple as an intrinsic part of that restoration. The happy ending inspired by order is often linked with the happy ending inspired by romance. So the typical Hollywood narrative ensures sexual as well as social order in the new equilibrium. Hollywood films 'have happy endings', Maltby suggests, because part of their cultural function is to affirm and maintain the culture of which they are part. That cultural function was, for example, inscribed in the industry's Production Code, which regulated the content and treatment of every Hollywood movie between 1931 and 1968. The fact that 85 percent of Hollywood movies feature heterosexual romance as their main plot device needs to be seen in the context of this regulatory framework.

(1995: 8–9)

If this is so, it suggests that the development of Hollywood and its influence has rested upon its economic and narrative structures. It also suggests that Hollywood performs an important ideological role through its typical narrative, which supports its power and ensures conformity and obedience in the wider society. The order entailed in the Hollywood narrative encourages a similar order in the society as a whole, which prevents the prevailing distribution of power from being disturbed. Hollywood cinema, like other institutions that hold power, benefits from this ideology of order. For example, it can promote the American dream if the social order and romantic couple in the typical Hollywood film are defined by the American dream.

However, is it possible to attribute such an apparently dominant ideological role to Hollywood? For example, it is not clear that major Hollywood genres, such as the gangster film, follow the narrative form or support the American dream in quite the way they should. It has been argued that other genres, such as *film noir*, depart radically from the orthodox approach of Hollywood cinema. It might therefore be useful to raise a few questions about the relevance of ideology. The view of the relationship between ideology and the Hollywood film we have described has indeed been called into question. In his more general critique of contemporary film theory, Carroll, for example, has argued that the equilibrium model is not the best way of understanding the Hollywood narrative. He argues it is not inevitable that this narrative will always have ideological intentions and effects and certainly not those usually described. It is perhaps more instructive to consider his critique of the ideological role of Hollywood film first, since it lies behind what he says about narrative.

The main object of Carroll's critique is the Althusserian-inspired theory of ideology which, he argues, dominates contemporary film theory. For our purposes, we need only note that the application of the theory to Hollywood narrative cinema suggests it is inherently ideological in the way we have noted.[3] He does not deny that 'many films may function ideologically to celebrate the values and assumptions of the status quo' (1996b: 277). However, this does not mean it is impossible 'to make a film from an oppositional position that mobilizes the resources of conventional cinema and that at the same time contests the ideology of the status quo' (ibid.). For example, a film does not necessarily become ideological because it 'tells a story with a beginning, a middle and an end' (ibid.). It is difficult to see why the adoption of the equilibrium model should always and inevitably be 'to the advantage of the status quo' (ibid.: 278). Also, as with most theories of ideology, we are not given any means of assessing empirically the effects of ideology on its target populations.

The typical mainstream Hollywood picture moves forward by asking questions which are then answered as the film advances. This feature is used by Carroll to characterise the Hollywood narrative structure. As we have seen above, this is one way of understanding this narrative, as a cause and effect sequence of events and it is a feature of the argument of Bordwell *et al.* (1985: chapter 3, e.g. 39). This is not inconsistent with the equilibrium model and it recognises the importance of narrative in social life. However, it is inconsistent with the view that these things are inevitably ideological. Films are accessible narratives because 'narrative is, in all probability, our most pervasive and familiar means of explaining human action' (Carroll 1996a: 87). This leads him to say 'that ... the core narrative structures of Hollywood-type films ... involve generating questions that ensuing scenes answer' (ibid.: 88). This is 'the question and answer model of movie narration – what I call the *erotetic* model of narrative' (ibid.: 89).

It is therefore plausible for Carroll to suggest that an alternative approach to ideology and the cinema should start from the content of films, since this is what film narratives involve. He argues that ideologies are 'either false beliefs or distorting categorical schemes that function to support some system of social domination' (1996b: 279; cf. Thompson 1990: 52–73). To determine whether a film is ideological we have to see how 'it promotes ideological ideas' as 'a function of its internal organization' (Carroll 1996b: 277). We cannot assume in advance that any film is ideological, but we can find out if it is by examining its 'internal organization'. This is what Carroll calls 'its rhetorical organization, i.e., the particular organization of its narrative and pictorial elements in such a way that it promotes or encourages ideological beliefs or frameworks in viewers' (ibid.). This means we can examine Hollywood films to see if their narrative tries to endorse ideologies. To do this, we do not need to assume that all films are ideological, nor that films can only accommodate one particular ideology. However, we can again note how in this argument the actual effect of ideology on its target audiences is purely hypothetical. No attempt is made to determine the effects of ideology.

It has to be recognised that any theory of ideology is fraught with difficulties which this theory only begins to register and which have yet to be satisfactorily resolved, if indeed they can. They certainly cannot be pursued here, though one or two questions can be raised. Not all films need be ideological. However, if we want to identify an ideological film by certain criteria, we can ask if its ideology is a result of its production, its consumption by audiences, or simply the conclusion of an analysis of the film. How does ideology get into a film? What puts it there? If it is put in the film as it is being produced, is this done consciously or unconsciously? Is it easy or difficult? Is it the result of a conspiracy? Or the consequence of taken-for-granted assumptions about the ideas films should deal with, criticise or endorse? Or the outcome of a struggle over ideas? What makes some films ideological and others non-ideological? How is ideology got out of a film once it has been put there, assuming it has been determined it is an ideological film? How does a film have ideological effects and can they be determined empirically and precisely? If a film can be said to have an ideology, how do we know it will even be recognised, consciously or unconsciously, by audiences, let alone accepted or rejected by them? How can we be convinced that a film has an ideological influence over the thoughts and actions of audiences? These questions should help clarify the difficulties with ideology that we need to be aware of in this discussion, which at best alludes to the ideology in films and only barely touches on how it may arise from the way they are produced.[4]

The equilibrium model and the Hollywood narrative do not necessarily prevent adversarial and radical ideologies and ideological dreams from being conceived and presented. However, it is still unusual for this to happen in the Hollywood film. Equally, it could be argued that alternative or oppositional film projects would find it difficult to get the necessary funding, or fail to be distributed properly for exhibition in cinemas. None the less, these possibilities would not be determined by the equilibrium model and the Hollywood narrative. They would arise from conscious and unconscious decisions made by those with financial and political power and with different ideological and normative assumptions about what constitutes a successful film.

To argue that 'the classical Hollywood film' is 'an ideological product', a 'representational commodity', involves recognising how this works through the standard narrative features of the Hollywood style. These include 'the stress upon goal-oriented individuals', 'an "objective" and inflexible story order' and the function of 'narrative closure' to 'transcend the social conflict represented in the film' by displacing it onto the 'individual', 'the couple', 'the family, or the communal good'. The latter point suggests how Hollywood cinema operates more generally to reconcile 'social antagonisms by shifting the emphasis from history and institutions to individual causes and effects' (Bordwell *et al.* 1985: 82–3). One example could be the emphasis in the American dream upon individual social mobility as the favoured path to material success. All the features mentioned entail assumptions about how the existing social order can and should work and why it should therefore be protected. They can thus serve to support and reinforce prevailing and dominant ideologies and the structure of the whole society.

The Hollywood narrative contains these ideological possibilities

because of the limits set upon what can be done within its framework of standardised norms and expectations (Bordwell *et al.*
1985: 82–3, 81). However, this is not the complete picture. For
example, 'narration can, however momentarily, break down the
ideological unity of the classical film' by concluding with an 'arbitrary happy ending'. When the happy ending 'is inadequately
motivated', as sometimes happens with *film noir*, then even 'ideological questions' can be raised. An arbitrary happy ending still
means a happy ending concludes the film, 'but to some extent the
need for it is criticised' (ibid.: 83; see also Chapter 5 of this volume
on *film noir*). An unconvincing romantic resolution of a film could
possibly encourage anxieties about the presumed harmony and
sanctity of the romantic couple. However, even here the explanatory stress remains confined to the influence of the Hollywood
narrative.

We have illustrated the narrative which has been argued to
typify Hollywood cinema and suggested how it may, and may not,
be linked to ideology. We have thus tried to identify some of the
difficulties associated with attempts to link together narrative and
ideology in an analysis of Hollywood cinema. And we have also
indicated briefly how difficult and complex the theory of ideology
is, especially when it is used to explain social phenomena. Notwithstanding these points, however, it remains the case that the
Hollywood narrative may often be found to refer to, sometimes in
admittedly complicated ways, the American dream and the conservation of social order.

Genre, popular culture and popular cinema

The formation of film genres has played an important part in the
development of Hollywood cinema and its film narrative. The idea
of genre is significant because it can complement the arguments
described so far and be used as a sociological category to study
popular cinema and television. It refers to a way of defining and
understanding films which have been shaped by the industrial,
narrative and ideological character of Hollywood cinema. The
production and distribution of popular films for a paying audience

have fostered its division into particular types, or genres. Hollywood cinema has always been a genre cinema. From its beginnings, 'the early film's economic dependence on vaudeville ... helped determine the genres and formal norms of the primitive cinema'. This meant that 'exhibition circumstances, short length and small-scale production facilities dictated the creation of films which modelled themselves largely on types of stage acts: the variety act, the fictional narrative, the scenic', 'the topical' and 'the trick film'. Such early genres 'reflect the type of appeal the producers and exhibitors exploited in selling them' (Bordwell *et al.* 1985: 159, cf. 159–61, 113–15).

Hollywood genres rest upon conventions and expectations that have been formed and developed within the unequal social relationships between producers and consumers. These genres are not relatively fixed sets of rules which can be used to make sharp distinctions between particular types of culture. This is the notion of genre to which much criticism aspires. However, it is not so instructive for sociology to view genres in this way, because its interest lies in social relationships, not textual rules. The argument here is that the idea of genre can be made relevant to the study of the social relationships associated with popular cinema and television, as well as providing another way of understanding Hollywood cinema. This argument can be developed by looking at some of the assessments made of the idea of genre. In the second half of this chapter we shall obviously concentrate upon popular cinema; television will be considered in Chapter 8.

There have been a number of interesting and useful attempts to get to grips with the idea of genre. One attempt to link the notion of genre to film is provided by Buscombe. He stresses the importance of formal details, such as the appropriate locations, but argues that, ultimately, the generic quality of a film depends upon 'conventions'. He writes, 'what kind of film a western is, is largely determined by the nature of its conventions' (1986: 15), the features which become associated with what is defined as the western. He continues: 'visual conventions provide a framework within which the story can be told ... what is more important is that they also affect what kind of story it will be' (ibid.). In the western, these stories are about the contrast between human beings and nature and the coming of civilisation; and its conventions are recognisable in that they enable these stories to be told successfully (ibid.: 15–16). However, whatever its merits, this approach still seems primarily concerned with the textual character of genre.

The difficulty this confronts can perhaps be seen more clearly if we look at Palmer's argument. He outlines some useful defining features of genre. He says, first, that the identification of a genre involves a 'horizon of expectations' for audiences. This is encouraged by the cultural industries' definition and promotion of their products by such things as advertising (1991: 114–15). Genre in this sense also serves as a 'norm', a set of rules and conventions, which helps audiences in defining their expectations. Lastly, he suggests that 'genre functions as a commercial device'. It is 'a labelling device' for the production and promotion of popular culture and 'a working method' for the creative producers of this culture (ibid.: 115–16).

Despite these highly useful suggestions, Palmer's study tends to remain text-bound. It goes into detail on a range of precise definitions and oppositions which are applied to the example of popular literature. However, little effort is made to understand the particular types of social relationships within which this literature is produced and consumed. This is surprising because the importance of these relationships is stressed by the definition of genre Palmer uses. It is presumed that these social relationships and how they work are already known because they are explained by a theory of hegemony (1991: chapter 6). This theory argues that people occupy specific positions of domination and subordination within economic and ideological relationships. Therefore, popular literature is merely an expression of this set-up and an example of the struggle for hegemony. This means that one need not go beyond this literature to understand it. However, the theory of hegemony is in need of more critical attention than that which Palmer lavishes on the texts he discusses. It is ahistorical, neglects the varying effects of social conflict, exaggerates the importance of culture, overstates the influence of ideology, underestimates the possibility of different 'textual' interpretations and minimises the role of production and audiences. However, these are not the issues that need directly concern us here. If we accept Palmer's definition of genre, we should examine the production and consumption of genre and not concern ourselves exclusively with texts. It also suggests we study the history of generic 'norms', how genres have become sets of conventions. We can only do what Palmer does if we assume texts carry hidden messages irrespective of their production and consumption, but this is a questionable assumption.

We can take this account a bit further by looking at another argument about genre. According to Neale (1990), the discussion of genre can become unnecessarily technical and rely too much on strict, textual definitions. These criticisms rely upon the view that genre is subject to significant social and cultural definitions and substantial historical variations. Neale bases his discussion on Todorov's understanding of the relationship between genre and realism. Genres do not only categorise films. They also embody expectations which attract audiences and allow them to assess the films they see as genre films. They are one way of enabling audiences to understand what is going on in a film. Therefore Neale argues that generic expectations 'involve a knowledge of ... verisimilitude, various systems of plausibility, motivation, justification and belief' (ibid.: 46). Verisimilitude means that ideas of plausibility and probability can be applied to films to make them intelligible to audiences and critics alike. A film is plausible and probable to the extent to which it corresponds to a sense of verisimilitude or 'realism'.

The meaning of verisimilitude can vary, however, and this is where Neale turns to Todorov, who distinguishes between types of verisimilitude. He defines two types apart from documentary or scientific realism or verisimilitude, which refers to a work that presents a reasonably accurate description of reality and aspires to the truth. The first type is generic verisimilitude, which refers to a work that conforms to the rules and conventions of a particular genre. What is plausible and probable here is decided by generic conventions. Films can only have verisimilitude in this sense if they conform to genre rules. This is close to the literary usage except that it refers more directly to the expectations audiences have about the films they prefer.

The second type is cultural verisimilitude. Todorov suggests that this type is close to 'public opinion'. Here people will regard a film to be probable and plausible if it conforms with what they believe to be true and appropriate in the society and culture which surrounds them. Audiences accept what they see at the cinema for this reason and not because a film conforms with generic realism, or is thought to be a true, documentary account. For example, the gangster film is closer to cultural realism since it deals with social concerns about crime and law and order. By contrast, the horror film is closer to generic realism since it relies more heavily on the genre's distinctive conventions. However, both types of verisimilitude can be found in these genres, even if one type is predominant (Neale 1990: 46–7).

The connections and variations between these types of verisimilitudes are discussed at some length by Neale, but what is of more immediate interest to us is his discussion of the formation and role of genres. He argues that the definitions and expectations of genres are formed by the film industry and other agencies that promote films, such as public relations companies, the press, critics and advertising agencies. These definitions and expectations make up what we understand as genre and promote both an individual film and its broader, generic status. Such understandings of genre which prevail at any particular time and identify specific films are obviously subject to the profitable, industrial production of films. They are therefore ideas produced by the industry and its promotional agencies, about the generic status of its films.

According to Neale, these factors suggest that genre is a process. This is a useful because it captures the historical character of genres. It suggests that they change, are part of wider social changes and are subject to the meanings constructed and circulated by producers and audiences. It equally makes it difficult to define the features of genre in a comprehensive and abstract manner. One indication of this is the quite widespread occurrence of hybrid genres which have developed out of, and in conjunction with, other genres. Definitions of genres have therefore to be historically relative and specific. While generalisations are valid, they are none the less limited by the empirical quality of genres (Neale 1990: 56–8). In this sense, there is no such thing as genre, only genres.

The historical character of genres has resulted from the way they are governed by the industrial and commercial development of profitable markets. As many observers have pointed out, popular culture is constrained by capitalist production, distribution and exhibition and genres have to be interpreted in this context. Genres are thus commodities shaped by the pressures of capitalism. Neale stresses 'the financial advantages to the film industry of an aesthetic regime based on regulated difference, contained variety, pre-sold expectations and the re-use of resources in labour and materials' (1990: 64). This demands that films be reasonably novel and distinct from each other, as well as familiar and common (ibid.). The idea of genre can capture such familiarity and novelty. As Buscombe notes, 'a genre film depends on a combination of novelty and familiarity' in its appeal to audiences (1986: 21). Genres are thus profitable because they offer a way of linking differentiation with standardised formats (cf. Bordwell *et al.* 1985: chapter 9, especially 110–12).

The points made so far suggest we should reject a quite common but misleading interpretation of genre films. This is what Neale terms 'collective expression' (1990: 64), or what Tudor refers to as 'dealing with … popular culture as a means of satisfying frustrated needs and as a way of confirming widely accepted attitudes' (1974: 182). In other words, the argument is that the popularity of film genres reflects the moods, sentiments and values to be found in the wider society. Both authors maintain that there are problems with this approach to genre study.

First, there is no reason why what is in effect 'consumer decision making' should be seen as a type of 'cultural expression'. Similarly, the motives behind consumers' choices, and the interpretations they can make of their choices, are greater and more varied than this approach suggests. It also fails to recognise that things such as production decisions, assessments of marketability and profits, and inequalities in consumption come between consumer choices and cultural values (Neale 1990: 64). Equally, it neglects the point that the culture presented by mass media may be misleading, false, or illusory, i.e. it may be ideological. Moreover, this approach tends to infer a type of mass psyche, or 'collective unconscious', in which everyone thinks the same and believes in the same things and which seems to be easily culturally expressed. Some of the dubious assumptions of psychoanalytic theory may have to be swallowed whole if this approach is accepted. Indeed, this 'extravagance' leads Tudor to suggest 'a more prosaic analysis' (Tudor 1974: 182–3).

Popular genres in film, television and other media are, as Rose points out,

> essentially commodities, manufactured for and utterly dependent on, public consumption and support. While popular culture theorists may argue about the hidden needs and desires genres reflect and fulfil, the formulas that have endured are those which manage to yield a regular profit for their producers.
>
> (Rose 1985: 5)

Like Neale and others, he therefore rejects the idea that genres, through some mysterious but none the less systematic process, reflect the cultural mood of the wider society. Again like Neale and others, he links development and changes in genres to their production and consumption.

Film genres can be understood as the economic products of a capitalist industry, but this does not mean they can simply be seen as the carriers of capitalist ideology. They are commodities, though not mere reflections of their production, distribution and exhibition. For example, it can be argued that they are also shaped by conflicts within and outside the film industry and by the need to find and retain an audience. According to Neale, film genres are not best understood as 'vehicles for "capitalist" (or "the dominant") ideology'. Criticisms can be made of this view that are similar to those which question the idea that genres are vehicles of cultural expression. Instead, he argues that

> the ideological significance of any ... genre is always to be sought in a context-specific analysis. It cannot simply be deduced from the nature of the institutions responsible for its production and circulation, nor can it ever be known in advance.
>
> (1990: 65)

None the less, genres can be explained, in part, by how they are shaped by their conditions of production and consumption. The familiar and novel features of popular genres provide an indication of these constraints. Genres have to be repetitive to allow production to be planned and organised effectively. This provides the standard product that audiences consume and accumulates the profits required for production to continue. However, genres also have to be sufficiently novel to ensure their continued popularity. They need to attract audiences and sustaining such markets equally accumulates the necessary profits. There is no guarantee that any particular film or genre will achieve this, but these are the basic conditions under which film genres are produced and consumed. These conditions mean that genres need to be both familiar and novel. If a genre becomes too familiar, the interest and attention of audiences will not be sustained. If a genre is too novel, production may be more difficult to calculate and audiences may be put off by seemingly experimental and eccentric films which fail to communicate clearly (Buscombe 1986: 21–2). Familiarity and novelty facilitate the production and consumption of genre films, as well as changes that occur, such as the mixing of genres and the emergence of new genres.

Changes therefore occur primarily for these reasons. For example, television genres are more likely to change as a 'result of network programming practices and production techniques than a sudden thematic reaction to new cultural concerns' (Rose 1985: 8). These conditions include regularity of production, competition between companies and the quest for high and stable audience ratings. They can lead to the increased use of popular devices, such as the representation of sex and violence, which is as likely to arise from these conditions as it is from changes in moral attitudes. They can also lead to innovations in popular genres. Rose cites an example from American television. He argues that 'like many other popular dramas of the late 1970s and early 1980s, "Hill Street Blues" incorporated the basic structural techniques of the daytime serial to provide night-time audiences with the satisfaction of intricate plotting and long-range character growth' (1985: 9). However, this does not mean that such genre products are purely cultural phenomena. According to Willemen, *Hill Street Blues* presents 'a carefully market-researched alternation of generically codified commodities transforming the programme into a kind of shopping mall where a customer may walk past one shopwindow in order to be caught by another one a bit further on' (1990: 109). Even the seemingly innovative generic change introduced by this programme is related to its status as a marketable and profitable commodity.

This example suggests how genres can be varied, how innovations can emerge and how genres can thereby evolve and change. This is a point Tudor makes in developing his 'prosaic analysis' of popular genres (1974: 183, 189). A prosaic analysis tries to gauge the 'potential meanings of a popular genre to its audience', 'to get some idea of the emphases and functions of popular culture' (ibid.: 183). As we have noted, popular genres are shaped by their production and consumption. Tudor recognises the limits these 'commercial reasons' impose on genres. As he argues, they tend to constrain the extent to which genres can be truly 'innovative and disturbing'. This means that 'a genre is a relatively fixed cultural pattern. It defines a moral and social world, as well as a physical and historical environment. By its nature, its very familiarity, it inclines toward reassurance' (ibid.: 180). A genre film is, after all, defined by the norms and conventions it contains. Genres can change, sometimes in innovative ways, but there are limits, imposed by production, consumption, narrative and ideology, beyond which change and innovation can rarely be taken.

Tudor illustrates these points by looking at the emergence of popular genres in the early film industry. He writes that 'producers experimented to find popular subjects, categorised them and used these categories to define their future efforts, finally giving rise to the elaborate classifications of Hollywood audience research'. It was 'inevitable' that 'this "what works once, works again" principle led to a cyclical tendency in the popular genres'. As a result, 'the pattern repeats itself at intervals considered commercially judicious'. Hence, 'the popular genres grew up with the cinema itself' (1974: 182).

Indeed, genres are dependent upon profitability and exemplify the standardisation associated with Hollywood cinema. The standardisation of innovations is integral to the way the Hollywood system operates. What has tended to happen is that 'if a genre or style or technique produces positive results (usually measured in box office receipts), other companies try an imitation of that success'. This has led to periodic cycles of genre films marking the history of Hollywood because 'one film that is successful spawns a host of others'. From 'within its circumscribed limits, Hollywood has attempted innovations and has standardized successes', which has meant that 'similar films often appear closely together and constitute cycles'. The cause of this standardisation thus lies, in part at least, in the 'economic practice of profit maximization' (Bordwell *et al.* 1985: 111).

Popular film genres, as we have seen, are sometimes argued to be meaningful. Tudor, for example, suggests they contain 'patterns of meaning' which are 'constitutive of the social world' and allow for the 'analysis of the relations between such patterns of culture and the societies in which they are manifested' (1974: 213). Social attitudes and behaviour cannot be read off from film genres. The meanings of genres cannot simply be equated with those to be found in the wider society. It is not possible to take either for granted and both need to be researched. However, there may be some relationships that can be unearthed. According to Tudor, 'reflection is too simple a concept' because popular film genres 'articulate for us the bases of our social lives; they give the underlying regularities of our societies' concrete form' (ibid.: 218). While this view may not amount to simple reflection, it still seems to be prone to the criticisms made above of the idea that film genres are vehicles of cultural expression.

Genre is also a useful sociological idea because it can capture an important aspect of the social relationships associated with cultural production and consumption. It conveys the prospect of individual choice since it appears that audiences can choose the types of film they like to watch by their generic qualities. Yet genre also suggests that cultural production and consumption are collectively shaped and determined. Through their respective activities, producers and consumers establish patterns of film genres that sell films, make money, provide viewing pleasures and leisure distractions and lead to the production of more films. These patterns are not created or reproduced by any single individual, but exist collectively and socially. Genre is an idea which can therefore combine certain individual and collective aspects of popular culture.

Conclusions

Apart from suggesting that genre is a useful sociological idea, we have, in this section, also related it to the preceding discussion of Hollywood. As such, we have tried to argue that the idea of genre can help us understand popular cinema and television. In particular, three points have been stressed: first, how relevant genre is as a way of linking production and consumption; second, how historically varied genres are; and, third, how this is bound up with the standardisation and differentiation, or familiarity and novelty, associated with popular Hollywood cinema. These points are comparable with those Ryall makes in developing a framework for studying genre, which brings together production, the audience and the text and which recognises its social and historical character (1979: 3–5, 21–5).

Ryall's argument can stand as a critical alternative to that of Altman (1999), who has taken issue with this way of understanding genre. Genre may not be that useful for textual criticism, but this is not our concern here. Altman seems to have three basic criticisms to make which relate to the above argument and we can deal with them in turn. The first is 'how does' the 'public recognition' of genres 'come about'. For Altman, the claim that 'genres are defined by the film industry and recognized by the mass audience' rests on 'the somewhat dubious assumption that genres shaped by the film industry are communicated completely and uniformly to audiences'. Consequently, little attention is paid to 'the constitution and naming of genres' (ibid.: 15).

It seems, though, that this is precisely the point about genre. It is difficult to define specific genres independently of their social and historical circumstances. There is little doubt in this view that the film industry shapes its genres. The problem is seen to lie in the way audiences are thought to recognise them. The communication of genres to them is seen to be automatic and to work irrespective of how diverse they are. However, to what extent does this challenge the approach in question, apart from saying it requires more empirical support? The diversity of audiences need not be a problem, as Chapters 7 and 8 below suggest. The criticism would seem to result in a plea, which few would disagree with, for studying the process of public reception. Also, there is nothing in the production and consumption approach to genre that means it is inherently tied to the idea that the reception of genres by audiences need be 'complete and uniform', or automatic.

Second, Altman argues that this approach assumes 'a quasi-magical correspondence between industry purposes and audience responses'. It is 'quasi-magical because the mechanics of the relationship between industry and audience have been described in only the most primitive manner' (1999: 16). Again, this does not appear to be a particularly damning criticism. The ideas we have about this relationship may well need to be refined, clarified and made more specific, but a historical and sociological approach could begin to do this. Equally, it is difficult to think of how genre could be the subject of a significant and relevant discussion without this relationship being at its centre. We are trying to understand a powerful industry with established methods of production, distribution, exhibition and narration, as well as patterns of audience recognition, viewing choices and ideology. Genre is, therefore, one useful way of trying to understand the crucial links between industry and audiences.

Third, Altman claims that genres do not always have 'clear, stable identities and borders'. He argues that the approach in question is 'challenged at every turn by the historical dimensions of film production and reception'. It 'assumes coincidence between industrial and audience perceptions', but 'history furnishes example after example of disparity', of 'crossbreeds and mutants' (1999: 16–17). We have already noted above the existence of hybrid genres and argued they could be included in the analysis of genre.

This criticism would seem to raise a problem only if we did want a clear and fixed idea of genre. The key word in the quotations above may be 'assumes'. It seems that what the 'industry–audience' approach needs to do is 'demonstrate' its arguments and there is nothing to prevent it from doing this. If it can be put in this way, genre is the 'dependent variable'. Therefore, if our interest lies in explaining popular cinema and how it develops and changes, then one of the things we would focus upon would be the emergence, establishment and mixing of genres. Moreover, it must be possible to think of distinct genres, if reference can be made to hybrid and mutant genres.

There are thus a number of things we can say about our discussion of Hollywood cinema. Genre is very important for understanding Hollywood film production since it represents another instance of how it has fostered standardisation; in this case, the formation, consolidation and variation of genre conventions. For example, we have noted above how genres were first developed in the early days of cinema, often following the example of vaudeville, and became standardised by the profit motive (Bordwell *et al.* 1985: 111, 159, cf. 145). Genre is equally important for the Hollywood narrative because it is another aspect of how this narrative works. For example, it provides another type of motivation, shapes the 'story action' and helps define the boundaries in the typical narrative (ibid.: 20, 72, 371). Moreover, genres attract audiences and serve to standardise, while also differentiating, popular patterns of consumption. The potential presence of ideologies in the typical Hollywood film also prevents genres from being understood as straightforward responses to audience demand.

These points suggest that genre is a significant idea for understanding popular Hollywood cinema. Like narrative and ideology, it indicates that this cinema may be fundamentally determined by, but is not simply reducible to, the profit motive. It is about making money, but its narrative, ideologies and genres enable it to be profitable. Its power and popularity derive from its economics and from its culture, but, most importantly, from how the two come together (Bordwell *et al.* 1985: 83–4 and 367; Gomery 1986: xi, 1–2).

Chapter 3

The gangster film

The gangster film

There is only so much that can be said about genre in the abstract. We now need to look at some examples to develop our assessment of popular cinema and make use of the general points which have emerged from the preceding discussion. The examples to be examined will be the gangster film, the horror film and *film noir* in that order. However, before doing this we need to be clear about the reasons for choosing these examples and the lines along which each example will be surveyed. The examples chosen should help to illustrate different aspects of popular Hollywood cinema and assess the value of genre for studying popular culture.

The gangster film is a genre which conforms closely to what was called 'cultural realism' in the last chapter. This means it is worth considering because it relates, however indirectly, to attitudes, beliefs and values in the wider society. It is a good example of the cultural realism of genre and generic conventions, though this does not mean that its generic realism should be ignored. The main reason for choosing the examples selected is what they can tell us about Hollywood cinema. The ideas of cultural and generic realism and their relation to popular genres and generic motivation are helpful in initially distinguishing genres that can illustrate the study of popular culture.

The gangster film has a number of features which can usefully be explored.[1] These include its production, its relation to Hollywood and the studio system, its ideology and narrative structure and their relation to the American dream. However, to begin with, it might be useful to define briefly some of the themes to be found in the gangster film. The basis of the gangster film genre was laid down in the early 1930s. It was established, in particular, by three films which were produced soon after the introduction of sound and as the studio system became more dominant. These films were

54

Little Caesar (1930), *Public Enemy* (1931) and *Scarface* (1932), and they continue to inform discussions of the gangster film. They are now generally seen as forming the 'classic' shape of the genre. While there have obviously been some changes over time, they set down certain conventions and patterns which have continued to be relevant.

The gangster film is about law, order and crime, but, unlike other crime and police genres, it focuses upon the figure of the gangster. It may not always see things from the gangster's point of view, but it focuses upon gangsters and their stories. These include how they entered a life of crime, their reasons for doing so, their success as gangsters and their common and predetermined fall from power, usually their death, at the hands of the forces of law and order. The viewpoint often taken in the gangster film, notably in earlier examples, is one governed by the morality of the wider society. This means the film shows the gangster's fate to condemn him and warn others away from a life of crime.

Therefore, while the gangster film is about law, order and crime, it commonly takes a specific angle on this subject matter which is represented through the character and narrative of the gangster. It concentrates as much on power and corruption and the ambiguities of law enforcement as it does on the need for justice to prevail and for the gangster to be punished. This arises from its concern with the criminal rather than the police and how it treats the social world of crime and its relation to the institutions of law and order.

Cultural realism

Another thing we need to do before we continue is to define more precisely the cultural realism of the gangster genre. Here a number of authors have provided some useful guidelines. Remembering the general nature of cultural realism that we noted above, we can now see how it applies to the gangster film. It was indeed one of the points of origin for the classic films. Raeburn, for example, has indicated how the gangster genre emerged out of prohibition in America and the consequent, criminal organisation of the illegal production and supply of alcohol in the 1920s. He argues that 'prohibition and the notoriety of crime barons like Al Capone were the genre's most obvious precipitants' (1988: 47). Similarly, Ryall has pointed out that 'the gangster ... genre developed during the late 1920s and early 1930s at the time that its subject matter – manufacturing and distributing illegal liquor, gang warfare – was actually occurring' (1979: 32). He warns against drawing a direct parallel between historical events and popular films, but does suggest that 'the history of organised crime ... provides the historical "raw material" from which the genre is drawn' (ibid.: 15).

This raw material is not directly represented by documentary realism in a popular film genre. It is reshaped and imagined differently for the purpose of presenting fictional drama in a popular film genre. None the less, genres such as the gangster film are more immediately relevant to events in the real world than other genres, such as the horror film. Ryall notes that with the gangster genre 'the links between actuality and fiction were posed in a much more explicit way than in, say, the western genre where the historical backdrop has usually tended to be rather more generalised' (1979: 32). These links may not be so obvious now, but they usefully distinguish the gangster film as a way of illustrating some of the things entailed in studying popular cinema.

The Hollywood system and the gangster film

The gangster film as we know it was a product of the growth of the Hollywood studio system. Its emergence and development can be accounted for by the themes outlined in Chapters 1 and 2. However, while its classic patterns may have been established just after the introduction of sound, the significance of this can be exaggerated. It has been suggested, for example, that the gangster film only really flourished when sound could capture the realism of rapid machine-gun fire and the screech of a speeding car's tyres (Raeburn 1988: 48). However, we have noted above how important practices, such as the typical narrative, were already being consolidated in the silent era. The coming of sound illustrates the ascendancy of the studio system and it made storytelling easier, but it is difficult to think of a film genre which would not have bene-fited from sound.

Thus, as with any Hollywood film genre, the gangster film has first to be understood as a commodity. To do this, however, we need also to refer to its cultural and generic realism and its narra-tive and ideology, since these features enable it to become a commodity. The determining influence exerted by Hollywood cinema and the studio system over the production of gangster films has usefully been highlighted by Ryall (1979: 28). Ryall suggests that 'the ways in which the studios were organised to produce films can be seen as determining factors on the final pattern or form of the individual film'. This is because the system imposed 'limits, constraints' on the types of films produced (ibid.: 28). Thus, gang-ster films have been shaped as genre products of this system. Hollywood popular cinema has been the context in which they have been produced, distributed and exhibited and the key influ-ence upon the general pattern they have taken.

As an example of this, Ryall points to the 'close relationship between Warner Brothers in the 1930s and the gangster film' which reflects 'the way … certain studios … are historically identi-fiable with certain genres' (1979: 28). We have already noted that Warner Brothers was one of the big five corporations which domi-nated the film industry and the studio system. Its association with the gangster film arose, in part, because the system relied upon the development of film genres for the reasons already discussed. However, it also arose, in part, because of the stars contracted to this studio. Warners had actors such as James Cagney (the star of *Public Enemy*) and Humphrey Bogart under contract who had become identified with the gangster film. For Ryall, there 'is an economic logic' at work here (ibid.). Studios put much time and money into grooming their stars and tried to use them as frequently as possible in their films. They even lent them out to other studios when work within a particular studio was not avail-able. So, if 'stars were normally suited to particular genres those would be the kind of films that the studio would be obliged to make' (ibid.; cf. Cook 1990: 308). The same considerations applied to other assets, such as available locations and sets that had already been constructed. The Hollywood system conforms to 'the general pattern of commodity production within a capitalist economy'. This involves 'the maximum exploitation of resources for financial gain, economies of scale, standardisation of product', among other things (Ryall 1979: 29).

The significance of the relationship between the Hollywood system and the gangster film also relates to the audience. Roddick suggests 'there was an identifiable audience need to be met and the studio system was designed to meet it economically – and therefore as profitably – as possible' (1983: 10). As we have noted, Hollywood film genres provide a profitable way of matching the needs of production with those of consumption. Roddick goes on to point out that Warner Brothers' commitments to realism and dealing with contemporary issues led it to favour the gangster genre as well as the social problem film. He, like others, argues that sound played a key role in allowing these commitments to be fulfilled because it made films appear more realistic (cf. Cook 1990: 293). This meant Warners could bring social realism and crime together in the gangster film which concentrated upon contemporary issues and events, such as the depression and prohibition and their relation to the rise and fall of the gangster.

As a Hollywood film genre, the gangster film could combine realism and popular entertainment. Since the classic gangster film proved very popular, more films were made and the cyclical character of the genre was set in motion. According to Roddick, these films were 'relatively cheap to make, since they used contemporary dress, sets ... and exteriors'. Also, 'once the formula was perfected – as early, basically, as 1931 – the scripting and pre-production process was ideally suited to Warners' streamlined studio methods' (1983: 99). D. Cook has also noted that Warners' drive to maximise economic efficiency fostered a 'fast-paced, disciplined narrative construction' well suited to the gangster film (1990: 307–8). The points we have considered so far have allowed us to understand some major aspects of the relationship between the Hollywood system and the emergence of the gangster film. We now need to look at the subsequent development of the genre.

The gangster film's relation to the production and consumption systems of Hollywood cinema has received relatively little attention, compared to the discussions about its ideological and textual qualities. However, some indications can be provided of changes in the relationship between the gangster film and popular Hollywood cinema. While the industrial and financial constraints of this system have remained reasonably consistent over time, some variations in the gangster film can be noted.

The gangster film is a Hollywood film genre and a product of the Hollywood system. It entails, as we shall see, the Hollywood narrative and maintains a generic balance between standardisation and surprise. However, some authors have identified definite cycles in the gangster genre even if they are based on ideological and cultural themes, rather than the relation of the films to the Hollywood system. These historical summaries usually start from the classic films we have already mentioned. Ryall (1979: 16–17), for example, has used the work of McArthur and organised the cycles of the genre into decades starting with the 1930s. This decade witnessed the arrival of the classic gangster film and the reaction to them with films, such as *G-Men* (1935), which focused upon the FBI agent as the hero. It also saw films which, to some extent, attributed crime to poverty and deprivation, such as *Angels With Dirty Faces* (1938). The 1940s was a decade which saw the *film noir* (see Chapter 5), the police procedural, or 'police documentary', such as *The House on 92nd Street* (1945) and the 'morally-oriented gangster film', such as *Force of Evil* (1948), which has also been defined as a *film noir*. The 1950s saw the 'syndicate film', films about government investigations into organised crime, such as *Murder Inc.* (1951), as well as 'historical reconstructions', such as *Al Capone* (1959). However, a film such as *The Roaring Twenties*, which came out in 1939, can equally be seen as a historical reconstruction or 'period' film. Indeed, many gangster films can be viewed in this light (Whitehall 1964: 12, 22, 40). Even the classic films were made a few years after the events they depict. Lastly, the 1960s saw the 'forties thriller reprised', such as *The Moving Target* (1966), which can also be viewed as an example of the private eye genre.

Gledhill has updated the overview provided by Ryall. She suggests that the late 1960s and the 1970s saw the addition of the 'police movie', such as *Dirty Harry* (1971), and the '*film noir* reprised', such as *Chinatown* (1974), to the gangster cycle. The 1980s witnessed the ' "classic" gangster film reprised', such as *Scarface* (1983) (1985: 86). However, the films mentioned are not all obvious gangster films, such as the private eye film *Chinatown*. Equally, no reference is made to highly significant gangster films which also fall outside the stated categories, such as Parts 1 and 2 of *The Godfather* (1971 and 1974, respectively) and *Bonnie and Clyde* (1967) (Raeburn 1988: 55–7).

Even if this type of exercise is useful because it tries to chart changes in film genres, it also has important limitations which need to be recognised. It is clearly too schematic in playing down continuities, such as those arising from production, genre and ideology, and exaggerating changes, such as the historical reconstruction film. It tends to misplace films, confusing, as we have seen, the gangster film with *film noir* and the private eye genre, and sometimes confuses the crime film with the gangster film. It focuses on particular films without assessing how representative they may be. For example, the classic films may have been representative of the origins of the genre because they were among the first to be made. Conversely, the *Godfather* films may represent a summary of the genre because not many gangster films were being made by then. Also, Whitehall points out that the 'syndicate' sub-genre really begins in the mid-1930s (1964: 19, 20, 22). He sees the 1950s' cycle as an anti-syndicate one. Historical surveys do not usually seem to be based on samples of films made at particular times. This means that the reasons for the author's choice are often not made clear and the significance of the films chosen not established. This way of dividing the history of genre is also too neat, tying changes to particular decades in a way that is simply unrepresentative. Not only do features of genres persist, but changes are rarely encapsulated in and defined by specific decades. This is as relevant to the analysis of ideology as it is to the relationship between the gangster film and the Hollywood system.

For the moment, however, we need to be more precise about the historical outline of the gangster genre, noting that we are dealing with continuities as well as changes. If we pay lip service to this type of exercise despite its limitations, there are a number of things that can be said besides what has already been outlined. It is safe to say that the relationship between the classic films and the emergence of the Hollywood system has been established. We now need to say more about what happened subsequently.

Within the general constraints of the Hollywood system, one of the first changes noted by writers such as Cook is the effect of the moral reaction against the violence and the glamorising of the gangster in the classic films. By the mid-1930s the government, or FBI agent, had become the central protagonist of a number of films, such as *G-Men* (1935). When the gangster took centre stage, he was the fated victim of deprived social conditions, as in films such as *Dead End Kids* (1937) and *Angels With Dirty Faces* (1938) (Cook 1990: 293). This approach could, of course, have gained sympathy for the gangster. However, it made it as clear as the classics did that the gangster could not succeed and that being born poor did not necessarily justify a life of crime. Cultural realism and ideology play their part in this variation, but it can also be viewed as the type of change a popular genre can go through to retain popularity.

Films which related organised crime to social conditions did not cease to be made in 1939. Indeed, some *noir* films, such as *Force of Evil* (1948), did precisely this and can also be viewed as gangster films, along with *noir* films about organised crime, such as *The Big Heat* (1953) and the *The Big Combo* (1955). Also, there were *noir* films about the individual gangster which did not directly address organised crime, such as *High Sierra* (1941) and *White Heat* (1949). However, some so-called *noir* films, such as *T-Men* (1948) and *The Undercover Man* (1949), are best viewed as examples of the 1950s', organised crime, cycle of the gangster film. On the whole, *film noir* is a generic variation of the crime and police film, rather than a definite cycle of the gangster film.

According to Cook, the gangster film re-emerged in the 1940s as a darker form of crime film, associated with the shift from individual to organised crime (1990: 514–15). The films of the 1930s, especially the classics, focused upon the gangster as an individual criminal. They did not stress the role of organised crime, even when dealing with such events as prohibition and the illegal provision of alcohol. This is not a conclusion which applies to all films. *G-Men*, for example, does show some recognition of organised criminal in the 1920s. However, it was the 1940s and 1950s which saw more public awareness of organised crime as government investigations unveiled the scale and power of the role of the 'syndicate', or 'Mafia'. In this period, the gangster film concentrates upon criminal investigations and prosecutions of the gangster as an organised, bureaucratic unit, rather than as simply an individual. Examples of these films include *Hoodlum Empire* (1952) and *Murder, Inc.* (1960).

The focus of these films was upon organised crime, but their protagonists were police and government agents, often working undercover, and not gangsters. They told well-publicised, sometimes sensational and frequently violent stories about the inner working of organised crime and the successful attempts of government to bring it under control. These films began to provide the studios with pictures which attempted to compete with television and resist the decline in cinema-going. Cultural realism and ideology clearly played their part in this, but changes in the studio system and the structure of Hollywood cinema were crucial in changing the gangster film. This change did not so much alter the classic format as turn the genre into another variant of the blockbuster film.

Before we deal with this point regarding films which illustrate this process, such as *Bonnie and Clyde* (1967), *The Godfather* and *The Godfather, Part 2*, we have to consider more directly the 'historical reconstruction' film. Some commentators have suggested that this type of film emerged in the 1940s and 1950s, as a sub-cycle of the gangster genre and has reappeared periodically ever since (Ryall 1979: 17; Gledhill 1985: 86). Examples include films such as *Al Capone* or *The Rise and Fall of Legs Diamond* (1960) (Cook 1990: 514–15). These films are 'historical reconstructions' because they explore an earlier phase in the history of the gangster. Both the examples cited are biographical pictures about famous gangsters who came to prominence in the 1920s and 1930s. However, the significance of this type of film can be exaggerated. *The Roaring Twenties*, which came out in 1939, is, as we have noted, a gangster film about the prohibition era and an individual gangster very much like the protagonists of the classic films. This means it can, as a period film, be linked to the earliest cycle of the gangster genre. In a way, the formative, classic cycle of the gangster film can be defined as a phase of historical reconstruction films because it was about an earlier period of history. Therefore, rather than seeing the historical reconstruction film as a recent and novel departure, it is perhaps better thought of as an intrinsic feature of the gangster genre and its cycles (Whitehall 1964: 12, 22, 40).

Along with these variations, Cook points to two other notable developments in the gangster film during the 1950s. The first is the 'caper' variant of the gangster film. This focused upon 'the mechanics of pulling off a big heist' and could be serious or comic in tone. Examples include *The Asphalt Jungle* (1950), *The Killing* (1956) and *Odds Against Tomorrow* (1959) (Cook 1990: 515). It is a sub-genre which has remained popular unlike the other variant, the 'anti-red' gangster film, examples of which include *I Married a Communist* (1950), *Big Jim McLain* (1953) and *Pickup on South Street* (1953).[2] In this type of film, 'the criminal figure is a communist spy and the syndicate is the "international communist conspiracy," but the traditional iconography of the gangster film is maintained' (ibid.). This type is another example of the organised crime film which emerged most clearly in the 1950s, here linking the fight against organised crime with the Cold War. However, it lacked the popularity and staying power of other types of gangster film and was a product of the overtly political, rather than the popular cultural variation of genre. Interestingly enough, Cook (ibid.: 517) argues that the James Bond films displaced the gangster film for much of the 1960s by setting criminal conspiracies on an international stage, again initially combining the Cold War with organised crime.

The next major change in the genre seems to have occurred in the late 1960s with the release of *Bonnie and Clyde*. This film has been given a significance which goes beyond the changes it is said to have introduced into the gangster genre. For many commentators it signalled the emergence of a 'new' Hollywood cinema, as well as reviving the gangster genre. For Cook it was more than just a violent gangster film. It was rather a 'sophisticated blend of comedy, violence, romance and – symbolically at least – politics' (1990: 878). It included 'anti-establishment' sentiments and presented the gangster as almost a 'romantic revolutionary'. Although still fated to die, the gangster represented a spirit of independence and freedom opposed to the prevailing system. In the context of its time, it was about America's military involvement in Vietnam. Aimed at the 'new youthful audience', it hinted at the part played by romantic rebels in fighting the 'military-industrial complex', to bring an end to the war (ibid.: 877–8).

Interpretations such as this ignore much of the actual substance of the film. How do Clyde's impotence and violence, for example, square with the putative sexual liberation and peace movements of the time? Or how do you transform nihilistic gangsters into freedom fighters? This interpretation also tends to play down the generic status of the film, whose structure follows the rise and fall narrative of the classic gangster films. It also ties the film too closely to its historical time and place, being content to read off its significance from some aspects of its immediate historical and public context.[3] Films produced at this time are often seen as illustrating the development of a more sophisticated and artistic American cinema. For example, it is argued that *Bonnie and Clyde* allowed the gangster film to return 'to the mainstream of American cinema as the vehicle for serious artistic and social expression ... that it was during the 1930s' (Cook 1990: 518, 877–80). Most of these films, though, including *Bonnie and Clyde* and *The Godfather*, remain obvious genre pictures as far as their production and consumption are concerned: that is, generic products of the Hollywood system (Bordwell *et al.* 1985: chapter 30).

However, Cook also points out how *Bonnie and Clyde* helped revive the gangster film in so far as it remained within its traditional generic conventions. It represented the gangster as a tragic, heroic figure and drew upon the example provided by earlier and similar films such as *You Only Live Once* (1937), *They Live By Night* (1949) and *Gun Crazy* (1950) (Cook 1990: 879). *Bonnie and Clyde* was a major hit and set in train a cycle of 'criminal couple' on the 'road' pictures that clearly referred to earlier phases of the gangster film (ibid.: 877–80). As such, like *The Godfather*, it can be seen as an example of the type of 'big picture' that Hollywood became reliant upon from the 1960s onwards (see Chapter 1). It was also yet another example of the 'historically reconstructed' or period gangster film.

'Hollywood's faith in the big-budget, mass-appeal feature' was restored by 1970, according to Cook. It might be added that it has not been severely tested since then. This decade saw a massive increase in the production costs of films, as well as the profits which could be made from their box-office success. Cook cites *The Godfather* as a leading example of this type of picture (1990: 887–8), a point enhanced by the success of its sequel, *The Godfather, Part 2*. These films, which showed 'the dark side of American business', indicated a return to some of the themes of the organised crime films of the 1950s (ibid.: 514–15, 891). Notwithstanding the artistic and sophisticated quality of some of these films, as well as their social commentaries and their kinship with European art cinema, they remain intelligible as genre products of the Hollywood system. In particular, these 'big-budget, mass-appeal' films are one way Hollywood began to cope with the decline of the studio system. Thus films such as *Bonnie and Clyde* and *The Godfather* have first and primarily to be understood in this context.

This argument is not meant to undermine the significance of *The Godfather*, even if it is open to interpretation as a genre film. Apart from anything else, it is one of the definitive gangster films, providing a cinematic summary of the genre. It can also be located in the cycle of vigilante films which characterised the gangster and the crime film in the early 1970s. As such, the Godfather dispenses the justice which those who respect him, or are under his influence, cannot get from the courts and the police. The courts may not hand down the proper punishment for rapists, but the Godfather will, in return for respect and an oath of loyalty. Like the 'rogue cop' in *Dirty Harry* and *The French Connection* (1971), or the embittered private citizen turned avenger in *Death Wish* (1974) and its sequels, the gangster takes the law into his own hands. This refers to a historical function of the gangster which is underlined in *The Godfather, Part 2*, but it also highlights a generic variation of the 1970s.

From the 1970s to the present day, the gangster film has witnessed the continuity of such traditional themes as organised crime, the control and profitability of illegal substances and the success and failure of the gangster. At the same time, the gangster film has remained a generic product of the Hollywood system, continuing the patterns represented by *The Godfather* and *Bonnie and Clyde*. One thing which has not been considered so far is the issue of race and ethnicity. Clearly, this has been a central feature of the gangster film from the classic period onwards. However, the 1970s saw the introduction of 'new' ethnicities, along with the 'old', into the framework of the gangster film. This has become an important aspect of the subsequent development of the genre.

One side of the gangster film's cultural realism and generic popularity is about the criminally organised supply of illegal but marketable goods. Another side involves ethnicity, the family and their relationship to American society and the American dream. The extent to which more recent gangster films have radically altered the number of ethnic groups represented, as well as the quality of these representations, can be exaggerated. However, bearing in mind that the gangster film has to be seen as a generic product of the era of the Hollywood blockbuster, this theme does provide a useful way of summarising some of its most recent developments. It has helpfully been outlined by Winokur.

'The contemporary gangster film', he argues, 'best embodies the ambivalence of film-makers towards ethnicity and race' in that it values the ethnic minority family, but suggests it breeds gangsters (Winokur 1991: 10). For example, 'the *Godfather* films suggest a connection between ethnicity and upward mobility' (ibid.). The family wants economic rewards and improvements for its members, particularly its future generations, but usually achieves this by organised crime and violence (cf. Raeburn 1988: 56; Bell

1962: chapter 7). This makes it 'the scapegoat for social ills', while 'the ethnicity celebrated as the cement holding the family together is in fact responsible for its destruction. Hence the critique of American politics and business is undercut by a critique of the ethnic family' (Winokur 1991: 10–11).

Winokur points out that the contemporary gangster film covers 'the same ethnic groups as their predecessors: Italian, Irish, Jewish and WASP' (1991: 11). He says this despite counter examples such as *Boyz N The Hood* (1991), or the so-called 'Blaxploitation' cycle of the early 1970s, which deal with African Americans, or *Scarface* (1983), which deals with Cubans. Instead, he argues this 'masks the continuing racism of US society behind the convenient half-truth that the traditional immigrant groups have made it' while 'those groups that would show how America still discriminates are not represented' (ibid.). The number of gangster films which deal with previously excluded ethnic minority groups would surely question this simplistic, conspiratorial view of the role of popular cinema. *Scarface* and *Boyz N The Hood*, for example, raise this issue, as Winokur seems to recognise implicitly later in his article. However, his argument does show how the significance of recent trends can be exaggerated and how the genre is still closely tied to the traditional, ethnic minority groups.

In conclusion, however, he points out one interesting contrast between the classic and contemporary gangster films. He says the former 'tended to see the nuclear family as a site of values apart from the gangster's activities', which 'defined itself in part by its rejection of the gangster'. Conversely, 'contemporary gangster films, in a pattern established by the *Godfather* movies, tend to conflate the values of the gangster and his family'. This is something to be found in gangster films involving African Americans such as *New Jack City* (1991)(Winokur 1991: 11), but not, interestingly enough, in *Boyz N The Hood*. For example, in *Public Enemy*, the gangster, Tom Powers (James Cagney), has a brother, a war hero, who remains morally resolute in his hostility towards Cagney's criminal career. By contrast, in the first *Godfather* film, Michael Corleone (Al Pacino), initially returns home as a war hero who will have nothing to do with his family's criminal business.

67

His status and position are accepted by the other members of the family, including his father, the Godfather. However, as the plot unfolds, he and not one of his brothers, becomes the true heir apparent to the Godfather. He takes over as the Godfather, the successful head of the family's gangster empire and the focus of the cycle of *Godfather* films.[4]

Ideology and the gangster film

The main argument about ideology and the gangster film tends to focus on the ambiguity of the gangster and appears to derive from a short but famous essay by Warshow, originally published in 1948. Even if the subsequent discussions do not directly refer to this work, it can still be seen as providing a source of inspiration (see Gledhill 1985). Therefore, to understand what has been said about the ideology of the gangster film, it is useful to clarify Warshow's argument.

Warshow starts by assuming that modern, democratic and egalitarian societies work to make people happy. They are 'committed to a cheerful way of life' (1964: 83). This is also true of their mass cultures: 'it is the function of mass culture to maintain public morale and certainly nobody in the mass audience objects to having his morale maintained' (ibid.: 84). However, there is another, more marginal and less prevalent, side to this optimism which expresses a 'sense of desperation and inevitable failure which optimism itself helps to create' (ibid.). By some mysterious process, the role for expressing this 'current of opposition' falls to the gangster film, which 'fills the need for disguise', but 'without requiring any serious distortion' (ibid.).

The gangster is a product of the city and the film's gangster is a product of the imaginary city created by cinema: 'the real city ... produces only criminals; the imaginary city produces the gangster' (Warshow 1964: 84). For reasons which are never made clear, this means that 'the gangster speaks for us, expressing that part of the American psyche which rejects the qualities and the demands of modern life'. The gangster 'is what we want to be and what we are afraid we may become' (ibid.). This works through the character of gangster films such as the 'classic' *Scarface*. 'The typical gangster films present a steady upward progress followed by a very precipitate fall.' The gangster's success and failure rest upon 'the unlimited possibility of aggression', since the gangster's life of crime is identified with 'the practice of brutality' (ibid.: 87).

In a later but related essay, Warshow suggests the gangster 'appeals most to adolescents with their impatience and their feeling of being outsiders'. Also, 'more generally he appeals to that side of all of us which refuses to believe in the 'normal' possibilities of happiness and achievement'. Thus, 'the gangster is the "no" to that great American "yes" which is stamped so big over our official culture and yet has so little to do with the way we really feel about our lives' (Warshow 1964: 90). Quite how Warshow knows this is unclear since no evidence is produced, but he is none the less led to conclude, in his main essay on the subject, that the gangster is ultimately 'doomed'. This is so because 'in the deeper layers of the modern consciousness ... every attempt to succeed is an act of aggression, leaving one alone and guilty and defenceless among enemies: one is *punished* for success'. The gangster film embodies 'our intolerable dilemma', which is 'that failure is a kind of death and success is evil and dangerous, is – ultimately – impossible'. It is resolved by the vicarious death of the gangster because 'it is *his* death, not ours' (ibid.: 88).

This is an unsubstantiated if not fanciful argument, which reads like a forerunner of much that now passes for cultural journalism and film studies. It has perhaps survived because relatively little has been written about the gangster film. To establish some guidelines it would be useful to outline here my misgivings with Warshow's argument.

First, Warshow does not prove his argument at key points. How does he know what people are thinking and how they react to gangster films? Like many writers about film, he uses what is tantamount to the 'royal we', the presumption that it is possible to speak on behalf of others without studying them first. How can he fathom 'the deeper layers of consciousness', know that the gangster film 'appeals most to adolescents', or assume that we share 'an intolerable dilemma' resolved only by the gangster film? What about people who do not like gangster films? Do they have an intolerable dilemma which is never resolved even though help is always at hand at the nearest cinema and, nowadays, can also be found on the television screen, or at the video shop?

Second, it might be possible to defend his stance by saying that he is really talking about the deeper, subconscious levels of the audience's mentality which are not obviously, or readily apparent. However, this does not mean they need always remain hidden like this, for how can knowledge of their existence be arrived at unless they sometimes come to the surface? Also, no mention is made of the methods used to gain knowledge of 'the deeper levels of modern consciousness'. These could, if outlined, tell us how the author knows what he claims to know. Since they are not mentioned, are we left with having to accept that he is a uniquely gifted individual who possesses privileged insight into what people are thinking?

Third, the significance of the Hollywood film's narrative struc-ture is neglected by Warshow and others who put forward similar arguments. We have noted above the main features of the typical narrative structure of the Hollywood genre film. While Warshow does note, for example, the rise and fall of the gangster in the gang-ster film, he does not address the substance of the genre's narrative. For example, a film such as *Little Caesar* is not just about the success and death of Rico. It is also very importantly about the achievement of his initial partner in crime, who leaves Rico and small-time crime, to pursue a successful career in show business. Could we not therefore say that the narrative of this film is saying 'yes' rather than 'no' to the American dream, provided it is achieved by a legitimate, rather than a criminal career? Equally, why can't his death be seen simply as representing the moral condemnation of the gangster and his violence? There are two ways by which Warshow and those who present a similar argu-ment can say it has more significance than this. They can make unwarranted assumptions about popular consciousness of the kind we have noted. Alternatively, they can draw out esoteric and peripheral, textual niceties marginal to the narrative of the films.

An example of this is the way the death of the gangster is

treated. The death of the gangster is obviously important in providing a typical and conclusive ending for many gangster films. The problem is rather that this death can easily be over-interpreted and more can be read into it than is necessary. For example, Gledhill cites the example of Jenkins, who argues that the significance of the gangster's death lies in how it invites an official and an emotional definition. Put somewhat simplistically, the scene is generally one where the gangster dies between the police officer 'who stands over the body and the woman, who often kneels by it or cradles the dead man's head'. The problem is that this scene is made to bear an interpretational weight it cannot carry. It is supposed to distinguish between two representational figures. The first is the police officer, who represents 'the official "meaning" of the death (public enemy dealt with)'. The other is the woman, who represents 'the audience's emotional investment in the character, the spectator's interest in the gangster's human qualities, which is developed through the woman's romantic interest' (Gledhill 1985: 90).

We cannot, of course, know that the audience have this emotional investment. It is again merely an unfounded assumption, which may be related to the fact that the audiences for films see them much less frequently than those who write about them. Equally, it is difficult to apply this interpretation of romantic interest to misogynistic gangster figures, such as Rico in *Little Caesar* who has no girlfriend, or Tom Powers, who is violent towards his in *Public Enemy*. It also appears irrelevant to the 'syndicate crime' cycle of the gangster genre. Even if we concede that there was some popular appreciation of the heroic status of the gangster, it appears to have been very short-lived, lasting only until 1933 (Whitehall 1964: 11, 40).

The deaths of gangsters also vary. In the first *Godfather* film Vito Corleone dies of a heart attack while playing games in a garden with his grandson. His son, Michael Corleone, stays alive but is alone and isolated at the end of the second film of the trilogy and he dies a natural death alone in his garden at the end of the third. There are other gangster films which do not have the ending referred to above. In one seemingly relevant example, *The Roaring*

Twenties, the woman has only an unrequited romantic interest in the gangster, a somewhat distant, emotional investment. Also, her closing comment at the end of the film, as she looks at the dead gangster – 'he used to be a big shot' – suggests a fatalistic regret that he wasted his time trying to succeed, for he has ended up a dead failure. His one, true, heroic act is to reject violently his life of crime and he dies, not because he is a gangster, but because he has ceased to be one. That he dies on the steps of a church may have more symbolic significance in that religion here 'transcends' all other meanings. It is also the gangster's only real salvation, as the end of *Angels With Dirty Faces* also suggests. This ending would tend to support, rather than contradict, the official line that crime does not pay. Neither the ideal ending the gangster film is presumed to have to express its contradiction between official and emotional definitions, nor the contradiction itself, are necessary. All that is required is that the gangster be punished, usually by his death. The view of writers such as Gledhill and Jenkins over-interprets what is only a particular instance of the death of the gangster in the gangster film.

Lastly, Warshow's argument – although he could not have realised it at the time – does not apply to later cycles of the gangster film (Ryall 1979: 16, cf. 11–12, 30). For example, the 1950s' cycle dealt with the bureaucratic organisation of crime, while *The Godfather* films located the gangster within the family. Of course, it is not obvious that Warshow's argument could accommodate the collective aspects of the gangster film.

Much of the subsequent literature which suggests that the gangster is an ideologically ambiguous figure has been usefully summarised by Gledhill (1985: 88–9). This often draws upon Warshow's argument and tries to present it in more sophisticated terms, while revising and extending its claims. Warshow's argument has been used to reject the idea that there are direct and immediate links between the gangster film and its social and historical reality (ibid.: 86; Ryall 1979: 15). It is also used to develop similar types of interpretation. The 'tragic hero' thesis is advanced, along with subsequent variations, which boil down to the theme of the ideological ambivalence of the screen gangster (Gledhill 1985: 86, 89–90).

Gledhill's discussion of the literature is helpful in noting some interesting points about the representation of the gangster. However, they are not always as prevalent, or as accurate, as is sometimes thought. The Hollywood system and its narrative and generic structures are rarely incorporated fully into the argument. For example, Schatz does try to link the genre to its technical and aesthetic limits, as well as to production and consumption. However, he suggests the industry's interest in maintaining the prevailing social order is compromised by the need 'to engage our sympathy for the criminal'. This results from the way 'the promulgation of safe ideologies is complicated by the technical and aesthetic requirements of the 'product'. Producers and consumers co-operate to refine 'genres that examined the more contradictory tenets of American ideology' (Gledhill 1985: 89). (Note that precisely what is contradictory is not made clear.) The death of the gangster is not a concession to the censorship groups lobbying Hollywood to observe the morality of the status quo. It is rather 'an aesthetic and ideological necessity, which recognises both sides of the contradiction that provides the dynamic of the genre'. This contradiction is clarified, in so far as it can be, by the 'appeal of the gangster'. This lies 'in his ability to grasp those goals for which the status quo says we should strive despite the minimal options it offers' (ibid.).

Even if we were to assume that this is indeed a function of the gangster film, there might be better ways of achieving it than a supposedly appealing representation of the gangster. There is no obvious link between the generic conventions of the gangster film and the need to portray the gangster in a sympathetic light. The concern with the role of censorship lobbies seems equally misplaced. They appear to have been more worried by the films' depiction of the official corruption of the police, the courts and business, than by the glamour and violence of the gangster (Whitehall 1964: 11).

However, what is perhaps most significant about these interpretations is how they neglect the influence of the typical Hollywood narrative upon the gangster film. For example, the claims made about the death of the gangster would appear to contradict the idea that the Hollywood narrative allows order to be restored at the end of the film. The popular appeal of the gangster, even when he dies, must, in these accounts, weaken the film's support of the status quo. However, this argument can be questioned since the death, or decline, of the gangster can be seen to provide the decisive ending Hollywood cinema has come to rely upon.

The gangster film developed early on as a distinct Hollywood genre, based upon the rise and fall of the gangster, as Warshow and others recognise (Warshow 1964: 85–7; Gledhill 1985). However, it is not as different from, or as contrary to, the ideology of Hollywood cinema as they seem to suggest. The gangster film can be fairly easily fitted into what has been argued above about the ideology and narrative of the Hollywood film. This ideology can cover not only the classic films, but also subsequent cycles of the genre. We cannot claim to know how intentional the production of this ideology has been. Nor can we pretend to know what, if any, influence it has had on audiences or how far, if at all, it has reflected their consciousness. None of these things can be inferred from the ideology and structure of film genres. We can, however, try to show how the gangster film, and not just the figure of the gangster, is consistent with the ideology and narrative of the Hollywood film as it has been described in Chapter 2.

Another way of making this point is to look at Raeburn's interpretation of the gangster film. He argues that the first films in this genre – his main example is *Little Caesar* – dealt directly with the gangster and his place in a wider ideological framework. What they thus did was to present, through the representations of gangsters such as Rico in *Little Caesar*, a critique of society and its values. He bases this on the claim that the gangster is outside society. 'Because, by definition, the gangster is beyond the boundaries of conventional society, he perforce presents a critique of that society' (1988: 48). This idea seems to figure to greater or lesser degrees, and in different guises, in a number of the arguments mentioned above.

We can question this interpretation, however. It is because the gangster is 'beyond' conventional society that he can become the focus of the moral anger of that society. It can be suggested that, even with the *Godfather* films, it is the gangster family which is outside normal society. The representation of the gangster would be far more dangerous if he were socially and ideologically integrated into society. This eventuality would suggest that the society as a whole was corrupt, potentially the real concern of moral censors as we have noted. The social order is supported and not criticised because it has no place for the gangster. Therefore, the gangster film can still represent the dominant morality and its critique of the gangster and his activities.

There are gangster films, such as *Angels With Dirty Faces* and *Dead End*, which hint at the possibility that poverty and deprivation can lead to crime and the gangster. However, the former indicates that this does not excuse the gangster; its ending, like that of *The Roaring Twenties*, shows how religion and individual salvation, but not social and political reform, can save even the gangster. There are other films, such as *Little Caesar* and *Public Enemy*, which suggest that the gangster has a warped view of the American dream and the path to fortune and fame. However, they usually contrast the gangster with someone who possesses a clear-sighted view of the dream and whose success does not entail a violent death. There are also films which see the gangster as representing a universal and timeless force of evil, such as those to be found in the *film noir* and syndicate cycles of the genre, as well as *Scarface* from the classic cycle. These clearly place the gangster outside society.

In conclusion, we can thus see how the gangster film does convey the typical ideology of the Hollywood film narrative. As we described earlier, this rested upon a three-fold development of the narrative: order, disruption and the restoration of order. This narrative entails an ideology which suggests that social order can be maintained. Social order is disrupted but is, in the end, restored. The narrative pattern and ideology indicate that the prevailing structure of power can be protected, even if it may have to accommodate aspects of the disruption for order to be effectively restored. The order restored at the end of the film remains largely consistent with the one at the start of the film. It has also been noted how the typical narrative pattern of the Hollywood film involves a number of features: psychological causation; unified, individual characters with a few, clear traits, who pursue specific goals, often in conflict with other individuals; a linear order of cause and effect sequences within which these matters advance; and a clear-cut ending which ties up all the loose ends and presents a fitting conclusion (see Chapter 2).

The gangster film is consistent with these ideological and narrative patterns. The Hollywood narrative can be related to the gangster film and its characteristic cycles, though it is not possible to prove this claim fully here. For example, the death, decline, or successful prosecution of the gangster, provides the conclusive ending the typical narrative demands. Likewise, the threads of the narrative, the crimes, the culpability of the gangster, the police and government agents' quest, are linked by the linear, cause and effect structure to lead up to this ending. Also, the focus upon specific, individual gangsters does not only indicate the prominence of psychological causality. It also reduces the social and political problem of organised crime to individual character traits, though in doing so it may often equally reduce it to specific ethnicities. This occurs even if lip service is paid to social conditions, for they usually serve merely as exotic background.

A similar argument can be applied to the ideology associated with this narrative. The problem the social order has to deal with is posed by the gangster and his criminal activities. A social order exists which is disrupted by the rise of the gangster. The gangster disrupts the social order by his extensive criminal operations that flout the law, by his callous violence that harms the non-criminal world and by his corruption that threatens to spread throughout the society. Various forces then have to come into play to deal with this disruption. They may involve the police, government agents and the law courts, but they can involve 'ordinary people' with grudges against the gangster because they have been crossed by him in business, or in love. They may involve weaknesses in the character of the gangster such as his pride; his desire for things he cannot have, for instance status and respect; and his obsessive pursuit of money, power and the American dream. Whatever their precise shape, they lead to the death, decline, or capture of the gangster. From this point of view, the death of the gangster represents the restoration of social order. The foundation of a new equilibrium may mean changes have to be made, such as making it less easy for gangsters to flourish. However, what is important is that the gangster film represents the return of social order. These narrative and ideological features characterise the gangster genre and can be applied to many of its examples. The contradictions and subtleties which many critics have noted can, from this point of view, be regarded at best as secondary, local and derivative variations of the genre. This chapter has tried to show how the gangster film is a product of the Hollywood system.

Chapter 4

The horror film

The horror film

Like the gangster film, the horror film raises issues relevant to an introduction to the sociology of film and film genres.[1] An indication of these issues has already been given in the general outline of genre contained in Chapter 2. To introduce the horror film, a number of points need to be made clear. Unlike the gangster film, the horror film relies more heavily on generic, as opposed to cultural realism. Genres do not usually exclude one in favour of the other, but clearly one can predominate. We tried to show how cultural realism has been characteristic of the gangster film and linked this to its production and consumption. By contrast, the horror film has been more reliant on generic realism and this is similarly linked to its production and consumption. For example, generic realism can allow us to make sense of certain cycles in the horror genre, particularly those in which it becomes increasingly self-conscious and self-referential.

The origins of the horror film are not as closely identified with America and mass culture as those of the gangster film. The horror film was consolidated as a film genre by Hollywood in the early 1930s and equally has important roots in American literature – the work of Edgar Allan Poe being one notable but not isolated example (Jancovich 1994: 9–10). However, it also has roots in European culture and English literature. Two of the main myths of horror, those of Frankenstein and Dracula, derive from novels published in Britain in the early and later parts of the nineteenth century. Mary Shelley's *Frankenstein* was published in 1818 and became also an equally successful stage play, while Bram Stoker's *Dracula*, which drew upon eastern European history and myth, was published in 1897. One important forerunner of the latter was Polidori's *The Vampire* which was published in 1819. Furthermore, Pirie has argued that gothic horror is a specific and

80

peculiarly English contribution to the horror genre. His case is that Hammer's production of horror films, which started in Britain in the late 1950s, revived the mythology of the English gothic tradition that had its roots in eighteenth-century literature. This, in turn, helped revive horror as a popular film genre (1973: chapter 1).

The narrative order of the popular horror film tends, in outline, to conform to that of the typical Hollywood film. This appears to apply whatever the theory held about horror and whatever the historical period at issue. Of course, emphases may differ and some endings may be more ambiguous than others. However, the order, disorder, restoration of order narrative remains the pattern that is followed. With the horror film, social order is disrupted by a monster who is usually, but not always, nonhuman or inhuman. This monster normally engages in murder and mayhem. It threatens the community by killing people in gruesome ways which are far from normal and which take on supernatural and incomprehensible qualities that characterise the monster itself. Eventually, usually through the acquisition of knowledge that can comprehend and combat the monster, the monster is confronted and killed. Since it is a monster from the supernatural world, this need not prevent it from returning for a sequel or two. Quite often the issue or dispute in the literature seems to concern how this narrative order is to be interpreted. Is it, for example, repressive or progressive? This type of question may arise because the horror film has attracted more theoretical attention than the gangster film and it will emerge again below when relevant.

These points will thus be returned to in the subsequent discussion. First, we shall consider how horror can be defined. Here, questions will be raised about what the horror film genre consists of, how it has been understood and how it relates to ideas about realism and to similar genres, such as science fiction. Second, we shall look at the cycles that have been said to characterise the history of the genre. This historical survey will indicate how the horror film genre, like all genres, has to be understood as a product of the Hollywood system. Finally, we shall consider some theories of horror which have tried to account for the significance, popularity and influence of the genre. This will necessarily draw upon the historical outline of the genre.

Definitions of horror

Attempts to define horror rest to some extent upon the arguments of which they form a part. For example, the horror film will be defined as a genre that represents the need for suppression if the horror shown is interpreted as expressing uncomfortable and disturbing desires which need to be contained. The best way to define horror would be to use the changing definitions with which the film industry tries to sell its products and audiences try to make sense of their consumption. Systematic evidence of this sort, however, is not available and a relatively independent set of criteria may still be needed to analyse the horror genre.

The commercial character of the genre needs to be recognised since it influences how films are defined in specific historical circumstances. For example, as Doherty has shown, the horror-cum-science fiction films popular with teenage audiences in 1950s America were called 'weirdies' (1988: 146–7). By contrast, not to present some guide to the definition would leave too many questions hanging in the air. For example, in his book on American horror films in the 1950s, Jancovich usefully contests attempts to separate horror from science fiction films. However, he then seems to fail to establish what horror consists of, so that both types of films are lumped together as horror, when differences clearly remain (1996: 10–18). He also fails to deal satisfactorily with the ambiguous status of a film such as *Psycho* (1960). This is defined as a horror film, but precisely why it should be is not made clear. It may be intended to invoke fear, but then so do thrillers, murder mysteries and action films. Fear is not the key.

A general view has developed that the horror film shows the monster, or the 'monstrous', and makes horror explicit and visible, rather than something merely hinted at and present through its absence (Pirie 1973: 41–2; Gledhill 1985: 101–5). This is not a bad start at distinguishing horror, but it only takes us so far. We need to be more systematic and to cover more of the substance of the genre. One useful way to start to do this, while not straying too far from the importance of commercial and popular definitions, is to turn again to Todorov's work. This work has been used by Murphy in his study of 1960s' British cinema (1992: 194–200) and his examples can be used to illustrate the points Todorov makes, noting that the latter is talking about literature.

Todorov distinguishes three forms relevant to horror as a genre: the uncanny, the marvellous and the fantastic. All three, to varying degrees, are categories of horror as a genre of popular culture. Todorov argues that at the end of a story which involves elements of the supernatural, or events which appear unreal, impossible or irrational, the reader can be led to one of three conclusions. The reader can decide 'that the laws of reality remain intact and permit an explanation of the phenomena described' (1973: 41). This defines the first category as the uncanny. With the uncanny, 'events are related which may be readily accounted for by the laws of reason, but which are ... incredible, extraordinary, shocking, singular, disturbing or unexpected' (ibid.: 46). Also, 'it is uniquely linked to the sentiments of the characters and not to a material event defying reason', unlike the marvellous (ibid.: 47), although it has also to be linked to the reactions of the reader or viewer. We can note here that, although it is not what is often thought of as horror, the uncanny is still associated with evoking fear.

Examples of the uncanny, 'the supernatural explained' (Todorov 1973: 41), would include any story or film in which seemingly strange and inexplicable events were the outcome of human agency, or open to rational explanation. It would cover what has become known as 'the psychological thriller'. Murphy cites the examples of films such as *Taste of Fear* (1961) and *Nightmare* (1964) in which victims are the subject of conspiracies to send them mad for financial gain, or other secular interests. It could also be argued to cover conventional science fiction. In this genre, for example, the monsters (aliens) encountered can be considered part of the natural order. Whether they come from millions of light years away and far distant planets, or whether they are met by humans travelling to these outer reaches of the universe, they are not supernatural. Rather they are still part of the natural order and represent the limits of human knowledge. Aliens may be non-human, but they are not unnatural. They do not depend upon the existence of the supernatural, which includes phenomena such as 'the undead'.

This category would also include *Psycho*, which is often seen as a horror film (Buscombe 1986: 20; Jancovich 1996: 220–32) though it is equally a psychological thriller, the genre most popularly associated with Hitchcock. In this film, Norman Bates, a young man apparently possessed by the spirit of his dead mother, commits a number of gruesome murders. Though human, he is the monster in the film and if his actions were not accounted for, then we might clearly be in the realm of horror. However, at the end of the film, a psychologist presents a rational account of Bates's behaviour, attributing it to a form of schizophrenia. One of the last shots in the film is of the murderer looking as monstrous as ever, but since it ends with a rational explanation, it counts as an example of the uncanny.

This contrasts with Todorov's second type, the marvellous. With this form, seemingly irrational or incomprehensible events can only be explained by accepting, for the purposes and duration of the film or story, the existence of another level of reality: the supernatural. This reality differs radically from normal experience. Unlike the uncanny, the reader is lead to conclude that 'new laws of nature must be entertained to account for the phenomena' (Todorov 1973: 41), the inexplicable and seemingly supernatural events described in the story or film. This is what defines the marvellous, the acceptance of another level of reality to explain 'events ... which are ... incredible, extraordinary, shocking, singular, disturbing or unexpected' (ibid.: 46). It is linked to 'the mere presence of supernatural events, without implicating the reaction they provoke in the characters', unlike the uncanny (ibid.: 47). This means that the supernatural events are meant to exist and to be seen to exist and are not subject to, or dependent for their existence upon, the perceptions of the characters. In the marvellous, the supernatural is visible. This is comparable to Pirie's idea that the horror film is defined, in part, by the visibility of horror (Pirie 1973: 41–2).

What is popularly and conventionally thought of as horror is usefully equated with the marvellous. This can help to distinguish horror from science fiction and the psychological thriller. 'In the marvellous', Murphy writes, 'events which we would think of as impossible (a man being made from dismembered corpses, a creature that sucks human blood and can only die by having a wooden stake driven into its heart) are accepted as part of the normal order of things' (1992: 194). The marvellous is synonymous with a common understanding of horror and with the generic realism which characterises this genre.[2] Horror films, 'where zombies, vampires and werewolves exist and only unenlightened fools question that brains and even souls can be transferred from body to body, can be classified as marvellous' (ibid.: 194–5). Demonic horror and the Dracula and Frankenstein myths can be considered examples of the marvellous.

We can introduce and clarify Todorov's third category, that of the fantastic, by referring to his literary example, Henry James's story, *The Turn of the Screw*. This is, he argues, 'a remarkable example ... which does not permit us to determine finally whether ghosts haunt the old estate, or whether we are confronted by the hallucinations of a hysterical governess victimised by the disturbing atmosphere which surrounds her' (1973: 43). Murphy treats a film version of this story, *The Innocents* (1962), in much the same light. He suggests the film conjures up 'a subjective world which may signify the drift of ... [the governess] into madness but may equally indicate the presence of supernatural forces' (1992: 195). Other examples Murphy mentions include 'Tourneur's 1940s films *Cat People* and *I Walked With a Zombie*' in which 'it is impossible to determine whether the bizarre events which occur are figments of a fevered imagination or manifestations of the supernatural' (ibid.).

This is what Todorov means by the fantastic. The reader is not lead to any definite conclusion about the causes of the inexplicable and supernatural events in the film or story. They are attributable neither to rational explanations, as with the uncanny, nor to an alternative level of existence, as with the marvellous (1973: 157, cf. 41). The fantastic, according to Todorov, leads the reader 'to hesitate between a natural and a supernatural explanation of the events described', a hesitation which can be shared by a character in the story or film (ibid.: 33, cf. 157). However, there is no resolution of this hesitation, otherwise the form will become either uncanny or marvellous. This is because, 'by the hesitation it engenders, the fantastic questions precisely the existence of an irreducible opposition between real and unreal' (ibid.: 167). Another example would be *The Shining* (1980), at the end of which we are not sure whether the man who has become the axe monster is clinically mad, or possessed by demons from the past.

While it is obviously not the last word on the subject, Todorov's distinctions do seem to make some sense of the types of stories and representations which have been included within horror and related genres. It describes many of the different films which have, at one time or another, been defined as horror films. Clearly, his scheme lacks any direct relation to the production and consumption of popular film genres. We shall need to assume the importance of this context, as well as indicate its relevance, as we go along. However, as we have seen, Todorov's scheme does describe themes, images and myths which are typically associated with horror, as well as science fiction and psychological thrillers. It also describes notable cycles in the horror genre, such as 1940s psychological horror, along with leading examples of the genre, such as *The Shining* and the defining myths of Dracula, Frankenstein and the Werewolf. While Todorov's overall analysis is not necessarily ahistorical, it does not relate the scheme as a whole to historical changes. Therefore, we now need to consider the cyclical changes the horror film has undergone, as it has developed as a popular film genre.

Cycles of horror

Universal and the 'horror classics'

The formation of popular cinematic horror is usually seen to lie in the cycle of films made by Universal in the early 1930s. The argument is similar to that made about the 'classic' gangster films of the same period which we considered in the previous chapter. The estab-lish-ment of the studio system and the arrival of sound helped shape the development of Hollywood's film genres. The horror genre is no exception.

Sound was important for the development of the horror film. Cook suggests that strange sound effects and literary dialogue could be introduced into the filming of the original, classic horror novels (1990: 296). As we have already noted, sound emerged along with the entrenchment of the Hollywood system. However, film horror itself has its roots in German cinema and German expressionism, even if the first Hollywood versions were less dark and less focused on internal, psychological states than their silent forerunners. Many films about the main horror myths were made before the coming of sound. For example, six films based upon Robert Louis Stevenson's *Dr. Jekyll and Mr. Hyde* were released between 1908 and 1920 (Maltin 1991; Wood 1988: 212–13). The German film industry produced some of the earliest examples of horror, including *Nosferatu* (1922), based on the Dracula myth, and *The Golem* (1915 and 1920), which has some things in common with the Frankenstein myth. In addition, for many *The Cabinet of Dr. Caligari* (1919) is the source of film horror, as well as a leading example of German expressionism (Prawer 1980: chapters 1, 6; Cook 1990: 112, 117–21, 124–6; Robinson 1997). Thus, 'artistically, the major influence came from Germany as first the styles of *Caligari* and *Nosferatu* were imitated' and 'the artists themselves immigrated to the Los Angeles area', notably to 'Universal Pictures, where the most influential films were produced' (Wood 1988: 213; Cook 1990: 132, 231–3). Hollywood's first and major horror classics – *Dracula* (1931), *Frankenstein* (1931) and *The Mummy* (1932) – were all sound films produced by Universal in the early 1930s (Cook 1990: 296).

Universal 'united the visual style of the German horror film with a strong grasp of popular narrative form' and turned it into a commercial success (Jancovich 1992: 55). This starts with the Dracula and Frankenstein films and includes other examples such as *The Bride of Frankenstein* (1933), which makes explicit the origins of the Frankenstein myth in Mary Shelley's novel, and

Dracula's Daughter (1936) (Cook 1990: 313–14; cf. Jancovich 1992: 53–8; Huss and Ross 1972). Cook sees a resurgence of this cycle in the late 1930s with *Son of Frankenstein* (1939) and *The Wolfman* (1941). However, he says it 'quickly lapsed into imitation and self-parody with titles like ... *Frankenstein Meets the Wolfman* (1943)' and then petered out (1990: 313–14). Jancovich notes that 'by the 1940s, Universal's films had become largely moribund and relied on poor rehashes of the 1930s formula or direct self-parody' (1992: 59).

This cycle is often thought to consist of a set of conservative or reactionary films. It is argued that it portrays the monster as a threat whose death is necessary to restore and maintain social order. We shall consider this theory more fully below. However, it is useful to note here that this cycle has been associated with the view that horror is a reactionary genre. Of course, this view is not limited to this cycle. Nor does this cycle have to be interpreted in this way, but it does provide a useful way of beginning to discuss these films.

The first Dracula film made by Universal can be interpreted as a repressive film. It shows how the social and sexual order is restored when the threat posed by Dracula to society and its women is eradicated by his destruction. Dracula is an outsider, an 'exotic' and dangerous foreigner and the harm and devastation he can bring to his victims are, thereby, all the more damaging. His death therefore restores order to society and ensures safety for its women. For example, as G. Wood puts it, 'sexual temptation in the form of European outsiders like Dracula must be overcome in the interest of the family and church. Heterosexual love and sexuality sanctified by marriage ... were the norms that had to be upheld in times of disorder' (1988: 213). He makes a similar argument about *Frankenstein*, which he sees as a warning about 'the dangers of' science 'tampering with the natural order' (ibid.).

This view is to some extent shared by R. Wood, whose influential psychoanalytical theory, based on the ideas of repression, the repressed and its return, will be discussed below. Here it will be enough to see how he interprets this cycle of films. His theory focuses most closely upon modern horror, in particular the 'progressive' horror films of the 1970s, but he does see it offering 'a comprehensive survey of horror film monsters from German expressionism onwards' (1986: 75). His theory also relies on identifying 'repressive' horror as well, such as the films from the 1930s.

Interestingly, he views *Frankenstein* as representing the repression of the threat posed by the proletariat, 'partly on the strength of its pervasive class references but more on the strength of Karloff's costume' (Wood 1986: 76). Presumably, industrial capitalism's science creates the proletariat (the monster) which threatens its existence. To prosper, bourgeois capitalism relies on the repression of the proletariat. The monster's destruction has then to be represented on film to indicate and secure its repression.

One point to note is that in the original Universal film, the whole society is mobilised to destroy the monster. So we have to assume either that these people are not working class (so what are they?), or that we are seeing a pre-class, pre-capitalist society. Also, Tudor has offered an interpretation of *Dracula* which also relies on class representations to make sense of what we see in the film. In his view Dracula, the decadent and dying aristocratic parasite, feeding on the blood of the peasants, is usurped and destroyed by the rational and scientific, urban middle class portrayed by Dr Van Helsing. He argues 'the bourgeois comes to the aid of the people against the aristocracy' (1974: 210), thus linking the story to the transition from feudalism to capitalism (cf. Jancovich 1992: 48–52). R. Wood stresses as well the foreign and external nature of the monster in 1930s' film horror, which makes its repression all the more urgent (1986: 76).

A problem with relying on a rigid application of this interpretation concerns the appeal or attractiveness of the monster. After all, Dracula has to have a seductive appeal for women which enables him to turn them into his victims. Similarly, it is Frankenstein the scientist who is the central monster in these films, not just the monstrous artificial life form he creates: the monster is human and the monster he makes is also a victim (Tudor 1974: 210). The appeal of the monster is emphasised to varying degrees by some theoretical approaches and it is said to indicate tensions in these films which the restoration of order does not completely obliterate.

Psychological horror

The recognition of this tension and the more subtle uses to which horror can be put, is often thought to characterise what is commonly seen as the next cycle of the popular horror genre. This is what Cook refers to as the 'atmospheric, low-budget horror cycle of RKO producer Val Lewton' which lasted from 1942 to 1946 (1990: 470). 'Beginning with *Cat People* and concluding with *Bedlam*, these films, by Lewton's own definition, were films of "psychological horror"' (G. Wood 1988: 214; cf. Farber 1972). They were films which relied upon 'atmosphere and suspense' and the idea that horror might 'even be imaginary' (Jancovich 1992: 59). They thus conform closely to what is called the 'fantastic'. They present strange, bizarre or puzzling events without accounting for them rationally, or indicating that they are obvious products of the supernatural. What they represent might be open to a rational, or a supernatural, explanation, but it is not clear which is appropriate. A good example is *Cat People* (1942) in which 'a woman believes herself to be descended from creatures who transform themselves into murderous cats when they are kissed. It is never clear if her belief in the supernatural is justified, or whether the explanation for the story could be psychological' (ibid.).

The films of Lewton were clearly products of the studio system as it began to change in the 1940s. They were 'B' pictures produced on low budgets (G. Wood 1988: 215). But they were therefore able to use, as did *film noir*, the limited autonomy this afforded to be more creative with the material available. This leads Jancovich to conclude that these films were the 'only significant' contribution to the horror film between the 1930s and the 1950s, dealing as they did with the 'themes of alienation, paranoia and fantasy' (1992: 59–61). At the very least, themes such as these could be represented and explored by the horror film as a result of low budgets and a consistent production cycle.

The next cycle of the horror film appears to contain a number of related elements. The 1940s saw the contraction of the original cinematic cycle and the turn to psychological horror, particularly the fantastic. By contrast, in the 1950s, horror with a science fiction slant, the rise of the teenage audience and Hammer film's rejuvenation of the horror classics were all significant developments of the genre. These changes need to be set in the context we have already established. Because of declining cinema attendances and the increasing popularity of television, Hollywood had to become more competitive. This meant its products had to be different from those offered by television: hence, for example, the spectacular effects afforded by horror and science fiction. It also meant defining the audience as a specialised set of consumers, rather than as a homogeneous mass: for example, marketing 'weirdies' for the growing number of teenage cinema-goers. Hammer films in the UK drew upon the English gothic horror tradition, as well as the horror myths initially used by Universal in the 1930s and the latter eventually provided financial backing for such films. Hammer also provides a good example of how a small, independent studio operated in producing 'B' films. It was characterised by low budgets, strict financial control, tight shooting schedules, cost cutting and efficient production techniques. Moreover, the box office success in America of Hammer's first horror film, *The Curse of Frankenstein*, in 1957, led American producers to return to the horror myths and monsters of Universal's classic cycle.

Horror and science fiction in the 1950s

The use of special effects became one way by which Hollywood tried to hang on to its audiences in the 1950s. Both science fiction and horror films were well placed to exploit some of the special effects of the time, such as 3-D, a leading, if short-lived, technique used in this struggle to retain audiences. Science fiction films such as *It Came From Outer Space* (1953) and *The Creature From the Black Lagoon* (1954), and horror films such as *The Maze* (1953) and *Phantom of the Rue Morgue* (1954), were all first shown in 3-D (Cook 1990: 486).

There are, indeed, examples of science fiction films made before the end of the Second World War. However, according to D. Cook, it was in the early 1950s that 'the modern science fiction film, with its emphasis on global catastrophe and space travel, began to take shape' (1990: 518). As we have noted, one main reason for this was that Hollywood made use of 'state-of-the-art special effects' in these films to attract audiences (ibid.: 519). Also, the cycle was initially a product of the majors, but the potential for independent producers to make a commercial success of low budget science fiction films was quickly recognised.

However, for authors such as Cook, 'with the war and the threat of nuclear holocaust came a widespread recognition that science and technology were in a position to affect the destiny of the entire human race' (Cook 1990: 518; cf. G. Wood 1988: 215–16). This recognition played its part in the emergence of the cycle of 1950s' science fiction films, which incorporated the horror film's representation of the monster into their conception of the alien invaders. They generally concerned a terrestrial or extra-terrestrial threat of some kind and introduced monsters created by nuclear radiation or a similar cause, as well as aliens from outer space, into the cycle. They also supplied representations of Cold War politics, since the threat of alien invasion was said to invoke anxieties about invasion and annihilation by the Soviet Union. It may therefore be no accident that the planet thought to contain the greatest threat to the earth was Mars, the 'red' planet named after the Roman god of war, a good example being *Red Planet Mars* (1952). The relevant examples cited by D. Cook include, other than those already mentioned, *The Thing* (1951), *Destination Moon* (1950), *The Day the Earth Stood Still* (1951), *Invaders from Mars* (1953), *War of the Worlds* (1954), *Forbidden Planet* (1956) and *Invasion of the Body Snatchers* (1956) (1990: 518–19; cf. G. Wood 1988: 215–16; Hodgens 1959).

It is this invasion narrative which Jancovich (1996) is particularly critical of in the interpretations made of the horror and science fiction films of the 1950s. However, his critique is directed at the content of these interpretations rather than at the theory of representation they imply. He does not question the value and relevance of interpreting films as reflections of a wider culture and ideology. Instead of seeing films as the products of their conditions of production, consumption and the consequent interplay of varying ideologies, he tends to explain their significance by a specific ideology. He thus substitutes the emergence of an ideology of 'Fordist' rationality for that of the Cold War. He argues that these films are just as much about American society as they are expressions of fears about foreign invasion and global devastation.

In particular, Jancovich contests the argument that 1950s' American horror (he sees these films as horror films) was necessarily and consistently repressive and reactionary. One of the targets of his criticism is R. Wood's thesis about repressive horror which we have already mentioned and which has been applied to the 1950s, as well as to the 1930s and 1980s. According to Jancovich, Wood 'dismisses the 1950s as an essentially reactionary period in horror' (1996: 2). In response, Jancovich makes a number of points which he develops at various stages in his book on this topic. First, the 'invasion narrative', the alien, Cold War interpretation we have mentioned above, does not characterise many of the horror films of this period. Second, even invasion narratives differ from film to film. Third, very different conclusions to those drawn by the invasion narrative interpretation can be arrived at by a broader look at a larger number of examples, including horror in other media. Fourth, these films 'were at least as concerned with developments within American society as they were with threats from without' (ibid.).

In this, they display a concern with the rationality of modern society, which the 'invasion narrative' interpretation fails to recognise. The 1950s horror film can therefore be understood as an examination of the rationalisation of American society. Jancovich defines rationalisation as 'the process through which scientific-technical rationality is applied to the management of social, economic and cultural life ... in an attempt to produce order and efficiency' (Jancovich: 1996: 2–3; cf. part 1). More specifically, he claims that 'Fordism', a precise type of rationality, became 'the context of American life in the 1950s' (ibid.: 18). By 'Fordism' he means 'a system of centrally ordered administration which relied on an elite of experts. It was their task to regulate social, political, economic and cultural life and they did so through the use of scientific-technical rationality' (ibid.: 19).

There are two related problems with this interpretation. First, the evidence for the rationalisation process is drawn from theoretical rather than empirical sources. This means, second, that the films are interpreted as an expression of ideology rather than of people's social experiences at the time. Rationality is something that theorists have argued about in a number of different ways. As Jancovich notes, it has been conceived of as 'the Power elite', 'the Technocratic society' and 'Mass Society', as well as 'the Postindustrial society' (1994: 11). The theorists assumed the appearance of some sort of rationalisation process, but disagreed about its value and effects. Some thought rationalisation should occur because a rationally ordered society is a good society. Others criticised it because they thought it eroded individuality and encouraged collective conformity, or enabled capitalism to dominate society and shape it in its image. Yet others bemoaned the onset of rationalisation, but thought it might bring economic and other benefits.[3]

The point is that these were usually theoretical arguments or pleas for reform, which said very little about the actual presence of rationalisation in America and other comparable societies. Also, such views did not gain universal approval. For example, the relevant work of the Frankfurt School is hardly weighed down with empirical evidence, while Mills's work was concerned to establish the existence of, and the control exerted by, 'the Power Elite' in America (Strinati 1995: chapter 2; Mills 1956). Critics have suggested Mills exaggerated this power anyway (Bell 1962: chapter 3). Other critics have argued that mass society theory and the post-industrial thesis misconceived the nature of social change (Strinati 1995: chapter 1; Giddens 1973: 255–64). The former has been criticised for over-emphasising the power of central institutions and the fragmentation of society and the latter for exaggerating the roles of rationality, the university and scientific knowledge. Also, some empirical sociologists questioned the extent to which bureaucratic rationality and control had been enforced in the workplace (Gouldner 1954).

Unless we can establish that rationality worked, we have to restrict it to a limited and distinct dispute over ideas. It does not appear to have been 'the context of American life in the 1950s'

(Jancovich 1996: 18), for which the Cold War seems as least as relevant. And would we not have to demonstrate the empirical emergence of 'Fordism' if it had the effect on the horror film Jancovich suggests? It may have been a current concern of the time but for whom? Although it may not be not a conclusive point, no evidence is presented to show that film makers or audiences necessarily shared the fears of the theorists. These films are understood as ways of representing and dealing with the ideology of rationalisation, rather than as expressions of Cold War ideology. Another interesting way of looking at these films may be the result. However, apart from a partial reading of some of the films, we are not told why one interpretation may be preferable to the other. Perhaps both say something about the content of these films. But they do not take us very far when it comes to understanding how and why they were produced and consumed. No theory is advanced, for example, to explain why popular film should indeed be the place in which ideological concerns are aired and assessed.

Teenage horror

We now need to consider the growth of the teenage audience for the horror and science fiction films of the 1950s. This will make even clearer the lack of context in interpretations such as those offered by Jancovich and the writers he criticises. The discussion of these films can be linked to some of the changes in the cinema audience which occurred in the 1950s. As we have noted, science fiction and horror films became popular and successful in the 1950s. The majors were important producers, but low budget films made by 'independents' gained a foothold in the market. The most notable example of the latter was AIP, which involved Roger Corman as a producer, director and writer. AIP found it was profitable to make monster and 'teen rock' films for the teenage audience. Television and the Hollywood 'A' picture tended to attract the adult audience, while teenagers were drawn to science fiction and horror. These films were initially 'B' features, but were soon sold as double feature packages to control the market better and make more money simply because two films could be sold rather than one. The majority of low budget monster films were seen as part of double bill features which were promoted together. The success of AIP led other independents to copy their formula (D. Cook 1990: 524).

The science fiction horror film was an effective way for Hollywood to distinguish its films from television by the use it made of special effects, wide screens and better sound, make-up and models. This obviously depended on the size of the budget allocated, but it was possible for even low budget films to use these developments successfully. The more serious and adult science fiction film was one result, a leading example being *Forbidden Planet* (1956). But the most profitable product was the low budget, high profile, 'exploitation' film aimed at the teenage market (Doherty 1988: 145–6, 156, cf. chapter 6 *passim*). While many of these films did not contain the expensive special effects of 'A' features, they were still able to profit from the increasing level of technical sophistication possible even with low budgets.

These films began to be called 'weirdies' by producers and consumers alike and became a distinct sub-genre. The term itself, it appears, was initially coined by the trade papers of the time, but it is at least indicative of some degree of popular understanding (Doherty 1988: 146). The term 'weirdies' provides a good example of the importance of the social context in determining the genre status of a particular set of films. 'Weirdies' were cheaply financed and produced science fiction, fantasy and monster films, exploitatively titled, aggressively promoted and designed to shock. They were also highly profitable and blended the horror and science fiction cycles of the 1950s; for example, a double feature might contain a science fiction and a horror picture (ibid.: 146–51).

AIP thought that the teenage market had become the mainstay of the film industry and thus began to produce a large number of low cost and luridly promoted 'weirdies' to meet its demands (Doherty 1988: 153–60). One of the best examples was *I Was a Teenage Werewolf* (1957), though there are a large number of examples, many of which have already been mentioned above (ibid.: 160–7, 150–1, 155). They were often made quickly, with the title and advertising frequently decided before the script was commissioned or written. They received aggressive and exploitative advertising and promotion, which played on the elements of fear and shock, as well as humour. Saturation booking and television and radio were used to promote the films. The foyers of cinemas were decorated in keeping with the films being shown so that coffins splashed with imitation blood, grotesque monster dummies and dancing skeletons greeted the incoming audiences. This even involved producers offering to insure members of the audience against their dying as a result of seeing the film, or paying 'fright victims' to collapse in terror at selected screenings (ibid.: 147–8, 156, 167–72). The merchandising of related products, such as monster masks, fanzines, comics and books, was also an important feature of the economics of this genre (ibid.: 171–2).

The content of these films was often ostensibly violent, gruesome and horrifying, but it is argued that both producers and audiences treated them as examples of humour or comedy. They were deemed to be fantasy films, not, unsurprisingly, realistic slices of life. They were 'tongue-in-cheek' films, not to be taken too seriously. The horror – the blood, the gore, the monster, the acts of violence – was meant to be funny not frightening. This was one of the defences the producers put up when accused by moral and censorship lobbies of using the horror in these films to exploit and corrupt the nation's teenagers, warping their minds and inciting them to violence and other acts of depravity. This is, of course, a convenient and protective ideology for the producers because it means that the films could be considered safe and therefore could continue to be produced and distributed. However, there is evidence that audiences also saw them in the same, humorous and facetious light. Doherty notes that 'teenagers seemed to agree there were often more "titters than terror" at a horror teenpic' (1988: 160, 156–60, 172–5).

At the very least, these conditions, which marked the production and reception of these films, must have affected the influence of any ideology they are thought to have carried. An awareness of this level of analysis should perhaps be taken into account when trying to assess the ideological content, intent and consequences of a set of films. It could be argued that in this case, since the films were not taken that seriously, their ideological impact would have been diluted and ineffectual. Moreover, it does not follow that just because films may concern a particular topic they have anything of substance to say about it and that it is this subject matter which attracts audiences. Nor does this necessarily provide the key to the meaning of such films. For example, as Hodgens remarks of this cycle, 'a twelve-ton, woman-eating cockroach does not say anything about the bomb simply because it, too, is radioactive or crawls out of a test-site' (1959: 37).

This cycle also witnessed the return to the horror myths that figured in the earlier phase initiated by Universal in the 1930s. This was the result of the American success of Hammer's *The Curse of Frankenstein* in 1957 and the screening on television of the classic horror films (Doherty 1988: 142, 147–51). Dracula, vampires, werewolves and Frankenstein and the havoc and terror they invoked therefore became stock characters and events in horror films during the late 1950s. Hammer's success, which continued with the subsequent horror films it made, occasioned a shift in the 'weirdie' from science fiction to gothic horror, though the USSR's launch of the Sputnik in 1957 led to a series of science fiction related films (ibid.: 152–3). The gothic horror phase was further developed by Roger Corman with a succession of films based on the stories of Edgar Allan Poe in the early 1960s, starting with *House of Usher* (1960) and ending with *The Tomb of Ligea* (1965) (D. Cook 1990: 525–6).

Hammer horror

Hammer did not start out making horror films, but played an important role in this period of the horror film. Hammer made an interesting contribution to the science fiction genre with the *Quatermass* trilogy, which comprised film versions of the television series. Indeed, television becomes more relevant to genre developments from the 1950s onwards. However, Hammer is best known for reviving the classic horror myths by returning them to their gothic origins and producing them as commercial successes, using an independent studio structure.

Pirie has suggested that 'the most obvious analogy' Hammer shares 'is with one of the small Hollywood studios of the 1930s and forties like Republic or Monogram'. He argues that 'almost overnight Hammer became a highly efficient factory for a vast series of exploitation pictures made on tight budgets with a repertory company of actors and a small, sometimes over-exposed, series of locations'. Hammer 'established a consistent "B" feature pattern whereby the credits changed only a fraction from film to film with perhaps one variable factor, script or direction or camera, among the constants'. This may well have meant that 'even in the early 1950s ... Hammer proved unusually flexible in coming to terms with the idea of genre, which the American cinema had been manipulating successfully for about thirty years. Financially this was reflected in the fact that they were the first British company to participate in American co-production.' It is also evident in the way Hammer 'reintroduced into Britain, the cinema of action and spectacle, of imagination and myth' (1973: 42–3, 26–7, 48, cf. 25–49; Gledhill 1985: 44–7; Jancovich 1992: 73–7).

Hammer started as a low budget film producer. This involved adapting radio programmes as well as turning out standard 'B' features, with American actors in lead roles and distribution rights for the American market. In the early 1950s, American companies were confronted with a particular problem. Production in Hollywood was becoming increasingly expensive, but they were earning money in Britain from film distribution which an agreement prevented from being fully repatriated. They thus looked to Britain as a place where cheap films could be made and co-production deals could work. At the same time, television was becoming increasingly popular, the X certificate, introduced in 1951, was used only sparingly and the double bill began to fade out. Therefore, horror in the UK could attract audiences, particularly the youth audience, to the cinema because it could exploit the relaxation of censorship afforded by the X certificate and provide an alternative to television (Street 1997: 76). However, Pirie says that even by the time Hammer started to produce its first horror film, X-rated films still faced censorship difficulties from censors, local watchdog committees and the cinema chains (1973: 39).

Whatever the precise weight given to specific factors, this context led Hammer to look for a new and distinctive type of film. The result was the cycle of colour and X-certificate horror films based upon the English gothic tradition. Pirie focuses upon the 'uniqueness of English gothic cinema' as the 'fundamental source' of Hammer horror's phenomenal financial and international success. This is a horror which works because of its visibility and its vividness and which has an aesthetic quality at the heart of its appeal (1973: 10, 9, 22).[4] Interestingly enough, Hammer's initial financial success came with the science fiction films *The Quatermass Xperiment* (1955) and its sequel *Quatermass II* (1956). However, these films did incorporate elements of horror, particularly with the bodily and psychic transformations which eventually produced the monsters.

Hammer switched to producing straight, gothic-inspired horror in 1956 with *The Curse of Frankenstein* (1957), an international box-office success which led to the series of Dracula films, starting with *Dracula* (1958). Warner Brothers had agreed distribution rights in America for *Frankenstein*, while Universal agreed them for *Dracula*. Universal had already made film versions of these and other horror myths and held the copright to their visual representations. This meant they could not be used by Hammer. So, for example, it had to reinvent the representation of Frankenstein. However, due to the huge success of *Dracula*, Universal gave Hammer the remake rights for all their old horror films while retaining distribution rights. (Indeed, Hammer produced the first colour film versions of both *Dracula* and *Frankenstein*.) The financial success of Hammer films was thus ensured by their popularity in the American market. This continued with remakes of, and sequels to, the original horror classics, which were given the distinctive gothic horror treatment, such as *The Mummy* (1959).

It lasted in the UK and America until the late 1960s. Then American companies began to withdraw from film production in

Britain even though Hammer's films still performed well at the box office. Hammer retained its American distribution deals, but found it more difficult to get regular finance in the UK. Eventually the size of the audience was not large enough to encourage and secure distribution in America, while competition from Hollywood in the fields of horror and science fiction increased. *The Exorcist* (1973) introduced a newer and more spectacular dimension to the horror film, while *Star Wars* (1977) signalled the rise of the blockbuster and linked it with the science fiction film. The former, in particular, is thought to have made Hammer's films look increasingly pale and dated.

The cycle of Hammer films had always relied upon the need for generic variation. It had used the established conventions of horror, but introduced variations as the development of the cycle demanded. By the late 1960s, when signs of financial decline began to appear, self-parody became more evident, one good example being *Taste the Blood of Dracula* (1969), which was advertised with the slogan 'drink a pint of blood a day' (Gledhill 1985: 47). This turn to self-parody had also eventually emerged in the Universal cycle of the 1930s. A more explicit approach to representing sex and sexuality, which had been apparent earlier in the cycle, also became more obvious. A good example of this was the female vampire and lesbian sub-cycle of the late 1960s and early 1970s: *The Vampire Lovers* (1970), *Lust for a Vampire* (1970), *Countess Dracula* (1970) and *Twins of Evil* (1971). Along with this, attempts were made to bring the genre up to date by setting Dracula and the vampire myth in the modern world, examples being *Dracula A.D. 1972* (1972) and *The Satanic Rites of Dracula* (1973). However, these attempts appear to have been unsuccessful in reviving the fortunes of Hammer horror.

Modern horror and modern society

There have been a number of developments in the horror film from the 1960s onwards. Some of these, such as the rise of Hammer horror and Corman's cycle of American gothic films, have been noted above. Not all of these developments, notably the debate about *Psycho* (1960), can be pursued at length here. In any event, we have already noted how *Psycho* can represent the uncanny variant of horror and Jancovich has also questioned the uniqueness of its contribution to the development of the horror film (1996: 220–32).[5] There are, however, a number of issues which are relevant to the cycles of the horror film genre. These include the emergence of new types of horror in the 1960s, the so-called 'slasher' and related cycles of the 1970s and the rise of the horror/science fiction blockbuster in the 1970s and 1980s.

It has been argued that, in the 1960s, the horror film began to focus more specifically on modern society. Some have seen this in the greater prominence given to the family as a social institution. This is a key aspect of R. Wood's theory (1986) and it has been regarded as something *Psycho* introduced into the horror film. However, Jancovich questions this view. He concedes that the 'concern with the family and with the instability of identity ... was to become one of the central problems within contemporary horror' (1994: 19). Yet this was not confined to the influence of *Psycho*, but was equally attributable to Corman's films based on the work of Edgar Allan Poe. Also, despite what Wood suggests, the family is not necessarily represented as the most basic unit of American society. Instead, it takes its place as 'only one element in a more general series of institutions and processes which penetrate and shape one another' (1986: 20). He mentions *Rosemary's Baby* as an example here because it focuses not only on the family, but also the Catholic Church and the media.

But whatever can be said about the family, it may be true that horror has become more concerned with the contemporary world. For example, as noted, Hammer began to set Dracula in the modern world in its search for ways of rejuvenating the vampire story. One argument which has some relevance here is the way Denne has linked the world of the horror film's monsters to the social world. He identifies three distinct types of monster film. The first type is the 'atmospheric' film where the world represented is that of the monster or 'of society as distorted and changed by the monster and his forces' (1972: 125). A good example of this is the *Dracula* film. The second type is the 'bipartite' film where 'the struggle occurs between and among two distinct environments' (ibid.). The best examples here are 1950s science fiction films. Lastly, there is the 'social monster' film where a recognisable society is represented as the place in which the monster intervenes and where the need to maintain social order is stressed. The world depicted is modern society, not the world of the monster and Denne cites the examples of the *Gorgo* and *Godzilla* films (ibid.). We could also cite some of the teen horror films of the late 1950s, *Psycho* and some films mentioned below as other examples. He continues: 'chronologically, the atmospheric had its heyday until the early and mid-forties; the bipartite from then until the mid-fifties; the social until now' (ibid.: 126). The point is that the focus of the horror film becomes increasingly and recognisably social and modern.

This argument is exaggerated, but, in a purely descriptive way, it captures a trend towards locating horror in modern society. Films are usually set in some form of society, but the suggestion is that the society in modern horror is clearly contemporary. One good example of this is the way society itself becomes the monster, supposedly bringing out the dark side of ordinary people, as in *Night of the Living Dead* (1968). Jancovich, like others, sees this film as an example of apocalyptic horror in which the social order as a whole is under threat from the zombies. The zombies seem so capable of easily increasing their number that they become a social force in their own right. Their inexorable power, from which there appears to be no escape, brings communal disaster and social disintegration. He argues that its sequel, *Dawn of the Dead* (1978), also represents the zombies as a threat to the consumerism which is integral to the modern social order (Jancovich 1994: 22–6). Other writers, such as G. Wood, have cited Hitchcock's *The Birds* (1963) as another typical example of the apocalyptic horror film and suggest that the apocalypse 'became an accepted part of the form of horror by the end of the 1960s' (1988: 217).

This type of textual interpretation, as we note at various stages in this book, is not necessarily in tune with that of audiences, or even producers. *The Night of the Living Dead* provides another instructive example. Grant recounts how at a horror film retrospective organised by Robin Wood for the Toronto film festival, 'George Romero, the director of *Night of the Living Dead*, was asked about the ideological implications of his work'. However, 'the audience ... was impatient with such talk, became rude and shouted for him to leave the stage so they could enjoy the movie ... have a good time and ... see the "good parts" '. He concludes that this reception 'brings into focus ... the discrepancy between textual interpretation and actual viewer reception' (1991: 128).

A variant of apocalyptic horror has added the devil to the forces of evil the horror film represents. Clearly, the devil has appeared before in the horror film, Dracula being one possible guise. None the less, the 1960s and 1970s saw the emergence of horror films which made direct and explicit references to the devil and his work. A film like *Rosemary's Baby* (1968) combines the demonic with the apocalypse since it is about the birth of the Antichrist (G. Wood 1988: 217). Further examples of this trend in horror include *The Exorcist* (1973) and *The Omen* (1976). Jancovich views the latter as evidence 'of the 1970s' preoccupation with demonic forces' (1994: 25).

Some of these films gained critical and artistic approval because they were the work of respected film makers. Most importantly, however, they were early examples of the blockbuster film which has become such a feature of contemporary Hollywood cinema. D. Cook has noted that by the mid-1960s science fiction had become a more respectable genre, which attracted more 'serious' film makers (1990: 528). This, in turn, was connected with the emergence of science fiction and horror as technically sophisti-cated, big budget and mainstream films. Early examples of science fiction films made by 'serious' directors include Godard's *Alphaville* (1965), Truffaut's *Fahrenheit 451* (1966) and Kubrick's *2001: A Space Odyssey* (1968) (ibid.). To this we could add Polanski's *Rosemary's Baby*, a horror film which may have given the genre some respectability and paved the way for such films as *The Exorcist* and *The Omen* (cf. G. Wood 1988: 217–18). However, the next phase of the horror film we have to look at concerns a sub-genre which has been far from respectable. This is the 'slasher' film, which also involves the serial killer as the monster.

The 'slasher' film

This sub-genre has attracted much attention, due to moral anxieties over its graphic violence and the changes in representation it is supposed to achieve. Its novelty may be exaggerated, for 'horror' has become a 'teenpic perennial' and the 'teen body count "exploitation" cycle of the late 1970s' merely another example of this (Doherty 1988: 240). An indication of this, one not always acknowledged, is the inclusion of teenagers in the adult horror film market (the 'R'-rated film in America) (ibid.). Before we discuss this more fully, we need to consider the context in which this type of film emerged and developed.

According to D. Cook, by the late 1970s and early 1980s, Hollywood had become more reliant on sequels of films which had already been successful, including monster and science fiction films, such as *Jaws* (1975) and *Stars Wars*. At the same time, it also became more reliant on 'films containing graphic sex, violence, or, preferably, both combined' (1990: 896). Arguably, both of these formulas have been standard and reasonably constant features of the Hollywood system. By the late 1970s, 'sex and violence' were manifest in the ' "psycho-slasher" films that glutted the domestic market in the wake of John Carpenter's ultra-successful *Halloween* (1978)', a low budget film which made an enormous profit (ibid.).

The success of the slasher formula was confirmed by the 'record-breaking profits' of *Friday the Thirteenth* (1980). This formula involved a series of murders committed by a psycho killer, with plenty of sex, violence and blood thrown in for good measure. The films derived to some extent from earlier examples such as *Psycho* and *The Texas Chainsaw Massacre* (1974). While Hollywood has often turned to the sex and violence formula when it has seemed profitable, this has been limited by the technology and censorship prevailing at any particular time. Also, the exploitation of blood and violence has existed at the margins of the industry since the early 1960s (Cook 1990: 896).

The slasher, serial killer sub-genre took such exploitation into 'the R-rated mainstream' with numerous 'spin-offs' from the *Halloween* and *Friday the Thirteenth* films. Other contributions included films such as *Driller Killer* (1979), *Prom Night* (1980), *The Slumber Party Massacre* (1982), *The Evil Dead* (1983) and *Nightmare on Elm Street* (1984), which has itself led to a number of sequels (Cook 1990: 896). Twenty-five slasher films were among the top fifty box-office successes of 1981, a year in which they comprised almost 60 per cent of all films released. Their popularity reached its peak soon afterwards, but they remained 'a regular feature of the annual production schedule and their porno-violent chic has become obligatory for many first-rate horror films' (ibid.). These include *Poltergeist* (1982), *The Hunger* (1983) and *The Serpent and the Rainbow* (1987), as well as films which also deal with science fiction, such as *Alien* (1979) and *Aliens* (1986). The slasher films 'are now an important staple of the video-cassette and cable television markets, owing to the sheer number in which they were (and are) produced' (ibid.: 896–7).

For Jancovich, slasher films 'concern a serial killer who tracks down a group of teenagers, killing them off one by one in various grisly ways and it is usually argued that its attacks are primarily directed against women' (1994: 29). Even if men are killed in these films in sufficient numbers, it is claimed that they none the less concentrate upon and linger over the murders of women, who are anyway the real targets of the killer (ibid.).

However, this interpretation can be contested by *Halloween*, 'the most discussed of the slasher movies' and the most obvious initiator of the cycle (Jancovich 1994: 29). After all, one of the intended female targets of the serial killer becomes the protagonist of the story. She successfully combats his attempts to make her his next victim more or less without male help. This story-line can also be found in other films, such as *Nightmare on Elm Street* and is prefigured, in a less obvious fashion, in *Carrie* (1976). In view of the number and range of films it has produced, it would be wrong to see this as a feature of the cycle as a whole. However, it can be found in a number of leading examples. In these, 'it is the female who refuses her role as victim and rejects the positions of powerlessness associated with femininity who is the hero' (ibid.: 33; cf Clover 1992).

These interpretations have figured prominently in the debates which have arisen within feminist theory on the issue of horror and gender (Gledhill 1985: 104–5). Indeed, Clover has argued that this 'female victim-hero' stands in marked contrast to the 'sadistic misogyny' often associated with the horror film. She argues that this 'female victim-hero' became the major protagonist of the independently produced, low budget, slasher film cycle which lasted from the mid-1970s to the early 1980s. It thus met the masochistic needs of its mainly adolescent male audience because they could experience being victims, besides the more common hero status they are usually offered (1992: 4–18 and *passim*).

Modern horror and modern Hollywood

The main thing that needs to be noted in this section is how the horror and science fiction film have become fertile ground for the type of big budget, mass audience, blockbuster film which Hollywood now favours. This type of film has already been described in Chapter 1 and some indication of its relevance to horror and science fiction has been given above. It was, arguably, developed by the science fiction film *Star Wars* and its two sequels. Drawing on the increasing respectability of the genre in the late 1970s, *Star Wars* became the first, successful science fiction blockbuster, combining state-of-the-art special effects with vastly increased merchandising opportunities. It showed the way for Hollywood to exploit new openings for markets and profits, as well as its more traditional ones.

The continuing popularity of science fiction as a vehicle for the Hollywood blockbuster may well arise from these conditions. It allows film makers to use the latest and most sophisticated special effects technology, while greatly increasing a film's merchandising opportunities. The latter includes products such as toys, replica monsters, sunglasses, watches, T-shirts, books, CDs, fast food specials, computer games and anything else on which the film's logo can be stuck. Science fiction – and, indeed, horror – can be readily exploited for these purposes, as the more recent examples of *Jurassic Park* and *Men in Black* show. Even a film such as *Armageddon* is basically a disaster film, but it is set mostly in outer space. Therefore, it can be suggested that Hollywood's 'fascination' with these types of films lies fundamentally in their technological and marketing potential (see Chapter 10).

D. Cook describes the significance of *Star Wars* and its two sequels, *The Empire Strikes Back* (1980) and *Return of the Jedi* (1983) in these terms. He notes that it 'combined sophisticated computerized effects, ... Dolby stereo sound and a fantasy-adventure plot containing folkloric elements to create a new breed of American science fiction' (1990: 529). This led not only to the sequels mentioned and the *Star Trek* series, but also to such films as *Close Encounters of the Third Kind* (1977), *E.T. The Extraterrestrial* (1982), *Ghostbusters* (1984), *Gremlins* (1984) and the *Back to the Future* trilogy starting in 1985 (1990: 529, 897). Cook argues that 'during the 1980s, this emphasis on high-tech special effects and sound continued in science fiction films which, successful or not, often had a more serious edge' (ibid.: 529). These were often films which drew upon the horror film genre as well as science fiction. As a whole, they include *Alien* (1979), *Blade Runner* (1982), *Starman* (1984), *Brazil* (1985), *The Terminator* (1984), *Aliens* (1986), *Predator* (1987), *Robocop* (1987) and *Terminator 2* (1991) (ibid.: 529). A number of these films, which combined horror and science fiction, 'contain strong female leads; an interest in the family; concerns about scientific-technical rationality and the military; killing machines which lack conscious motivation; and forms of body/horror' (Jancovich 1994: 33).

Horror has thus featured in the modern Hollywood blockbuster through its combination with science fiction. However, there have also been recent remakes of classic horror films, *Bram Stoker's Dracula* (1993) and *Mary Shelley's Frankenstein* (1994), which provide yet more examples of the modern Hollywood film. They made extensive use of big budgets, special effects and heavy promotion to provide purportedly faithful renditions of the original novels, but also succeeded in updating the original Universal films.

Due to its reliance on generic realism, it is possible to see the contemporary horror film as another example of postmodernism (Wood 1988: 218–19). The most recent examples of this include

In the Mouth of Madness (1995), *Wes Craven's New Nightmare* (1995), *Mars Attacks!* (1997), *Scream* (1997) and *Scream 2* (1998). These films are self-reflexive and knowing about the conventions of the genre in the way postmodern theory suggests. They rely on the tacit understanding that both film makers and audiences know how such films work and they therefore produce and appreciate them because of this self-conscious knowledge. This does not mean to say they are not frightening, but it is argued that people are very aware of how fear can be evoked. The characters in the *Scream* films, for example, openly discuss the conventions of the horror film as they become enmeshed by the horror which erupts around them. The horror they come across is typical of the plot of so many horror films, although the knowledge of genre conventions itself leads to a trick ending. In another film, *Wes Craven's New Nightmare*, itself another sequel to *Nightmare on Elm Street*, the plot hinges upon the making of a film.

Of course, this is not necessarily new. Earlier modern examples that provide irreverent parodies and stress knowledge of the genre's conventions can be found. These include such films as *The Rocky Horror Picture Show* (1976), *An American Werewolf in London* (1981), *Gremlins* (1984), *Gremlins 2* (1990) and *Love at First Bite* (1979). However, as we have already seen, this seems to be a feature of other cycles in the history of the genre and is not something unique to the contemporary period as postmodern theory claims. It seems to be another instance of the cyclical regularity with which the genre parodies itself and may be a feature of genres whose standardisation is heavily dependent on generic realism. In any event, postmodernism will be dealt with more fully in another part of this book.

Modern horror has equally seen the 'teenpic horror' of the 1950s reworked with modern techniques, while a number of the science fiction blockbuster films, such as the *Back to the Future* trilogy, have been geared to the teenage market (Cook 1990: 897). High-profile horror films set in the contemporary world, but drawing on established film traditions and building on the success of the horror/science fiction formula, have become prominent in modern cinema. These include *Alien Resurrection* (1997), *The*

Devil's Advocate (1998), *The Fifth Element* (1997), *Godzilla* (1998), *Independence Day* (1996), *Interview with the Vampire* (1994), *Jurassic Park* (1993), *The Lost World: Jurassic Park* (1997), *Men in Black* (1997), *Scream, Scream 2, Species* (1995), *Species II* (1998), *12 Monkeys* (1996) and *The X Files* (1998). There have also been smaller scale, lower budget variants of this development, such as *Anaconda* (1997) and *Event Horizon* (1997). The point is that all these films can be seen as the products of the modern Hollywood system.

Theories of horror

It is perhaps evident from the above that there are probably two distinct theoretical approaches to horror: one sociological and political, the other psychological and psychoanalytical. Each contains different theories but they tend to share much in common. The first approach sees horror as a reflection of prevailing social, political and cultural conditions. One or more of these conditions may be stressed at the expense of the others, but the point is that the horror film is reduced to the prevailing conditions it is supposed to represent. Although we cannot go into detail on the claims and limitations of all the theories which make such an argument, they include a number of variants. One important example is the work of Jancovich, which we have outlined and criticised above and to which we will return briefly below. There are others which can be noted in passing. These include those arguments which relate horror and science fiction films directly to the social and political concerns of the 1950s and 1960s, such as the Cold War, fear of invasion by the Soviet Union, nuclear war and ecological devastation (Jancovich 1994, 1996). Also relevant in this context is Derry's attempt to relate modern types of horror to such concerns (Gledhill 1985: 100–1), as well as Tudor's idea of 'patterns of sociation' (1974: chapter 8).

The second approach tends to reduce horror to an imputed and general psychic need or state of mind, be it conscious or unconscious, which it is designed to respond to or fulfil. Again, we cannot go into detail on all the theories that can be grouped together here, though we will use one variant as a good, illustrative example below. None the less, there are a number of theories which can be noted at this juncture, some of which have been referred to above. These include post-structuralist theories (Gledhill 1985: 103–4; cf. Neale 1980), Clover's analysis of the slasher and rape revenge films, theories which see horror as an essentially conservative genre and some feminist theories (Gledhill 1985: 104–5), as well as those which attribute horror to a universal, human need to be scared.

A useful example to consider briefly, since it is often quoted and has cropped up a few times above, is R. Wood's psychoanalytical theory of the horror film. As we have seen, he argues that the horror film is typically repressive. For him, 'the true subject of the horror genre is the struggle for recognition of all that our civilization represses or oppresses' (1986: 75). The horror film represents the restoration of social order, which involves the repression of anything that can conventionally be considered 'abnormal' or 'deviant'. It functions to meet this need for order by repressing into the psychic unconscious these deviations from the norm, which include female sexuality, the working class, other 'exotic' cultures and bisexuality and homosexuality (ibid.: 74–7, cf. 77–80). The horror film 'dramatises the re-emergence' of these 'others' as 'an object of horror', 'the happy ending (when it exists) typically signifying the restoration of repression' (ibid.: 75). The theory therefore states that the horror film functions to fulfil this psychic need for representation and repression. According to R. Wood, this theory offers 'a comprehensive survey of horror film monsters from German Expressionism on' (ibid.).

Historically, the horror film has usually been repressive in the manner described. However, in the 1960s and 1970s it was equally capable of working in a different, though comparable manner. It functioned to represent the 'return of the repressed', rather than merely its repression. R. Wood suggests, using 'Freudian themes', that there is 'an enormous surplus of repressed sexual energy' looking for an outlet in a very sexually repressed society (1986: 80). How this energy knew what to do is not clear, but it found what it was looking for in the horror film of the 1960s and 1970s. After

Psycho, the Hollywood horror film began increasingly to focus on American society and the American family, a claim questioned by Jancovich (1996: 221–3, 226–30). However, for R. Wood, some horror films, starting with *Psycho*, became 'progressive' and 'critical' in that they identified 'the monster with the fundamental institutions of American society' (Jancovich 1994: 16; cf. Gledhill 1985: 101–2). They also departed from the more typical horror film by not destroying the monster and, instead, making it generally more ambiguous. R. Wood argues such films suggest that 'the repressed can never be annihilated' (1986: 87). He illustrates this by the end of *It's Alive* (1974), 'another one's been born in Seattle', as well as *The Texas Chainsaw Massacre* (ibid.: 87–94). In the 1970s, the indestructibility of the monster became for a time the 'cliché' of the horror film (ibid.: 87). This cyclical departure from the typical horror film is, however, still interpreted by how it functions to allow 'the repressed' to be represented. This is, presumably, because a particular need for this arose and had therefore to be fulfilled.

It is perhaps less evident from what has gone before – although, hopefully, some hints have been recognised – that neither of these approaches and the theories they have fostered provide adequate explanations of the horror film. The horror film is, primarily, a product of the Hollywood system and a popular film genre. This affects what is produced and distributed. So it is difficult to see how it can reflect anything, or meet any psychic needs, independently of this system. Prevailing social, political and cultural conditions are not usually as clear, accurate and uniform as some theories seem to assume. Such conditions may also be deceptive in that, for example, ideologies may misrepresent what is actually happening. For example, Jancovich claims horror in American film and literature from the 1950s onwards reflects a concern with the scientific rationalisation of American society. This is confirmed by the work of leading social and political theorists. However, both horror and rationalisation theories may not have reflected what was going on in American society, or may have only been linked to some very specific and limited developments. Equally, rationalisation may have been the thwarted ideological project of a particular group. Usually, we do not learn very much from such theories about the social and historical contexts they think are significant, nor how their claims to knowledge might be supported and defended.

Similarly, the evidence for the psychic functions of horror – if any is given at all – is often confined to the films themselves, although occasionally a few disparate sources may be thrown in as additional support. However, the validity of the need, its extent and its satisfaction, are rarely established. The horror film becomes the focus of the psychic need and its fulfilment results from an unidentified, yet miraculous process.

Clover tries to deal with these problems by focusing upon a particular example (1992: 231–2). She argues that the slasher and rape revenge films of the late 1970s and early 1980s, with their 'female victim-hero', fulfilled the 'usually forbidden' masochistic needs of adolescent males (ibid.: 4–19, cf. 226–30). However, apart from confirming that adolescent males were the main audience for these films, her argument is confined to the properties of the horror film. She does not say how people and social institutions know how to relate to horror in the way her theory implies. Also, we are never told how representative the audience for these films was of adolescent males as a whole. Nor are we referred to any evidence which shows that adolescent males watched these films to fulfil their masochistic needs. Clover suggests that such needs could be satisfied only for the specified period by independently produced, low budget horror films because they could take more chances and be more creative than mainstream, conventional films. They had all but disappeared by the late 1980s as their concerns had been absorbed and made safe by the latter (ibid.: 235–7). But why should these films have worked in this way? The capacity to be creative is a long way from the fulfilment of masochistic desires and it is difficult to see how the latter can be implied from the former. And when these films ceased to be made, what then happened to adolescent males and their masochistic desires? We are given no idea why they turned to these films in the first place, nor what happened to them once the films ceased to be made. It is never made clear how and why these films managed to emerge and function in the ways identified.

This also indicates other problems. The Hollywood system treats audiences as consumers, so horror cannot be simply reduced to imputed psychic states or needs. When people go to see films they are, primarily, acting as consumers. As we thus noted in our general discussion of genre, what is being talked about here is the behaviour of consumers rather than some type of collective expression. There is therefore no reason why the choices of consumers should reflect social conditions, or be consistent with an imputed psychic need and its fulfilment. Commonly, of course, the audience is not discussed at all and the production and consumption of films are not given sufficient recognition. Wider social concerns, or psychic needs, are not guaranteed a place in consumer markets, even assuming they can be identified clearly.

If the horror film is a privileged place where deep-seated psychological desires, or social, political and cultural concerns can be managed, we are not told why. The horror film is said to function in a particular way to meet specific needs. It either reflects social, political and cultural concerns, or meets certain psychic needs. However, a number of questions can be raised to which such arguments appear to have no answers. Why should the horror film function in this way? Presuming, for the sake of argument, that it does, what makes it do so? Are there alternatives which might also perform this function? How are the needs which need to be met identified by the horror film, its producers, its audiences, or theorists? If there are functions why should they be fulfilled and if there are needs why should they be met? The question why popular film genres should be argued to work like this is one which has also emerged in the analysis of *film noir*. It may be that it is not the best way to understand films as popular culture.

Chapter 5

Film noir

T HE CHOICE OF *film noir* as the last of the Hollywood film genres to be considered rests on slightly different criteria from those we have used so far. *Film noir* is very instructive about Hollywood cinema, but it is not obviously a realistic or convention driven genre. These claims have indeed been made about *film noir*: some, including its practitioners, have said it offers a more realistic addition to mainstream Hollywood cinema; others have said it has a very identifiable and characteristic narrative and style.[1] Both of these points are important in assessing it as a type of film. However, in themselves, they are not as significant as *film noir*'s supposed radical difference from Hollywood genres and Hollywood cinema and its critique of American society and the American dream embodied in the Hollywood film narrative.

It is this critique that we shall be concerned with in this chapter. *Film noir* is said to be markedly different from the more orthodox Hollywood genres, so its assessment should allow us to come to some general conclusions about popular culture and Hollywood cinema. We shall therefore try to say what *film noir* is, what its major themes and tensions are and what the reasons are for its emergence and duration. However, we shall conclude by asking whether it is as distinct or as radical as is often claimed.

What is *film noir*?

This is a question often asked in the literature and it is possible to put forward a reasonably clear definition. We could say that the term refers to a cycle of mainly urban crime thrillers made in Hollywood between the 1940s and the late 1950s which dealt with the dark side of the American psyche and the bleak and forlorn nature of American society. It is said to have taken a cynical and pessimistic view of human nature and the progress of urban, industrial societies. It is thus argued to have represented a critique both

116

of American society and the American dream. It has also been said that it presented these themes through an appropriately dark, idiosyncratic and 'subversive' *noir* style. This picture needs to be filled out and we shall try to do this below. For the moment, it provides us with a serviceable definition of *film noir*, whatever we may want to argue subsequently.

However, any definition seems to raise as many questions as it answers. In asking 'what is *film noir*?' Bordwell *et al.* suggest it is neither a genre nor style. It is not a genre in the usual sense because it was not recognised and defined by film makers and audiences at the time as a distinct film genre. It is also not a style because 'critics have not succeeded in defining specifically *noir* visual techniques ... or narrative structure' (1985: 75). Instead, they suggest that an understanding of *noir* can be reached by seeing it as an exclusionary term – one which says what it is not rather than what it is – which refers to the 'repudiation of a norm' of film making. We shall return to this argument below. However, attempts have been made to distinguish both the style and narrative of *noir* films and the latter can help us establish the by now conventional argument about *film noir*.

The idea that there may have been something different about a segment of Hollywood's output in the 1940s is suggested by a complaint aired in *Life* magazine, a source of 'middle class, middle brow opinion' (Clarens 1980: 192). In 1946 it commented that

> whoever went to the movies with any regularity during 1946 was caught in the midst of Hollywood's profound post-war affection for morbid drama. From January through December deep shadows, clutching hands, exploding revolvers, sadistic villains and heroines tormented with deeply rooted diseases of the mind flashed across the screen in a panting display of psychoneuroses, unsublimated sex and murder most foul.
> (quoted in ibid.: 1980: 192)

This may be an exaggeration but, for the time being, it can serve as a sign that a recognisable difference in some of Hollywood's films may have started to become apparent.

This was certainly the view taken by the French film critics who first gave *noir* its name. Writing at the end of the Second World War, they likewise recognised the novel and distinct character of the American *film noir*, as Hollywood films started to become available again in greater numbers. Unlike other types of American films, the *film noir* went 'further into pessimism and a disgust for humanity' by portraying 'a fatal inner evil' (Chartier 1996: 25, 27). They argued that Hollywood had started to make *noir* films which were comparable to the more uplifting and politically conscious ones made in France from the 1930s onwards. The American *film noir* was equally distinct because it departed from the confidence and optimism usually associated with mainstream Hollywood cinema. This interpretation of *noir* as a cinema of scepticism and pessimism is one that continued to gain favour both in France and elsewhere. However, at least one French critic at the time suggested these films were just another extension of Hollywood's role in sustaining 'the three classic themes of capitalist propaganda – work, family and nation' (Rey 1996: 28); they did not represent anything radically different or new.

Some recognition was thus accorded to *noir* films at the time they were being produced. This has subsequently been developed into a considerable body of critical work which argues that *noir* represented a critical if not radical picture of American society and an alternative to mainstream Hollywood cinema. We have already noted some examples of this above. Therefore there has been some basis for regarding *noir* as a genre, even if it is not a genre in the usual or conventional sense. The significant questions are how important are the supposed features of *film noir* and how valid are its interpretations?

Defining *film noir*

There is a distinct type of film which can be called *film noir*, if the majority opinion in the literature is to be believed. There may not be that much agreement about whether it can be defined by its style, as a genre or sub-genre, or as a tendency or movement. There may also not be agreement about every film which is supposed to count as a *noir* film. None the less, there is a surprising degree of agreement both about what *film noir* is and about what count as the main *noir* films. We can use these points in the literature to describe *film noir*. This description can identify themes or tensions which define *film noir* and show how and why it is thought to be different from mainstream, Hollywood cinema and critical of the American dream and American society.

As a prelude to this we can note that a typical *fim noir* narrative has been identified. The idea that there is something new or different about the *noir* film has led Damico to define the narrative that distinguishes it as a film genre although, as we have seen, this possibility has been questioned. In general terms, for Damico, the typical *noir* film has a man who is unhappy, usually cynical and 'often bitter'. As a rule, he is 'sexually and fatally attracted' to a woman who has a 'similar outlook' on life. They meet initially either by chance or as a result of the man's job, which can often entail him being hired to investigate the woman. The man's attraction to the woman is fatal because it leads to his corruption and downfall. The woman may put him up to it or it may be 'the natural result of their relationship', but the man is led 'to cheat, attempt to murder, or actually murder a second man to whom the woman is unhappily or unwillingly attached'. This act can result in the woman's betrayal of the man, but it is certain to lead to 'the sometimes metaphoric, but usually literal destruction of the woman, the man to whom she is attached and frequently the protagonist himself' (1978: 54). This provides a useful starting point and a fair outline of the narratives of many *noir* films, such as *Double Indemnity* (1944), *Out of the Past* (1948) and *The Lady from Shanghai* (1954). However, it may not be unique to the *noir* film and it is difficult to apply to a number of films which have been defined as *noir* films such as *Murder, My Sweet* (1944), *Dark Corner* (1946) and *Touch of Evil* (1958).

We obviously cannot do justice to all the points made about *film noir* in the literature, but we can single out some of the most relevant ones for attention. The first such theme is fatalism and the tension between fate and individual human agency. *Film noir* is often seen as being different and radical because it adopts a fatalistic attitude towards human conduct. What happens in the world is the result of an impersonal and unknown force, which constrains individuals to behave in ways over which they have little or no control. Fate rather than agency determines the narrative of the *noir* film and the lives and deaths of its characters. It is not the relatively free and consciously determined actions of individual human agents, but the unseen, random and decisive hand of fate which determines what happens in *noir* films.

It is not that clear how this fate can be defined in more precise terms. However, apart from rare exceptions, such as *Body and Soul* (1947) and *Force of Evil* (1948), it is usually a universal and existential force and not one obviously attributable to the specific constraints of a particular society such as capitalism. Fate is not unambiguously and socially determined by capitalist society, but appears to be an inherent feature of the human condition. This means that the attributes of individual human agency – enterprise, initiative, hard work – needed to achieve the American dream are undermined by the inexorable forces of fate. *Film noir* is thus defined by the way it resolves the tension between fate and human agency; it is fatalism which prevails.

Characters in *noir* films utter dialogue which tends to confirm this point. One of the concluding comments of the male protagonist of *Detour* (1945) is that 'fate or some mysterious force can put the finger on you or me for no good reason at all'. In telling the audience how his troubles began, the male protagonist of *Criss Cross* (1949) says that 'from the start, it all went one way. It was in the cards or it was fate or a jinx or whatever you want to call it.' The private detective protagonist of *The Dark Corner* (1946) tries to give this force some substance, as well as justify the film's title, when he complains 'I feel all dead inside. I'm backed up in a dark corner and I don't know who's hitting me.' We can also refer to Damico's idea of the *noir* genre's narrative to make this point. The first and decisive trick fate usually plays upon the male hero is to get him to meet the fatal woman, more commonly known as the *femme fatale*. After this, as the male protagonist of *Double Indemnity* (1944) puts it, he is being taken for a ride from which there is no escape except destruction. After he has seemingly pulled off the perfect murder, this protagonist tells the audience, as he walks down a dark and deserted street at night, that he can hear his footsteps, 'the footsteps of a dead man'. True enough, at the end of the film he does die at the hands of his lover – they shoot each other. As he dies, he wryly comments that he 'did it for the money and the woman' though he 'didn't get the money or the woman'. Similarly, the protagonist of *The Killers* (1946) passively accepts his fate, to be gunned down by two contract killers, because he 'did something wrong once'.

The second major theme or tension we can find in *film noir* concerns the contrast between optimism and pessimism. The mainstream Hollywood film is seen as being optimistic in its view of the progress of society and human motivation, even if it admits that evil exists and influences events. This is expressed, most typically, by its happy endings, in which problems are resolved and the social order is restored. *Film noir* is seen to take the opposite view. It is pessimistic about the prospects for social and individual progress and improvement and cynical about human motivation, believing that money, above all else, ultimately drives human actions and inevitably corrupts society. This is the complete opposite of the beliefs embodied in the American dream. Indeed, the material wealth which is seen as the pinnacle of achievement in the American dream, is accused of being the root of evil in the *noir* film. Thus, pessimism, cynicism and despair, rather than optimism, belief and hope, are thought to characterise the content and conclusions of the *noir* film.

We should not be led to conclude (at least at this stage of the argument) that the *noir* film adopts a clear moral stance and unambiguously distinguishes between good and evil, simply because it refers to evil. This is the third theme or tension we need to consider: how *noir* films view the relationship between good and evil. It is suggested that they often blur the distinction between the two or ignore it altogether. The typical Hollywood film does recognise evil or comparable things, such as immorality and crime, but it does not usually let them succeed. Instead, goodness, morality and the law restore the social order and reign supreme in the end. It is not so much that *film noir* is argued to reverse this order, but that it does not recognise the dividing line between good and evil. In the *noir* world, the police are often as corrupt as the criminals; wrong-doers and murderers are frequently more attractive and charismatic than the morally correct and the innocent; and the fatal woman is inevitably more appealing, active and independent than the good woman. Characters, particularly the protagonists, are morally confused rather than simply good or evil and their confusion is often not resolved by the end of the film. The fatal woman and the male victim, like the gangster, pursue the American dream through illegitimate and illegal means, in their cases murder and sex, and not through the morally appropriate channels. These can also be called into question in *film noir*. For example, the corrupt lawyer who finances the professionally organised theft in *The Asphalt Jungle* (1950) describes crime as 'merely a left-handed form of human endeavour'.

There are many *noir* films which have been characterised in this way, most notably those which deal with the lack of a clear, moral dividing line between the police and the criminals. These include films such as *The Big Combo* (1955), *The Big Heat* (1953), *Cry of the City* (1948), *Kiss of Death* (1947) and *Where the Sidewalk Ends* (1950). A good example is *Touch of Evil*. In this film, the corrupt police chief catches criminals by indiscriminately planting evidence on those he suspects of the crime. He has no real evidence, merely the suspicion of wrongdoing. But he justifies his actions because, in his view, everyone is guilty of something. If they are not guilty of the crime they are being set up for, they are normally guilty of another one. This is found to be the case with the crime which the film describes, so the chief's method is vindicated. There is thus no real and sustainable dividing line between good and evil, while in the *noir* world few can escape the taint of moral weakness. This film illustrates how *noir* films are pessimistic and cynical about human motivation and behaviour and show fate, the consequence of immoral or illegal acts, eventually catching up with individuals however much they try to escape it. This is also exemplified by another film which some see as one of the most typical *noir* films, *Out of the Past*.

These points rely on the way *film noir* sees money and financial and sexual advantage as the reasons why people think and act in the ways the films describe. In this it stresses the American dream's goal of material and familial success. However, it tends to indicate that the pursuit of this goal does not lead to happiness, fulfilment and social harmony but to immorality, crime and social discord. *Film noir* suggests that social relationships and human ambitions and actions are dominated above all by money. This is why some critics, taking into account its fatalism, pessimism, cynicism and moral ambivalence, regard *film noir* as a critique of Hollywood, the American dream and American society.

A number of comments can be used to confirm this view. Schrader says that these Hollywood films of the 1940s and early 1950s 'portrayed the world of dark, slick city streets, crime and corruption' (1972: 8). According to Flinn, '*film noir*, like shoulder pads, wedgies and zoot suits, was an essential part of the Forties outlook, a cinematic style forged in the fires of war, exile and disillusion, a melodramatic reflection for a world gone mad' (1972: 11). In a similar vein, Hirsch argues 'noir unleashed a series of dark allegories of the national state of mind during the forties' (1981: 200). He also maintains that 'noir exposes the underside of the American dream in a mode that mixes German Expressionism with a native hard-boiled realism' (ibid.: 209). For Kemp, '*film noir* can be seen as a riposte, a sour, disenchanted flip-side to the brittle optimism and flag-waving piety of Hollywood's "official" output of the period' (1986: 270). Indeed, Kemp argues that *film noir* presents a very clear expression of how money and its relentless and amoral pursuit is thought to permeate social relationships in American society. He draws attention to three assumptions which animate *film noir*. First, there is the power of money, the dominance of cash and financial greed, which is portrayed as being normal. Second, there is 'class warfare'. In contrast to the typical Hollywood film, this is presented as involving oppression, hatred and violence. Third, there is the depiction of the 'land of the free-for-all', a society in which 'rampant individualism' holds sway. Loyalty to a wider collective good or a social conscience cannot exist in the *noir* world, in which almost everyone has their price (ibid.: 266–70). Kemp argues that *noir* is indeed about the effects of capitalism and not about an inevitable human tendency towards corruption. For the reasons he mentions, *film noir* can be seen as a radical critique of the American dream and American society.

It would be possible to extend this discussion of the themes or tensions to be found in *film noir*, even if we did not venture into the territory of visual style. There is, for example, the argument that *film noir* is based upon the tension between paranoia and normality, whereby the latter is constantly at threat from the former. The protagonists of the *noir* film are often potentially 'insane' or 'deviant' in their thoughts and deeds and threaten the normal world, which is often shown as being on the edge of paranoia itself. The films therefore deal with the tension between the two. Yet again, *film noir* is seen to address the contrast between the corrupt but exciting city at night and the pure but mundane small town or rural community. However, the points we have paid attention to above should have brought out some of the main features of the *noir* film. The quotations we have used indicate how the debate about *film noir* concerns the reasons given for its emergence as a type of Hollywood film genre, even if it is not a genre in the conventional sense. We now need to consider some of the explanations put forward for *film noir*'s appearance in the early 1940s. Before we do this, however, there is one aspect of *film noir* which we need to look at first, since it has received particular attention in the literature. This is how it deals with the representation of gender, for it is sometimes thought to be radically distinctive in the way it achieves this.

Gender and *film noir*

Unlike the gangster film, which tends to marginalise women, or the horror film, which tends to victimise them, it has been argued that the *noir* film tends to place them centre stage. This is evident in what Kaplan has to say. She suggests 'the *film noir* world is one in which women are central to the intrigue of the films and are furthermore usually not placed safely in … familiar roles'. Represented in this world and 'defined by their sexuality, which is presented as desirable but dangerous, the women function as an obstacle to the male quest'. The success of this quest therefore depends on the extent to which the male 'can extricate himself from the woman's manipulations'. If he is unsuccessful, he can be destroyed. However, 'often the world of the film is the attempted restoration of order through the exposure and then destruction of the sexual, manipulating woman' (1980: 2–3).

This analysis raises all sorts of issues, only some of which can be pursued here. One of the most notable is how Kaplan's understanding of *film noir* can be seen to conform to the general features of the typical Hollywood narrative. In this sense, the fatal woman represents a threat to the prevailing social and sexual order. She is the disruptive force which needs to be dealt with for order to be restored. The narrative of the *noir* film thus works to overcome the disorder caused by the sexual manipulations associated with the fatal woman's quest for power and independence. The social and sexual order can only be restored in these films by the destruction and, not infrequently, death of the fatal woman. The man may also be destroyed and may sometimes die, though often it is enough that he has learned his lesson, even if the experience does stay with him for the rest of his life. Examples of the latter include *The Lady from Shanghai*, *Pitfall* (1948) and *The Woman in the Window* (1945).

An equally notable issue concerns whether the representation of women in *film noir* can be considered progressive in any sense, or whether women are still stereotyped and kept in their place within patriarchy. Kaplan would seem to come down in favour of the latter, as her argument suggests. This may be the most considered answer to the question. However, she also shows how this type of film may differ from mainstream Hollywood films in the way it represents women, even if this difference is ultimately suppressed or destroyed.

One way of assessing how different the *noir* film may be in this respect is to look at gender as a whole. For if these films treat women differently, this must have consequences for the way they represent men. It can be suggested that the *noir* film sets up a tension between the male and the female, which is different from the more orthodox representations of gender in the standard

Hollywood film. This involves an apparent reversal of the qualities that normally define the female and the male in popular cinema. Indications of this are provided by Kaplan, as well as by Damico's idea of the typical *noir* narrative. We need to realise that the representations at issue are specific types of females and males and not ones which are more varied and extensive. In particular, we are dealing with the sexually manipulative woman, the fatal woman or *femme fatale*, and the man as the fated dupe, the doomed victim of this woman.

The first thing we can say about this is that the *noir* film can be seen to reverse the usual attribution of activity and passivity to gender roles. Put simply, in the typical Hollywood film, it can be argued that men are active and women are passive. This is not always or simply the case, of course, but it tends to be true of the overall development of the narrative. It is also supported by more general evidence on the representation of women in contemporary popular culture.[2] The *noir* film is argued to reverse this by making the male protagonist the passive victim and the fatal woman the active manipulator of events. In this sense, she may be the fatal woman, but she is not a mere victim of fate. We can appreciate this if we recall Damico's account of the *noir* genre's narrative and the examples which have been mentioned. The *noir* film is often about the initially covert schemes and actions of the fatal woman, which lie behind the events depicted by the narrative. These are eventually revealed during the film, leading as they often do to the subsequent demise of herself and her male victim. This male is usually a victim of a fate whose determinism he falls prey to when he is seduced by the fatal woman. He becomes her witting or unwitting accomplice in the pursuit of her schemes to acquire wealth and power. In this way, his fate typically comes to him in the shape of the fatal woman.

This change in the attribution of passivity and activity to men and women means a reversal in the gender identity of the major protagonist in many *noir* films. This point should be obvious from what has been argued so far. The leading male in the *noir* film may have a role, such as a private eye or a police officer, which suggests he is the major protagonist. However, this cannot always be taken at face value. As the narrative unfolds, he will often be revealed to be a mere pawn in the game being played by the fatal woman. A weakness such as this might be expected of the insurance agents in *Double Indemnity* or *Pitfall*, the cashier in *Scarlet Street* (1945), the ambulance driver in *Angel Face* (1953), or the doctor in *Where Danger Lives* (1950). But it is also a fate to which the private detective in *Out of the Past*, or the assistant district attorney in *The File on Thelma Jordan* (1950) are not immune.

While *noir* films often show police officers as violent, corrupt and ready for seduction, it is difficult to find examples in which they are victims of the fatal woman's schemes. In a film such as *The Big Combo* (1955), the police officer is sexually obsessed with the fatal woman, but she has no plan in which he is implicated. Likewise, the 'rogue cop' in *The Big Heat* (1953) resists sexual temptation since he remains faithful to the memory of his dead wife. The general point at issue here is that the prime mover in the *noir* film is often the fatal woman rather the nominal male hero. This is the case even if the film's conclusion leads to her destruction.

These considerations have led to the argument that the *noir* film opens up a space for women outside patriarchy and offers opportunities whereby it can be resisted. There are story-lines in some *noir* films, such as *Phantom Lady* (1944) and *The Reckless Moment* (1949), where, without the patriarch, the woman is, by design or default, the investigator or troubleshooter. There is even a *noir* film, *Raw Deal* (1948), in which the woman succumbs to a fatal man and falls prey to the doomed romanticism which normally afflicts the male. Unusually, this film, like *Mildred Pierce* (1945), also uses the woman's voice-over narration to tell the story. Notwithstanding these examples, this argument is meant to apply to the general run of *noir* films.

We have already noted Kaplan's claims regarding this point. Similarly, Gledhill argues that aspects of *film noir* 'structure, in an intermittent commentary, a discourse about women and sometimes, perhaps subversively, for women' (Gledhill 1980: 14). One such aspect is 'the suppression of the bourgeois family and centrality of women in the male world of action', which 'produces female representations outside family definition and dependency'. These tend to remain sexual in character – the woman 'is filmed for her sexuality' (ibid.: 19) – and they fail to be 'progressive' since 'female sexuality is ... juxtaposed ... to the law and the voice of male judgement' (ibid.: 15).

However, this does not necessarily displace the importance of women in *film noir*. Not unusually, 'the centre of the plot is dominated by questions about female sexuality and sexual relationships involving patterns of deception, seduction and unrecognised revelations rather than by deductions of criminal activity from a web of clues' (Gledhill 1980: 16). 'The plot of the typical *film noir* is ... a struggle between different voices for control over the telling of the story.' This means that 'the woman's discourse may realise itself in a heroine's resistance to the male control of her story, in the course of the film's narration' (ibid.: 16–17).

The way the heroine is depicted can support and extend this argument. Gledhill argues that the *noir* film does not represent the fatal woman, the heroine, as a consistently 'unstable' and 'treacherous' protagonist. This is particularly evident if she is contrasted with the 'marginal female figure representing the good woman' and the male who, despite his misfortunes, retains 'a consistency of values' (1980: 18). For example, 'not only is the hero frequently not sure whether the woman is honest or a deceiver, but the heroine's characterisation is itself fractured so that it is not evident to the audience whether she fills the [fatal woman] stereotype or not' (ibid.: 18).

The significance of these representations is underlined by the way *film noir* is argued to treat the family. Harvey, for example, suggests that the *noir* film 'is structured around the destruction or absence of romantic love and the family' (1980: 25, cf. 33), in contrast to the typical Hollywood romance and the American dream. 'The possession of' the '*film noir* women' is 'held up', for the male protagonists, 'as a tempting means of escape from the boredom and frustration of a routinised and alienated existence' (ibid.: 26–7). However, these 'women are not, finally, possessed' (ibid.: 27). There are thus considerable differences between *film noir* and the way romance and the family figure in the standard Hollywood narrative.

The main sexual relationship in these films does not become romantic love and lead to the formation of another family. Instead, the couple is destroyed by the relationship. As we have seen, the female's destruction is usually physical as well as moral, while the male's fate is, if not death, then melancholy. Since 'many of the films noirs depict a boredom and sterility associated with the married state ... both men and women seek sexual satisfaction outside marriage' (Harvey 1980: 29, 31). The irony here is that 'both pleasure and death lie outside the safe circle of family relations' (ibid.: 29). The sexual relationship between the fatal woman and her male victim in the *noir* film is, to some extent, sanctioned by the ways in which the family, marriage and romantic love are represented. Sometimes they are not directly represented at all. At other times they are presented, but merely as unexciting, predictable, claustrophobic and mundane institutions. In other instances, the secondary male character, whose wealth the fatal woman is after and to whom she is often married or involved with, is not infrequently impotent. All of this means that the actions of the *noir* couple acquire a rationale which rests upon escaping or defying convention and routine, rather than finding romance and the ideal marriage. It equally means that the fatal woman discovers a power and independence outside romance and the family that are not normally available to women within a patriarchal society.

'The strange and compelling absence of "normal" family relations in these films' indicates, for Harvey, that 'important shifts in the position of women in American society' were taking place (1980: 25). She has in mind here such changes as the temporary wartime introduction of greater numbers of women into the workforce, often to do jobs left by men who were instead fighting overseas. This gave women an important financial independence, as well as the experience of work and the sense that they could do jobs that were previously the province of men. We shall return to this point below when we consider the causes of *film noir*. However, we can note here that Harvey argues that these social changes lie behind some of the things she notes occurring in *film noir*, which we have looked at above. Therefore, *film noir* 'may be seen, in part, as an indirect response to this forcible assault on traditional family structures and the traditional and conservative values which they embodied'. She refers to *Mildred Pierce* as an example of this trend (ibid.: 25).

It can therefore be concluded that *film noir* has provided representations of the independence and power which are available to women, especially the fatal woman, outside the constraints of the traditional family and a patriarchal society. However, these representations are often confined and restricted by their focus on sexuality and manipulation and are subject to the forces of patriarchy which seem to prevail in the end. A brief but pointed example can be found in *The Big Heat*. In one scene, Gloria Grahame tells her boyfriend, Lee Marvin, about a new perfume she is wearing; one which 'attracts mosquitoes and repels men'. He, however, replies that it does not work on him and she complies. Also, later in the film, she becomes the victim of his horrific violence, though she does eventually get her revenge. As Gledhill points out, these films 'both challenge the ideological hegemony of the family and in the end locate an oppressive and outcast place for women' (1980: 19). This suggests that the *noir* film may be better seen as conformist rather than subversive in its representations of women. Gledhill and others have usefully shown how this type of film can be subversive and how it differs from the typical Hollywood film and the more conventional cinematic depiction of American society. However, they have equally indicated the limits to which these characteristics are subject. This can imply that the *noir* film is a morality tale which presents a warning about what happens when men and women stray from the path of convention. In this sense, we could argue that *film noir* conforms to the model of social and sexual order we described above. To be certain about any of these conclusions, we would require more knowledge than we have of the *noir* films' audiences and how they responded to the films and their themes.

Explanations of *film noir*

In this section we shall look at some of the reasons put forward for the emergence and eventual decline of *film noir*. With some explanations these are obviously connected. If the appearance of a certain phenomenon is said to induce the rise of *film noir*, then its disappearance will mean that *film noir* can no longer be sustained. For example, if, as Schrader argues, the emergence of *film noir* is attributable to a mood of postwar disillusionment then the gradual removal of this mood will lead to the demise of *film noir*. People will no longer need to see *noir* films because they are no longer disillusioned. As we have already noted at various points in this book, there are quite severe problems with this type of 'needs and gratifications' or 'mood of society' explanation. However, it is useful for making the point that explanations about the rise of *film noir* can also account for its decline.

This, however, raises another qualification. It can be suggested that since its establishment, *film noir* has never really gone into decline. Its critical recognition, first in France and then in America and elsewhere, has meant that *noir* films have continued to be produced ever since the earliest examples mentioned above. There may have been a short interruption in the making of *noir* films in the 1960s. However, even this is debatable and the self-conscious definition of *film noir* has ensured its presence ever since. For example, as Bordwell *et al.* point out, 'recent years have seen the release of such films as *Chinatown* (1974) and *The Big Fix* (1978), which clearly are responses to the critical canonization of *film noir*' (1985: 75). Certainly nowadays, most *noir* films that are made are explicitly acknowledged as such by their makers and the critics. *Film noir* has become a distinctive genre particularly in the consumer guides provided by newspapers and magazines. It may also now have a continuity simply because film makers are taught it in film school. This continuity means that explanations need not necessarily account for the demise of the *film noir*, though they may have to recognise the subsequent rise in its critical and aesthetic status (Hugo 1992).

A consideration of explanations of *film noir* should allow us to develop our assessment of some of the specific features of its nature and context and its relation to Hollywood and the American dream. It should also allow us to raise some more general points about the sociology of film. This will pave the way for the critical conclusion to this chapter. The explanations to be considered can roughly be divided into cultural, political and economic ones, though we shall not insist on any rigid division between the three. Before we look at these we need to consider a very popular way of accounting for *film noir*. This attributes its appearance and significance to the changing mood of society and sees it as a sign of the times. This is also a popular way of interpreting films more generally.

Film noir *as a reflection of society*

We have already seen examples of this above in our discussion of *film noir* definitions. As Kerr points out, this interpretation argues that *film noir* 'was the cinema's unmediated reflection of an all-pervading postwar gloom' and thus treats it as a 'symptom of social malaise' (1986: 222).[3] Schrader, for example, traces one of the sources of *film noir* to a widespread sense of 'post-war disillusionment' which 'was directly demonstrated' in *film noir*. He suggests 'the disillusionment many soldiers, small businessmen and housewife/factory employees felt in returning to a peacetime economy was directly mirrored in the sordidness of the urban crime film' (1972: 9–10). Thus, *film noir* directly reflects the disaffected mood of society.

We have already criticised this type of explanation of films, notably in the chapter on horror, and we can repeat but also extend that argument here. It is interesting to note, first, that some authors regard the 1940s in America as an era of hope and optimism, rather than one of cynicism and despair. Even Schrader sees the need for *film noir* to decline by the mid-1950s when 'Americans were eager to see a more bourgeois view of themselves' (1972: 12), though he continues to use a reflectionist theory of film. Quart and Auster take a more detailed view of the issue. They concede that *film noir* may have represented 'a revelation of some unconscious public despair'. But they also point to 'the war-inspired conviction that sufficient energy and good will existed in the society to solve any problem and triumph over any evil' (1984: 28). This defines for them 'the basic self-confidence' and 'the essential optimism of the 1940s'. Against this, '*film noir*'s evocation of evil may have served only as a delicious contrast: making the ultimate victory of goodness and justice that much more glorious' (ibid.). However, this conclusion does not only question the idea that *film noir* expressed a social sense of gloom and despair. It also raises suspicions about this form of explanation in general because here we have a radically different interpretation of the public mood to that which is more usually attributed to *film noir*. Severe doubts must be cast upon this reflectionist theory of film if Quart and Auster can have the opposite view of the mood of society to that perceived by Schrader and others. It suggests that reading off films as a reflection of some imputed social mood, which is either difficult to define or confined to the films themselves, is a limited if not futile exercise. Indeed, Quart and Auster suggest, as do Bordwell *et al.* (1985: 76–7), that *noir* films were also 'merely derivations from other popular arts such as the successful hard-boiled novels of Cain, Hammett and Chandler' and 'products of whatever genre films made a profit at the box office' (1984: 28).

Equally, the reflectionist interpretation relies upon a liberal and pluralist view of society (Kerr 1986: 220), which argues that its culture, including its films, can directly reflect a democratic consensus. Therefore, society's institutions, including its media, are sufficiently open and democratic to enable films to reflect society's mood or disposition. This view, however, ignores the effects of inequalities of power in the economy, politics and culture in determining not only what is shown, but also what is not shown. If the latter is the case, it severely limits the capacity of films to reflect, directly or indirectly, any widespread mood or consensus. Likewise, it suggests that the ideas to be found in films may be imposed upon their viewers; may be most consistent with the interests of the most powerful; and may simply be misleading, illusory or marginal.

The reflectionist model, as we have seen, mistakenly assumes that decisions made by consumers on what films to see add up to a mood or predisposition of society as a whole. It also fails to tell us how film makers acquire the knowledge to make films which reflect society. Kerr argues that it regards Hollywood as 'a monolithically conceived film industry'. Instead, he suggests we think of it as a set of 'particular, relatively autonomous modes of film production, distribution and exhibition in a particular [historical] conjuncture' (1986: 223, cf. 220). This, in turn, means, at the very least, that these modes must mediate between, or intervene within and therefore shape and influence, the relationship between films and the wider society. We will look at the detail of Kerr's argument below, but we can note here that he does provide a useful alternative to the popular reflectionist interpretation of *film noir*.

Cultural interpretations of film noir

First we need to look at cultural explanations: that is, arguments about the cultural influences that led to the emergence of *film noir*. We shall consider a number of those mentioned most frequently in the literature. However, their influence should not be exaggerated, for they do not take us that far in accounting for *film noir*. They tend to focus upon aesthetics rather than ideology, even though they refer to culture. Indeed, *film noir* has more often been interpreted as a critique of ideology – for example, that of the American dream – than it has as an aspect of the ideology of a capitalist society like America.

One of the most important arguments in developing the study of *film noir* has been that put forward by Schrader. In particular, he draws attention to a number of cultural influences upon *film noir*. The first is what he calls 'the German influence' (1972: 10). During the 1920s and 1930s, a large number of film makers – directors, writers, actors, cinematographers, composers, and so on – fled to Hollywood to escape political and racial persecution in Germany and Central and Eastern Europe. Working in the Hollywood system, these expatriates were able to inject into its products some of the style and content they had learnt and developed in their homelands. This effect was known as German expressionism and included such things as 'unnatural or expressionist lighting', 'chiaroscuro' or high contrasts between black and white, and a sense of doomed romanticism. Expressionism basically means the use of external features, such as darkness, to express internal states of consciousness, such as fatalism and despair (Hirsch 1981: 53–8). This approach was therefore seen to stimulate the emergence of *film noir*. Many of the film makers who worked in this vein were German and other European émigrés, such as Fritz Lang, Robert Siodmak and Billy Wilder. However, many of them were not, and while the style may have eventually flourished, it cannot be regarded as the direct product of a number of individuals (Kerr 1986: 220, 222). It is equally argued that it influenced other genres as well, such as the horror film (see Chapter 4). Also, this has not been the only cultural influence attributed to individual artists.

Schrader refers us also to the influence of the American detective and crime novel upon *film noir*: what he and others describe as *the hard-boiled tradition*. Having 'their roots in pulp fiction or journalism', a group of writers, which included Dashiell Hammett, James M. Cain, Raymond Chandler, Horace McCoy and others (a later but significant figure is Cornell Woolrich), created a 'tough' and 'cynical' type of detective and crime fiction (Schrader 1972: 10). This 'hard-boiled', pared down style read more like a film script than a conventional novel and emphasised dialogue, atmosphere and action more than description, plot and introspection. Those writers who fashioned it are credited with introducing a class-divided, urban realism to the detective novel and a 'tough and cynical, albeit protected, romanticism' to its hero. Many of these 'hard-boiled' writers had their stories and novels adapted for *noir* films and themselves went to Hollywood to work as screenwriters, contributing scripts for such films. Probably the most famous of these writers, though not the most 'hard-boiled', has been Raymond Chandler who created the proto-typical, cynical but romantic private detective hero, Philip Marlowe. A number of Chandler's novels were adapted as scripts for *noir* films, often with the explicit intention to directly film their '*noir*ish' atmosphere, as with *Murder, My Sweet* (1944). Chandler himself wrote a few original screenplays for *noir* films, such as *The Blue Dahlia* (1946) and, with Billy Wilder, *Double Indemnity* (1944). We must again be wary of attributing too much influence to a group of individual artists. However, as both Bordwell *et al.* (1985: 76–7) and Quart and Auster (1984: 28) point out, *film noir* shows Hollywood cinema 'taking over' the conventions, content and style of this type of popular literature. Also, as with German expressionism, the hard-boiled tradition can, despite the differences it contains, be seen as a cultural movement.

The last cultural influence mentioned by Schrader is 'post-war realism' (1972: 10). He and others have noted the influence of wartime film newsreels and documentary film making upon popular cinema. It has been noted, for example, how it encouraged the use of location shooting and hand-held cameras for point of view shots. This move towards greater realism influenced the development of *film noir*, although it did not directly shape some of its earliest and more muted examples. Schrader again ties this into his reflectionist, sign-of-the-times interpretation of film. 'The realistic movement', he argues, 'suited America's post-war mood.' Popular film had to meet 'the public's desire for a more honest and harsh view of America' which could no longer be 'satisfied by the same studio sets'. Therefore, this movement 'succeeded in breaking *film noir* away from the domain of the high class melodrama, placing it where it more properly belonged, in the streets with everyday people' (ibid.). Another cultural influence which needs to be mentioned is that exercised by 'the established film genres of the 1930s'. These are argued to have laid various aspects of the groundwork for *film noir*. For example, the gangster film is said to have established the more realistic representation of both crime and the city, while the horror film is thought to have introduced dimly lit interiors and the use of darkness to evoke menace and evil (Hirsch 1981: chapter 3).

As authors such as Bordwell *et al.* (1985) and Kerr (1986) show, and as we have tried to argue above, Hollywood is a historically specific film industry, whose products are commercially produced within typical and conventional technical, narrational and generic frameworks. Whatever the relative merits of the cultural influences outlined, they need to be understood and appreciated within this context. Political influences which relate to the industrial pattern of film, as well as to politics more generally, have been seen as being important for the development of *film noir*. It would therefore be useful to look at some of them here.

Political influences

One of these influences has been thought to be the involvement of politically radical and socially conscious film makers in the formation of *film noir*. Kemp notes that 'explicit political statements are rare in *film noir*' even though most of the films 'share a set of implicit, perhaps even inadvertent attitudes to society which readily lend themselves to interpretation as left-wing' (1986: 268). As we have seen above, Kemp argues *film noir* is open to this interpretation because it presents a critical, pessimistic and cynical picture of the American dream and American capitalism. '*Film noir* explores the symptoms of a deformed society ... cankered by greed', including 'the corrosive power of money', 'the callous cash payment', class 'hatred and violence', individual self-interest and habitual corruption (ibid.: 268–9).

Responsibility for this critique could rest with the political intentions of the film makers. Kemp notes 'there were ... avowed leftists, of various shades among the writers and directors of *film noir* and many of them introduced socialist views into their work, if not necessarily with the express aim of advancing the cause' (1986: 268). These were the ones who were most likely to fall foul of the investigation by the House Committee on Un-American Activities (HUAC) into Communist subversion in various areas of American society, including Hollywood. The post-war machinations of the committee covered the years between 1945 and 1954 and involved obtaining from witnesses the names of Communists, or sympathisers, working in Hollywood. Those identified could then become open to political persecution. The committee's acquisition of names led to those named being called as further witnesses and urged to give other names, and so on (ibid.: 270). Failure to name names or admit to being a Communist before the committee led to prison terms for a number of film makers. 'Most of the avowed leftists' working in the Hollywood film industry, according to Kemp, 'fell victim ... to McCarthyism'. He adds that 'some recanted (Rossen, Dmytryk); some were blacklisted (Howard Koch, Albert Maltz, Polonsky); some driven into exile (Losey, Dassin); some self-exiled (Welles, Huston)' (ibid.: 268).

These film makers thus had the political theory and social conscience to motivate them to make *noir* films. This is suggested by their politics in Hollywood, their membership of the Communist party, their participation in popular front movements in the 1930s, their involvement in radical theatre and their view of art as a political force for radical social change. Political experience and motivation would obviously have varied between them. An instructive if not completely representative example is Abraham Polonsky. He is famous for writing *Body and Soul* (1947) and directing and co-writing *Force of Evil*, two of the more radically inclined and socially conscious *noir* films. Equally, he is worth mentioning as he was 'one of the few writers' who went to Hollywood 'with previous experience in the CP [Communist Party] and a deep knowledge of Marxist theory'. Also, he was 'the only screenwriter to have had any involvement with non-literary trade union organizing' (Ceplair and Englund 1979: 191).

However, Kemp argues that *noir* films were also made by people 'with no known left affiliations' (1986: 268). For example, Kemp provides a detailed outline of *Where Danger Lives* (1950), arguing that it is representative of *film noir*'s radical view of society. But, as he goes on to note, its 'director, John Farrow, was a Catholic, devout to the point of excess', who never 'attracted the attention of HUAC' and was untroubled by the blacklist (ibid.). This suggests that the radical, left-wing implications of *film noir* must have existed as an unconscious 'set of political assumptions so widely held as to have become virtually undetectable' to supporters and opponents alike (ibid.).

Kemp therefore puts forward his theory about the politics of *film noir*. This argues that *film noir* was 'a riposte, a sour, disenchanted flip-side to the optimism and flag waving piety of much of Hollywood's "official" output of the period' (1986: 270). His case seems to be that the left-wing, oppositional and radical politics suppressed during the Cold War and the dominance of HUAC had to gain expression somewhere. To find an outlet, no matter how oblique, obscure or subtle it may have been, this politics chose to emerge in *film noir*. Thus the thawing of the Cold War and the retreat of HUAC led to its decline (ibid; cf. Schrader 1972).

There are at least three problems with this theory, apart from the fact that it is probably less plausible than that which attributes some influence to left-wing, political film makers. (After all, their role could have been influential in suggesting certain themes and styles, without necessarily being comprehensive or uniform.) First, it still relies upon a reflectionist view of the relationship between film and society. Here, films function to express a submerged and disaffected politics. Moreover, this theory reduces society to the level of the individual psyche, since it is based upon Freud's theory of the interpretation of dreams. This means the theory does not realise that these are different levels of reality, or what might be termed ontologically distinct phenomena. Likewise, it fails to recognise that functions need not necessarily be fulfilled and that politics may be effectively suppressed. Also, the theory does not tell us how political ideologies which are repressed manage to find expression in films.

Second, is *film noir* as critical of American capitalism and its ideology as is suggested? Many *noir* films present stories and characters which do not fit easily into the picture presented by Kemp and others. There remains a moral world of difference between the 'rogue cop' and the gangsters in even the most typical *noir* films. *Film noir* is more likely to be characterised by the ambiguity it expresses about the relationship between good and evil, than by the unambiguous portrayal of a corrupt society. Its critical interest is often seen to lie in this quality. Even if we assume for the sake of argument that the films are as Kemp sees them, audiences at the time may not have interpreted them in the way he suggests. They could, for example, have viewed them as morality tales, showing what could happen if money becomes everything in people's lives. What evidence there is suggests that the audience for many

'B' *noir* films shared much in common with their characters (Maltby 1984: 66).

Third, it follows from this that *film noir* may not have had the distinctive politics Kemp argues it had. Authors such as McArthur, whom Kemp cites (1986: 268), and Quart and Auster suggest that *film noir* is without politics because it has little idea of society. As the latter put it (and as indicated above), 'despite their sense of universal corruption', *noir* films 'had little sense of society'. Usually, 'they defined corruption in psychological and more often metaphysical terms, where human beings could only stand impotent and helpless in the face of evil' (1984: 27–8). In McArthur's words, *film noir* is metaphysical because it deals 'with angst and loneliness as essential elements of the human condition' (Kemp 1986: 268). Despite Kemp's criticisms, this is not obviously conducive to the politics he seeks to detect in *film noir*. Others might also argue that pessimism and cynicism led towards an isolated quietism and away from leftist politics.

Economic explanations

We shall now consider economic influences in concluding this section on explanations of *film noir*. Explanations which focus upon the history of industrial and economic factors in the formation and development of *film noir* are not that prominent in the literature. One important exception, which we have noted above in our discussion of gender, looks at the increased wartime employment of women in the American workforce. It is argued that this fuelled male anxieties about the financial and sexual independence of women, which were expressed in *film noir*. Eventually, this resulted in a backlash, with women being encouraged back into the home and the embrace of patriarchy (Harvey 1980). Viewing *noir* films as morality tales suggests they could, intentionally or unintentionally, have had this effect. There is still a reflectionist and functional feel to this argument, but it does at least identify some of the stories that found their way into *noir* films. Despite their relative absence, economic and related explanations are probably more systematic and substantial than some others that have been discussed. Provided their terms are not too rigid or narrow, they are perhaps more plausible and persuasive. For example, it would be simplistic, as Kerr shows, to explain *film noir* 'as ... an attempt to make a stylistic virtue out of economic necessity' (1986: 220), even if its clarity and relevance make it an appealing idea.

Kerr's explanation is the one we shall consider here as it is probably the most substantial and systematic attempt to relate *film noir* to the history of the American film industry. While political influences were not a major consideration in Kerr's original analysis, he does provide some illumination in a later preface. His argument is that *noir* films are best understood as 'B' films, arising out of the developments which produced them both. Thus, government action, 'the 1940 Consent Decree', 'eliminated both blind selling and block booking'. This 'encouraged' the use of 'trade shows for every film (and not just A films')' and 'an increasing differentiation of product especially at the most threatened end of the industry, that of the smaller independent studios and the B units' (1986: 221). This political influence combined with economic changes to play its part in the emergence of *film noir*.

The major argument put forward by Kerr is that 'the B *film noir*' was formed 'by a negotiated resistance to the realist aesthetic on the one hand and an accommodation to restricted expenditure on the other' (1986: 223). This occurred along with developments in production, distribution and exhibition in Hollywood during the 1930s and 1940s. The 'B' film arose in the early 1930s out of 'an attempt by a number of independent exhibitors to lure audiences back into their theatres at a time of acute economic crisis in the industry' (ibid.: 227). By the mid 1940s, the double bill had become a standard feature at cinemas. This had thereby fostered 'an entirely new mode of film production – the B unit' (ibid.: 228). The double bill combined 'one relatively expensive A film and one relatively inexpensive B'. The former came from 'the major studios', the latter from 'low budget units at the same studios' or one of the 'several B studios'. A cinema's rental of an 'A' film 'was based on a percentage of box office takings', while the 'B' film relied on a flat fee and so was less dependent upon 'audience attendance figures'. These fixed rentals would have formed the basis upon which the fixed budgets for the production of 'B' *noir* films would have been calculated, all 'B' films being produced in this way (ibid.: 228–9). Also, when shown outside double bills, 'B' films were more likely to be seen in less prestigious cinemas in less central and affluent areas than 'A' films (ibid.: 228). As Maltby points out, 'the *film noir* ... was a low status product, playing to the bottom end predominantly of the urban market' (1984: 66).

The budgetary constraints on 'B' film making tended to involve 'variable costs like sets, scripts, footage, casual labour and, crucially, power' (Kerr 1986: 230). These constraints combined with generic limitations and the demands placed on the 'B' feature in a double bill – that it not take too much time away from the 'A' feature – to distinguish the 'B' film. They meant that these films had relatively short running times, usually 'between fifty-five and seventy-five minutes'. What is more important, they had a degree of autonomy in production which may have furnished fertile ground for the *film noir* style. For example, 'the paucity of "production values" (sets, stars and so forth) may even have encouraged low budget production units to compensate with complicated plots and convoluted atmosphere'. It thereby pro-moted an expressionistic rather than a realistic style (ibid.: 231; cf. Hugo 1992).

Kerr's argument is that the 'B' *film noir*, 'like the B film gener-ally', 'was determined not only economically but also ideologi-cally'. It was formed 'not only by accommodation to restricted expenditure but also by resistance to the realist aesthetic'. For example, the double bill was not just shaped by the financial need to put any two pictures together. It came also to depend upon the contrasts between the 'A' and 'B' features. This rested on the com-mercial appeal that it had for producers, distributors, exhibitors and audiences alike, but it obviously also relied on the differentia-tion of the 'B' from the 'A' film. This led to 'B' films becoming more intricately hybrid and less obviously mainstream products. Kerr suggests that 'the curiously cross-generic quality of the *film noir* is perhaps a vestige of its origins as a kind of "oppositional" cine-matic mode'. For example, 'low key lighting' may not just have been 'more economic', but also more 'dramatic' and 'radical' than 'high key lighting' (1986: 232).

The Anti-Trust action of 1948 meant that the major Hollywood studios had to divest themselves of their control over cinema chains (see Chapter 1). This led to 'the demise of many independent studios which had thrived on providing films for the bottom half of the [double] bill' (Kerr 1986: 234). It also led to the eventual decline of the double bill: 'quite simply, low budget productions could no longer be guaranteed fixed rentals in exhibition' (ibid.). This process of divestment, which had been started by 'the Anti-Trust suit in 1938', was not completed until 1959, the period during which 'the B *film noir* flourished' (ibid.: 235). This, therefore, also explains why, at this point, the *noir* film may have suffered a relative decline.

It was during this period that the 'B' *film noir* emerged to negotiate 'an "oppositional space" within and against realistic cinematic practice'. This ideological process pushed the *film noir* to resist three contemporary 'strands of realism – Technicolour, television and the A film', a resistance which supported its differentiation as a 'B' film product (Kerr 1986: 237–8). The incorporation, for example, of 'a colour aesthetic within realism' created 'the space which *film noir* was to occupy' (ibid.: 241). This period thus 'saw the conjunction of a primarily economically determined mode of production, known as B film-making, with what were primarily ideologically defined modes of "difference", known as the *film noir*' (ibid.: 242).

This is a very useful and promising account of *film noir* which seems to get us further than many of the other explanations we have considered. However, it is not without problems and a discussion of these can introduce the conclusion to this chapter. First, while Kerr makes a convincing case for the emergence of a distinctive type of 'B' film, he is less convincing when he argues this 'B' film took the direction of *film noir*. The crime thriller, which is the conventional genre where we usually find *noir* films, was not the only popular 'B' film. Westerns were equally popular but did not take the same aesthetic direction, and while horror, another popular 'B' genre, shares more with *film noir*, there still remains a clear difference between the two. This point does not deny that there may have been an aesthetic opposition between *film noir* and cinematic realism, but it does ask why this was true only of the crime thriller. Kerr does not want to argue that *film noir* arose simply through the exercise of artistic ingenuity within the constraints of restricted expenditure. Yet it is difficult to exclude this completely if we are to make sense of what is thought of as an aesthetically oppositional genre, which is how he thinks of *film noir*. It may be even more important if we try to distinguish between the distinct genres associated with the emergence of the 'B' film.

We have conceded on the first point that *film noir* may have been opposed to cinematic realism. However, our second point is that *film noir* is often thought of as being more, not less, realistic than the mainstream Hollywood film (Bordwell *et al.* 1985: 77). This has, in part, been mentioned by those film makers responsible for *noir* films. They welcomed the opportunities that such film making gave them to present a more realistic portrayal of American society than Hollywood usually permitted. Think of the socially conscious films and film makers mentioned in the previous section on political influences. Think also of the influence that the realistic crime novel and cinematic realism are thought to have exercised over the emergence of *film noir*. Schrader (1972), for example, has linked *film noir* closely to what he calls postwar realism. This is not to argue that these views are necessarily correct, but it does indicate that the idea of realism at stake here needs to be identified, clarified and illustrated at greater length. The last point of criticism that needs to be made here is that Kerr has exaggerated the oppositional or radical nature of *film noir*. *Film noir* may not be as critical or as different as is often claimed in the literature. We can leave this as a question mark against Kerr's argument since it is the problem that will be discussed in our concluding section.

Conclusions

There are a number of fairly obvious difficulties with the idea of *film noir*, as may be apparent from the preceding discussion. These include disagreements over those films which are to count as *film noir* and those which are not and the historical period to which *film noir* is to be consigned. There is some agreement on both these questions. There is a body of films which contributors seem prepared to regard as *noir* films and there is a sense that the 1940s and 1950s were the times when they were most likely to be made. Also, it is now thought that *noir* films have appeared at frequent intervals since the late 1950s and early 1960s (see, for example, Gallafent 1992; Grist 1992). This means that the decline of *film noir*, which some authors try to account for, has not happened due to the critical acclaim it has subsequently achieved, its convenience as a consumer guide and its place on the curriculum of film schools and film studies.

However, disagreements remain over both the precise period in the 1940s and 1950s when *film noir* is supposed to have emerged and established itself and the films to be covered by this definition. There are indeed wide differences between critics over the number of films to be counted as *film noir*. For example, Spencer (1984) lists over 500 titles, Silver and Ward about 300 (1980: 333–6, 379), while Bourde and Chaumeton refer to only 22 (Vernet 1993: 24) and Tuska insists that only films with obviously unhappy endings truly count as *film noir* (1984: 151–2). There are also notable differences about the period which is to be identified with *film noir*. Some authors confine it to a very specific era, while others provide a much looser historical time scale. For example, Kemp (1986) and Schrader (1972) tend to confine *film noir* to the period between 1945 and 1955, though Hirsch (1981: 199) restricts it to the years between 1944 and 1950. By contrast, Durgnat (1970) extends *film noir* backwards and forwards in time.

Disagreements such as these must raise questions about the coherence and usefulness of the idea of *film noir*. However, they have to some extent always been apparent in its discussion. Perhaps more serious are those criticisms which directly question its status and explanations. Vernet, for example, refers to the disagreement over the historical period and scale of *film noir* (1993: 2–4). However, he takes the argument further. Like

Bordwell *et al.*, his approach emphasises the structural continuity of Hollywood cinema, rather than its cyclical discontinuity. Also, he argues that the initial interest shown in France and the historical and critical context this provided was crucially important in shaping the terms of the subsequent debate about *film noir* (ibid.: 4–5, 20–6). These points allow him to raise a number of issues.

He notes first that a number of film makers associated with *film noir* had 'nothing to do with Germany or even Austria' and that a number of film makers from these areas in Europe had 'nothing in common with expressionism' (Vernet 1993: 7). Moreover, he finds evidence of expressionism in Hollywood films prior to the emergence of the *film noir* and suggests that a number of the stylistic traits attributed to *film noir* have a much longer history (ibid.: 8–12). This raises serious doubts about the stylistic integrity and historical novelty often attributed to *film noir*.

Second, he raises questions about the role and influence of the hard-boiled detective novel. The key thing here is the time lag between the appearance in the 1920s and early 1930s of the first stories and novels of Hammett, the first hard-boiled writer, and the screening of the first *noir* films in the 1940s. (There is also a ten-year gap between the appearance of the first novels of Hammett and Chandler.) This raises the following question: why could the *noir* message not be obtained from this literature, if there was such a public need for it? Also, films were made from this literature before the 1940s and could be interpreted as *film noir* but usually are not. Vernet cites *Dangerous Female*, the first film version of Hammett's novel *The Maltese Falcon*, as an example (1993: 12–14). This came out in 1931, a year after the novel and ten years before what is usually deemed to be the *film noir* version.

A similarly radical view of *film noir* is taken by Reid and Walker. They contest one of the standard points of agreement in the literature, that the employment of women in the wartime workforce afforded them greater independence and fed the job insecurities and sexual anxieties of men. They point out 'it was not during or after World War Two but during the Depression that the prejudice against working women … was most acute' (1993: 63). They also raise other questions about the supposed links between *film noir* and the postwar period. They argue that if *film noir* was expressing a world-view audiences were eager to consume, why did the numbers going to the cinema begin to fall dramatically after 1946 (ibid.: 59)? They also note that the 'post-war forties reversed long-standing demographic trends of increased divorce and lowered fertility' (ibid.: 61, 93–4). This suggests a period of optimism and hope, a point also made by Quart and Auster (1984: 28).

In the end, Vernet is led to argue that 'numerous films are swept under the rug in order to attempt to maintain an artificial purity and isolation of *film noir*' (1993: 14). Vernet's radical view of *film noir* thus questions its very status by suggesting that it 'belongs to the history of film criticism' rather than to 'the history of cinema'. He concludes that it is an idea which 'for the moment, can only be found in books' (ibid.: 26). Similarly, Reid and Walker raise 'the more interesting matter of whether it [*film noir*] exists at all' (1993: 59).

In view of these criticisms, what are we to make of *film noir*? We have seen how the extent to which it can be presented as a critique of Hollywood cinema, the American dream and American society is more limited than is usually recognised. Equally, while there may be films which can be called *noir* films, they may not be as significant or as unique as is often claimed. However, *film noir* can still be related to the general concerns of this book if we return to the argument put forward by Bordwell *et al.* with which we started this discussion. This contends that *film noir* does not ultimately disturb the dominant mode of Hollywood film making, nor its typical narrative pattern. However, they qualify this by noting the impact of *film noir* in a number of areas. They suggest that '*film noir* has been considered to challenge the classical Hollywood cinema in four ways' (1985: 75). One of these is technique and style. For many authors *film noir* is its style, but it is not an area we have concentrated on in this chapter.

What then are 'these patterns of nonconformity' (Bordwell *et al.* 1985: 75)? The first is 'an assault on psychological causality'. *Film noir* characters are not psychologically stable, but are often morally ambiguous and the protagonists also usually suffer 'internal conflict'. This questions the 'logical action', clearly 'defined

characters' and the 'psychologically stable hero' of classical Hollywood cinema. The second is 'a challenge to the prominence of
heterosexual romance'. In *film noir*, the psychologically unstable
hero is confronted with the fatal woman, the seductive but manipulative heroine. Their sexual relationship is not romantic and does not
result in a happy marriage, as would be expected in the typical
Hollywood picture. The third is 'an attack on the motivated happy
ending'. This, to some extent, follows from the previous point. The
film noir does not end with the happy resolution of the relationship
between the male and female leads. Most consistently, 'the resolution
of the plot often expresses the working of the fate that has overseen
the entire action; in this event, the film ends unhappily'. However,
this can be 'too shocking', or an internal or external moral censorship
can be imposed. In these circumstances, the *noir* film will have 'a lame
and tacked-on' ending, which will usually not dull the sense of corruption, cynicism and evil the rest of the film has evoked (ibid.: 76).

These 'patterns of nonconformity' have been much discussed
'because they attack certain American values prominent in mainstream Hollywood cinema', such as the American dream. However, they can be managed by the Hollywood system. They 'adhere
to specific and non-subversive conventions', in particular 'those
derived from crime literature and from canons of realistic and
generic motivation' (Bordwell *et al.* 1985: 76; cf. Quart and Auster
1984: 28). The point is that *film noir* appears less critical and
subversive when it is located within the narrative and generic
patterns of Hollywood cinema and other aspects of popular
culture. Not only is there not a great deal of difference between
film noir and the popular literature from which it has often been
drawn, but the latter has directly shaped and influenced many of
the supposedly novel and radical features of *film noir* (Vernet
1993). In turn, these features were readily assimilated by the
typical patterns of Hollywood cinema.

According to Bordwell *et al.*, 'every characteristic narrative device
of *film noir* was already conventional in American crime fiction
and drama of the 1930s and 1940s' (1985: 76). Examples include 'a
new realism', 'first person narration', 'the relativity of right and
wrong', 'the city as a jungle of corruption and terror', 'the solitary

investigator walking down "mean streets" ', 'expressionist subjec-
tivity', 'abnormal mental states', 'psychological ambiguity' and 'an
atmosphere of fear and peril' (ibid.: 76–7). These features had
already become conventional in hard-boiled detective novels, spy
stories and psychological thrillers and 'were easily assimilated by'
Hollywood cinema. This means that 'the narrative "problems"
posed by *films noirs* are in fact conventions taken over by Hollywood from popular literature' (ibid.: 77). *Film noir* introduced
these conventions, but kept them within the unity of the standard
Hollywood film, thereby blunting their critical edge.

Another telling way of illustrating this point is the *noir* interpretation of the film *The Dark Corner* (1946). As evidence, this interpretation refers to what it sees as 'a cry of existential anguish'
uttered by the detective hero – 'I feel all dead inside. I'm backed up
in a dark corner and I don't know who's hitting me' (Silver and
Ward 1980: 82). However, this can equally be seen as an example
of generic motivation along the lines suggested by Bordwell *et al.*
The line of dialogue immediately preceding this outburst, which is
part of the same speech, goes something like 'I can't get a handle on
this case'. The detective's despair is not about his fate amid the
alienation and gloom of the human condition, but the difficulties
he comes across in pursuing his investigation. These include, as
Silver and Ward note (ibid.), being framed for murder, which can
only add to his investigative frustrations. *The Dark Corner* is a
detective film with an investigative structure and the detective's
thoughts, words and deeds are made intelligible by this narrative.
The detective's voicing of his frustrations could also be viewed as
the introduction of a more realistic motivation than that which
commonly animates the investigative, detective story. The detective's 'cry of existential anguish' thus has the same generic status
as Sherlock Holmes's resort to his pipe and violin, or Philip Marlowe's turning to the whisky bottle and a chess problem. These are
ways of presenting the difficulties encountered before the investigation is successfully completed. The detective knows who is
hitting him by the end of *The Dark Corner* because he finally gets
'a handle on the case'.

Film noir is usually traced back to the original debate among

French critics after the end of the Second World War. This exercise tends to confine itself to those critics who regarded *film noir* as something different and special. Vernet (1993), for example, sees this debate as playing an important role in forming what is understood today as *film noir*. It is, therefore, interesting that even then there were dissenting voices, which contested the idea of *film noir*. Rey, for example, published a critical piece in 1948 that relies on a rather exaggerated and mechanical view of Hollywood films as propaganda, but which none the less raises some relevant points. He sees Hollywood cinema upholding the virtues of 'work, family' and the 'nation'. Far from agreeing with the view that *film noir* challenges these institutions and the society and cinema which support them, he argues that all it succeeds in doing is endorsing them. The 'dark or *noir* film (as the fashionable expression has it)' may 'offer images of American society that are hardly flattering'. However, it still upholds the values of the society even if it 'works through absurdity' and 'perhaps through deliberate reversal'.

Rey takes the example of *Double Indemnity* and argues that 'at no point' in it 'does conventional morality surrender its claim'. It 'takes pains to illustrate how crime does not, cannot, in fact, pay'. This is achieved through the continued presence of the chief insurance investigator, the moral and rational centre of the film, to whom the male protagonist's confession is addressed. The fatal woman may give 'the devil his due', but this accords 'with Christian tradition, which does not hesitate to represent evil when necessary'. The *noir* film, like Hollywood films more generally, 'far from denying certain social problems, readily represents them so that they may be better stigmatized'. This is another way of evaluating and explaining *film noir*. In the end, it cannot go beyond 'the spirit that gives Hollywood life and the standing orders that regulate the cinema as an industry' (1996: 28–9). This is not that inconsistent with the arguments of Bordwell *et al.* and Kerr, which, taken together, appear to offer the most useful way of understanding the economic, narrational and generic place of *film noir* in Hollywood cinema.

Chapter 6

Popular television

Citizenship, consumerism and television in the UK

W E CONCENTRATED UPON Hollywood in our survey of popular cinema because it is arguably the most powerful institution involved in its production, distribution and consumption. It also has a prominent role in popular culture more generally. However, other media, such as television, are not subject to precisely the same influences. Caughie draws attention, for example, to 'the difficulty in television of generalizing across national systems in the absence of the kind of international standard which classical Hollywood cinema has provided for the understanding of cinema' (1991a: 135). This conclusion would apply to popular television in Britain, whose study we shall be concerned with in this and the next three chapters. These will consider the production and consumption of popular television, the television audience, popular television genres and the issue of postmodernism.

There is a reasonable amount of historical detail available about popular television in Britain and a number of different histories which can and have been written.[1] This chapter will try to consider the development of popular television and look at some of the factors that have influenced its production and consumption. However, justice can hardly be done to the relevant material in one chapter. Therefore, we shall focus upon the specific issue of the conflict between citizenship and consumerism. This conflict has been a crucial factor in shaping the development of television and it has become even more relevant in recent years. It has been one of the most significant issues affecting popular television as popular culture and is a useful starting point for an introductory outline of this area. The ideas of citizenship and consumerism will be defined before we look at the development of popular television. This chapter will present an outline of some of the major changes which have occurred in this medium and will assess them by the conflict between citizenship and consumerism. We are concerned here with the institutional rather than the generic basis of popular culture, the conditions under which it is produced and consumed, not simply its content. This outline should also provide some of the crucial background to the subsequent chapters on television.

Citizenship and consumerism

To clarify the terms of this conflict and to stress its significance we can use Murdock's work on the subject. He sees cultural rights as an essential component of citizenship, which refers to the capacity of individuals to participate fully in a democratic system. He identifies citizenship as 'the right to participate fully in existing patterns of social life and to help shape the forms they may take in future' (1994: 158). Citizenship in the area of broadcasting means defining the viewer or listener as, first and foremost, a citizen who has cultural, as well as political and social rights.

Cultural rights cover participation in the areas of information, knowledge, representation and communication. Citizens need access to the information which will enable them 'to make considered personal and political judgements' and 'pursue their rights in other areas'. The information they have a right to should be 'comprehensive and disinterested information on the activities and plans of public and private agencies with significant power over people's lives'. Information, however, is often processed as knowledge; it is interpreted, argued over and used in explanations. Citizens, therefore, need to have access to this knowledge as well (Murdock 1994: 158). They equally need their 'experiences, beliefs and aspirations adequately and truthfully represented in the major forms of public culture'. To back this up, they require 'communication rights' which 'entail the right to contribute to the circulation of public information, knowledge and representation, not simply as a consumer but as an active provider' (ibid.: 159).

The provision of these rights has radical consequences for the organisation and funding of the broadcasting system. Television, for example, would have to meet a number of requirements. It would need to 'be as open as possible and not subject to undue influence from any one power group'. It would have to offer 'the widest possible range of viewpoints, perspectives and expressive forms'. In promoting this diversity it would also need to be 'available to everyone at the minimal feasible cost' (Murdock 1994: 159). This definition of citizenship should, ideally, lie at the heart of public service broadcasting.

By contrast, consumerism treats the viewer or listener as a consumer, as someone who is there to buy the services and goods produced. It regards television as a business which is there to be exploited for its profitability. The context in which television should operate is the 'consumer market place' where 'individual consumers ... must be enticed to part with their money'. Television run by private enterprise is primarily a way of 'assembling audiences for sale to advertisers' (Murdock 1994: 156–7). The fundamental determinant of what is produced is not citizenship, but the search for markets and profits. In this sense, consumerism provides a 'public service', not because it serves the rights of a democratic public, but simply because it gives people what they want, or what they are told they want (ibid.: 165). The market, not citizenship, determines what is to be produced and consumed.

The economic bases of these systems, the sources of their finance, are crucial in shaping their character. 'Who gets to speak in this central public space [television], to whom, about what and in which ways', Murdock argues, 'depends in large part on how the system is paid for.' The BBC is funded by the licence fee which everyone has to pay. This provides one way of protecting public service broadcasting and 'is the "least worst" way to maximise the range of voices in play and to ensure that their conversations and arguments are accessible to every citizen'. This source of finance is thus linked to the provision and protection of cultural, citizenship rights. By contrast, for the market-dominated, consumerist system of television provision, 'there is no "public", only individual consumers who must be enticed to part with their money'. Television has to work like any other business. There is no public service requirement which should have a prior or principled claim on television, since it has to be produced and consumed much like any other commodity. In these ways, 'funding plays a crucial role in organizing production and consumption' (1994: 157).

There are a number of recent examples of how this conflict has become apparent in popular television in the UK. We shall return to this in more detail below, but it is useful to set the scene with these examples. Murdock himself provides the relevant context for this conflict and the trend towards commercialism, by underlining the fundamental importance of advertising. As he notes, 'an advertising-based system must address audiences first and foremost in their role as consumers (of the programmes and the goods advertised within them) rather than as citizens with an entitlement to the broadest possible range of representation and debate' (1994: 176). Therefore, it is difficult for an advertising-based system to accommodate citizenship and its increasing dominance is achieved at the expense of cultural rights.

A couple of recent examples can provide a preliminary illustration of these points. One example involves the almost constant concern about the effects of television consumerism upon children. In this case, the concern focused upon the 'dumbing down of children's television by programmes and techniques imported from America' (*Guardian* 16 February 1998: 9). Citizenship means that children should be helped by television to become informed citizens. This is essential to public service broadcasting. Instead, a 1998 survey, distributed by the Broadcasting Standards Commission, found evidence of an influx of American programmes which were mostly intent on selling toys and providing audiences for advertisers. American imports include cartoons and magazine-style programmes and it is these which tend increasingly to dominate at the expense of domestic dramas and educational programmes. Between 1991 and 1995, public service provision fell while children's programming increased. The shortfall was made up by American imports. The American pattern is, as a result, becoming increasingly common on children's television, not only in Britain but across the rest of Europe. This pattern is described by one of the authors of the study, who notes that in 'the US the name of the game is to entertain and then deliver children to advertisers, basically to help people sell toys on the back of popular characters. It's a system that caters for advertisers' and toymakers' needs' (ibid.). The report concludes that the 'public service tradition of serving children as all-round developing personalities and future citizens is under threat' (ibid.).

The other example is of another fairly constant source of concern: serious drama on television. The concern here is that consumerism will eventually prevent serious drama, which is challenging, unorthodox and complex, from finding a place in the television schedules. Economics already tends to favour the series over the single play because costs can be spread advantageously over a number of episodes. This issue came to a head when Michael Wearing, a respected producer of drama for the BBC, whose successes include *Boys from the Blackstuff* and *Our Friends in the North*, resigned in protest at the increasingly commercial and autocratic style of BBC management. He claimed the management at the BBC had introduced 'rampant commercialism' and 'stifled creativity' (*Guardian*, 6 February 1998: 3). His was not the only voice raised in protest. Tony Garnett, another drama producer noted for such successes as *Cathy Come Home*, *This Life* and *Between the Lines* (cf. Wayne 1998), argued the industry was now 'run by managers with the mentality of 18th and 19th century mill owners'. He went on to say that television had become an industry 'where workers are costs, not assets, where slashing overheads is more important than nurturing talent, where fear and loathing are poisoning creativity' (*Guardian* 6 February: 1998:3). One response to the resignation from a spokesman stressed that the BBC was 'going through a period of change' and that it had 'to be competitive' (ibid.). There are obviously other problems and viewpoints at issue here. However, the tension between the need for economic discipline and the desire for an open culture in which creativity and diversity can thrive is clearly brought out even within the BBC itself.

These are recent examples, but the tension or conflict they identify goes back to the origins of popular radio and television and the formation of the BBC. A concept which is central to the idea of citizenship rights, its opposition to consumerism and the examples we have briefly considered, is that of public service broadcasting. We need to be clear about what this means before we look at the development of popular television.

Public service broadcasting

This concept has usefully been defined by Scannell, and we can use his account to clarify its content. It is consistent with the outline of cultural rights presented above and is as much about how things should be as about how they are. It emerged along with the origins of the BBC and is often identified with the views of John Reith, the first director-general of the BBC, who held office from 1927 to 1938.

First, 'broadcasting' is 'a public utility', 'a national service in the public interest' (Scannell 1990: 13). Second, broadcasting has to maintain the highest standards in information, culture and knowledge. This means that 'it could not be used for entertainment purposes alone'. Third, most of the people had to be reached by as much as could be broadcast. 'Broadcasting had a responsibility to bring into the greatest possible number of homes in the fullest degree all that was best in every department of human knowledge, endeavour and achievement.' Fourth, 'broadcasting should give a lead to public taste rather than pander to it' since it has to educate the public. Both of these points mean that a 'high moral tone' has to be preserved and that 'the vulgar and the hurtful' has to be avoided (ibid.).

Scannell notes that these points present an argument for public service broadcasting which sees it as 'a cultural, moral and educative force for the improvement of knowledge, taste and manners'. However, it also 'had a social and political function' in that it 'might bring together all classes of the population', acting 'as a kind of social cement'. 'As a national service', it could promote 'social unity particularly through the live relay of those national ceremonies and functions', such as 'a royal wedding, the FA cup final, the last night at the Proms', which bind 'people together in the shared idioms of a public, corporate, national life' (1990: 14).

Linked to this is the important role broadcasting should play in keeping the public informed about the major social and political issues of the day. Broadcasting 'could provide the facts ... and the arguments for and against' on these issues. This is directly relevant to the relationship between broadcasting and citizenship rights. 'Broadcasting had an immense potential for helping in the creation of an informed and enlightened democracy.' Therefore, 'the concept of public service, in Reith's mind, had, as a core element, an ideal of broadcasting's role in the formation of an informed and reasoned public opinion as an essential part of the political process in a mass democratic society' (Scannell 1990: 14).

Lastly, public service broadcasting originally involved maintaining the BBC's monopoly in the UK. This, for Reith, was the best way of 'guaranteeing the BBC's ability to develop as a public service in the national interest', since 'universal availability was the cornerstone of the creation of a truly national service in the public interest' (Scannell 1990: 15). It also meant that a diversity of programming under one general and national policy could be achieved, while standards could be maintained and disseminated (ibid.: 15–16). This concept and its various implications were originally developed for radio as the BBC was formed and began to evolve, but it was equally applicable to television.

The BBC began the first regular transmissions of television in 1936, though its initial reach was very limited. Despite the curtailment of transmissions during the Second World War, this situation obviously changed, particularly from the early 1950s onwards. However, it was not until the late 1950s that most homes could receive television transmissions. Between 1946 and 1959, the television audience showed a 'fast but steady … growth … interrupted only once, when two years before the start of ITV [in 1955] the Coronation produced a dramatic rise in viewers' (Seaton 1997: 167–8).

The formation of the BBC

The setting up of the BBC involved a compromise which says much about the relationship between citizenship and consumerism and how it has changed over time. Initially, decisions had to be made about the broadcasting of radio but these were extended to television when it became available. This context is effectively outlined by Seaton. She notes that the formation of the BBC 'depended on the rejection of both market forces and politics in favour of efficiency and planned growth controlled by experts'. As such, the public broadcasting corporation 'made no profits', but 'the goods it made, programmes, were in theory accessible to an infinite number of consumers' (1997: 114).

The BBC emerged out of this tension between state monopoly and market forces. The service could be provided by the market, letting commercial forces operate radio and then television broadcasting. Alternatively, broadcasting could be provided directly by the state, which would have monopolistic control over the new media. It was intended that the BBC should, in theory at least, avoid these alternatives. It was therefore established as a public corporation and financed by a universally applied licence fee, precisely to achieve this. The licence fee funded the BBC so that it did not have to rely on market competition to make money and avoided the use of advertising or sponsorship (Murdock 1992). It was also granted a monopoly over the provision of broadcasting services (there were also technical reasons for this which rested on the management of the wavelengths available for transmission). These factors protected it from commercial pressures. Making it a public corporation, rather than a government department, meant that it was also kept at arms length from the state. Government had to decide the size of the licence fee and agree to any increases, but these issues would go before Parliament and be subject to parliamentary scrutiny. The BBC was thus the solution to the related problems of how broadcasting was to be paid for and controlled. It was on this basis that the idea of public service broadcasting began to take shape. It was also to remain more or less unchallenged for the next thirty years, after the formation of the BBC as a public corporation and a public utility in 1926.

As Scannell argues, 'the British solution, back in the early 1920s', to the tension we have noted, 'was the creation of a single company, the British Broadcasting Company, licensed to broadcast by the Post Office and financed by an annual licence fee charged on all households with a wireless' (1990: 12). The solution arose from within the state through its committee system (ibid.: 12–13). This gave the BBC the independence from commercial pressures it needed to fulfil the idea of public service broadcasting. Otherwise, it would have been more constrained to appeal to popular demand. This would have made entertainment its main focus of attention to the detriment of other types 'of programming with a more educative or culturally improving aim' (ibid.: 15). This was linked to the fear that trying to appeal to popular demand would lead to a lowering of standards. The BBC also needed to be free from government interference and state control, hence its status as a public corporation and its public service function. The independence of the BBC from the state and the market has been subject to changing and varying degrees of pressure during its history (ibid.; Seaton 1997). We shall look at a select range of these changes in this chapter, particularly those which concern the relationship between citizenship rights and consumerism.[2]

Between 1926 and 1955, broadcasting (first radio and then radio and television) was provided solely by the BBC as a public service which tried to avoid both commercialism and state control. It was to be a universally available service to which all the public were to have access and which covered the whole spectrum of public life through the range and variety of its programmes. It was primarily there to educate and inform, rather than merely entertain, and to promote, and to raise standards as opposed to being led by popular demand and succumbing to market forces. What happened to this idea and the pressures it faced, as popular television developed, are the subjects of the rest of this chapter.

Commercial television and public service broadcasting

The introduction of commercial television

We have seen how the BBC was formed to prevent it from being influenced and shaped by commercial pressures. As such, the licence fee meant that the BBC did not have to attract advertising and therefore did not have to lower the standards of its output, nor be controlled by the government of the day. This involved specific

limits being placed upon the ability of American culture to undermine the elevated, national culture the BBC was trying to construct
and protect. Also, the influence of American commercial practices
was limited in that television was not financed, as it was in the
US, by advertising and sponsorship. However, it was clear that
the profits and markets television could realise would soon be
exploited by commercial interests. Therefore, private enterprise
eventually found a place in the financing and programming of television. The example of the BBC and the influence of the public
service model meant that television in the UK need not necessarily
take the overtly commercial form it took in the US. Commercial or
independent television was introduced into the UK in 1955 as television audiences had already started to increase. This could allow
commercial television to perform one of its major functions, that
of delivering audiences for advertisers; this is one of the things the
funding of commercial television provides. However, the influence
of commercial pressures in the mid-1950s should not be exaggerated, even if they have become increasingly influential as popular
television has developed.

Nowadays, commercial pressures and consumerism are becoming increasingly important in shaping the financing and programming of popular television. Yet the position was somewhat
different when commercial television first arrived in the UK.
Scannell suggests that it is misleading to see the system in
Britain 'as a mixture of public service and commercial broadcasting, as represented respectively by the BBC and ITV' (1990:
17). This is because commercial television was introduced under
the supervision of, rather than in direct opposition to, public
service broadcasting. Commercial television may have subsequently started to move away from this framework, but in 1955
it was bound by its constraints. 'The terms under which commercial broadcasting was established by government', Scannell notes,
'made it part of the public service system from the beginning'
(ibid.).

This was due to the statutory creation of the Independent
Television Authority (ITA) to try to ensure that commercial television would be introduced within limits set by the public service

system. As a public corporation, the ITA was there to regulate independent television (ITV) and make sure that it, too, would 'inform, educate and entertain' (Scannell 1990: 17). Therefore, commercial television was first introduced within a framework of public service control. It 'was subject to state regulation and control by an authority charged with maintaining high standards of programme quality' and extended the scope of public service broadcasting (ibid.: 17–18).

This can be seen in a number of ways. The ITA was charged with a range of duties. It was to exert overall control of the transmissions of commercial television. It granted the franchises to the private companies which provided television programmes to the ITV regions. It regulated the advertisements run by the ITV companies. The type of advertising chosen to fund commercial television in the UK consisted of advertising breaks within and between programmes rather than the direct sponsorship of programmes. The latter was then the preferred model in the USA and it also included breaks for adverts. The ITA was there to ensure that the adopted advertising system was not subject to abuse. It also supervised the programmes put out by the ITV companies which meant, in effect, ensuring that they maintained a certain level of quality.

The introduction of commercial television also represented a break with the public service tradition. The BBC itself was not averse to more populist developments in broadcasting. Seaton notes, for example, that 'before the war the BBC had regarded the regular expectation of particular kinds of programmes as "lazy listening", but during the war and afterwards it 'made considerable efforts to develop such habits'. The reason for this was that 'regular programmes produced predictable audiences' (1997: 148). Also, the BBC had already started to screen imported American programmes before ITV was introduced.

However, ITV was more clearly geared towards providing entertainment on a consistent and lavish basis and more readily adopted the formulas and style of American television. For example, greater prominence was given to the 'star qualities' of the television personality, and the advertising format was more influential. Commercial television attracted its audience through more populist programmes, such as 'the giveaway shows, *Double your Money*, *Take your Pick* and *Beat the Clock*' (Seaton 1997: 169). It also screened a large number of American imports, though the BBC was not inactive in this area. By contrast, it was more regional than the BBC in both scope and character and was supposed to produce a designated number of locally based programmes. Also, ITV is credited with some important developments in quality television, such as *Armchair Theatre*. None the less, ITV clearly represented the emergence of an explicitly populist form of television in Britain.

This interpretation is the one which informed the conclusions of the Pilkington Committee when it reported on the workings of television in 1962. Its report led to the third channel being given to the BBC rather than ITV. It concluded that 'the public was passive', which 'led it to consider audience preferences as little more than the expression of commercial manipulation'. Thus, it attempted 'to mitigate the impact of advertising by giving the third channel to the BBC and by strengthening the power of the ITA' (Seaton 1997: 178–9). The ITA was criticised by the committee 'for equating quality with box-office success' (Scannell 1990: 18). However, over time its main role (it eventually became the IBA, the Independent Broadcasting Authority) 'was to license television franchises and to reallocate these periodically'. It had to ensure '"balanced programming", "due impartiality" in the treatment of controversial issues and a high quality in programme production as a whole'. It could 'enforce its recommendations' by shaping 'the broadcasting schedule', prohibiting 'the transmission of particular programmes' and revoking 'the franchises of offending companies'. It 'monitored and controlled the amount, timing, quality and content of advertisements'. Also, it required that at least 'one-third of all' programmes 'shown on commercial television' should be 'serious non-fiction, sensibly distributed over the week as a whole in appropriate times' (Seaton 1997: 182–3).

The Pilkington Committee clearly favoured the BBC and wished to foster public service broadcasting. This provided the measure by which commercial television could be judged and found wanting.

In particular, the committee felt that commercial television pro-grammes, 'designed to get the largest possible audience', had 'to achieve this' by appealing 'to a low level of public taste'. This meant 'a lack of variety and originality, an adherence to what was safe and an unwillingness to try challenging, demanding and, still more, uncomfortable subject manner' (Scannell 1990: 118). Despite this, some might argue that the influence of the Pilkington Committee was probably the last evident sign of the overall domi-nance of the public service tradition. Subsequent developments have tended to favour consumerism and commercial television.

By the 1970s, the system had evolved into a duopoly shared by the BBC and ITV. While the introduction of commercial television had occurred within the framework of public service broadcasting, this did not necessarily place exacting limits on the further com-mercialisation of popular television. This duopoly meant that the BBC had to become more like ITV to compete with it, just as it meant that ITV had to face some of the responsibilities of a pub-lic service broadcaster. The Annan Committee on broadcasting reported in 1977. It found that the BBC's 'monopoly had given way to a cosy "duopoly" between the BBC and ITV who had both come to terms with competition by providing a broadly similar programme service with a roughly equal share of the audience'. Broadcasting appeared to have become unaccountable and 'was no longer representative of the increasingly diverse tastes, interests and needs of an increasingly diverse society' (Scannell 1990: 19). It was increasingly argued that the coherent national identity, which the BBC had once represented, had started to breakdown and diversify. It was therefore this change that had to find representa-tion on television. The committee recommended that the fourth channel should not go directly to the BBC or ITV. Instead, it suggested it be granted to a new organisation which would repre-sent 'those interests ... underrepresented or excluded in the output of the BBC and ITV'. This new channel 'would not produce any of its own programmes'. Rather, much 'like a publishing house', it 'would commission its programmes from a wide range of sources, including independent programme makers' (ibid.: 20). This is what became Channel 4.

Scannell notes that this period saw the breakdown of the consensus on the value of public service broadcasting. For him, 'the defence of the original monopoly had been linked to a claim to a unified policy for programming that rested on a presumed social, cultural and political consensus whose values were widely shared' (1990: 20). Once this began to decline and pressure increased from interests which favoured the further commercialisation of television and questioned the value of state regulated broadcasting, the public service tradition became increasingly open to challenge. Also, up 'to the end of the 1970s', the BBC's monopoly could be defended on purely technical grounds. 'The scarcity of suitable wavelengths for broadcasting necessitated the intervention of the state to regulate their allocation and use' (ibid.). However, the development of video, cable and satellite transmissions has undermined this necessity. Instead, from the early 1980s onwards, it has ushered in multi-channel broadcasting, subscription services and pay per view television, as well as moves towards deregulation. This has strengthened the hand of those interests which argue television should be shaped by consumerism and not citizenship rights. We shall return to this, the emerging context in which Channel 4 was introduced.

Channel 4

This context is important because it shows the growing power of commercial forces and brings out the continuing significance of public service broadcasting. Indeed, Scannnell suggests that 'the establishment of Channel 4 must be seen as the expression of a continuing political commitment to regulating broadcasting as a public good and in the public interest' (1990: 25).

Channel 4 does not make its own programmes. Instead, it broadcasts programmes made by independent production companies, many of which it has commissioned (Seaton 1997: 196). As noted, it acts much like a publishing house, which distinguishes it from the BBC's traditional 'in-house' form of television programme making. Now, however, with deregulation, the BBC and ITV have also come closer to the publishing model. By 1993 independent productions are estimated to have accounted for 25 per cent of their output (ibid.: 197). The idea, introduced with Channel 4, was that independent production should be developed by having television channels commission or accept programmes made by independent production companies, rather than have the channels make their own. The transition is similar to that described in Chapter 1, when the Hollywood studio system gave way to independent production, though with British television it appears that the 'majors' may be divested of their production facilities. The consequence with Channel 4 has been that production is achieved by 'out of house', independent production companies.

Channel 4 was originally 'financed by the existing commercial companies who supplied much of its material. As it did not sell its own advertising time it was somewhat removed from the direct pressures experienced by the rest of the commercial sector' (Seaton 1997: 197). Initially, the ITV companies financed Channel 4 in return for selling its advertising time as well as their own. The idea was that Channel 4 would be less concerned with the demands of selling advertising and less constrained by the interests of advertisers. This has been changed by the 1990 Broadcasting Act (ibid.). Channel 4 now sells its own advertising, which makes it more vulnerable to commercial pressures. These come not only from advertisers' interests, but also from the need to make sure enough of its programmes are sufficiently popular to attract audiences for advertisers.

There are thus obvious commercial pressures on Channel 4, but its introduction and development have also had public service implications. Channel 4 was supposed to provide a way of representing the emerging diversity of British society we referred to earlier. It had a specific remit to furnish an outlet for minority interests. Its publishing house style of production allowed some small independent producers to make programmes they might otherwise have had difficulty in making. Increasing cultural diversity, be it ethnic, racial, gendered or generational, was also to be accommodated by the new channel. It could provide access to television for such groups as ethnic minorities, women and youth, which had previously been underrepresented, misrepresented, or ignored. It could also schedule minority interest programmes, such as those on the arts, particularly experimental ventures, which might not find a place on other channels. In these ways, Channel 4 represented 'an important (and perhaps the last) reinterpretation of the public service role of broadcasting' (Seaton 1997: 197).

However, questions can be raised about the extent to which these conditions have been, or could be, realised in practice. Seaton, for example, points to survey evidence showing that many independent production companies are 'financially precarious with low profit margins' and heavily 'dependent ... on the patronage of the established channels' (1997: 197). Diversity of production may therefore be more apparent than real. Equally, the development of Channel 4 may afford a different and more profitable representation of 'minority interests'. A channel such as Channel 4 'can offer programme incentives' which appeal to 'discriminating' and 'selective television viewers' and so 'sell them the things' they are interested in consuming. Such a channel can 'deliver higher concentrations of the more affluent consumers that advertisers want' (ibid.: 196). It can, through its programming, attract a particular minority, the affluent, and provide this desirable section of the audience for advertisers. This occurs because in the end 'the limitations of commercial broadcasting are largely the result of the economic pressures to which it is exposed' (ibid.: 197). By contrast, the extent to which Channel 4 can represent minority groups and minority interests and provide access for independent programme makers is evidence of a continuing commitment to public service broadcasting (Scannell 1990: 25). Channel 4 is thus caught in the conflict between television as a private commodity and television as a public good.

Consumerism, citizenship and video, cable and satellite television

The Peacock Committee, which reported in 1986, was 'set up to consider alternatives to the licence fee as a means of financing the BBC'. It regarded broadcasting as 'a commodity – a marketable good like any other – provided for consumers'. The aim of its report was 'the establishment of consumer sovereignty in broadcasting through a sophisticated market system'. This entailed 'the greatest freedom of choice for individuals via the widest provision of alternative broadcast goods' (Scannell 1990: 21). It was consumers who would decide through the free market what should be on television. The idea of public service broadcasting would not find a place in such a system. However, the committee wanted to defend a conception of this service which it identified with 'the production of a wide range of high quality programmes'. It therefore suggested the setting up 'of a Public Service Broadcasting Council to secure the funding of public service programmes' since it envisaged the abolition of the licence fee. Instead, television was eventually to be funded by consumers paying directly 'for particular channels or programmes' (ibid.: 21–2). Thus, this committee expressed the growing dominance of consumerism. It 'placed public service a long way second to commercial considerations and consumer choice' (ibid.: 22).

Public service broadcasting relies upon 'a policy of mixed programming on national channels available to all'. Commercial interests, market forces and consumerism undermine this policy in at least two ways. First, they lead broadcasters to 'go only for the most profitable markets – which lie in densely populated urban areas that can deliver large audiences without difficulty'. Within the public service framework, both the BBC and IBA reached areas with their broadcasts that 'strictly economic considerations would' have led them to 'simply neglect' (Scannell 1990: 25). Consumerism, by contrast, cannot guarantee a universally available service. Second, mixed programming inevitably gives way to generic programming. This is a broadcasting 'service in which all or most of the programmes are of the same kind', for example 'MTV (music video)' and 'CNN (Cable News Network)' (ibid.: 25–6). The problem with this is that 'it fragments the general viewing public', which is still identified by the mixed programming transmitted by the terrestrial television channels in the UK. The consequence of generic programming is to undermine 'the principle of equality of access for all to entertainment and informational and cultural resources in a common public domain'. The likelihood is that this domain will 'shatter into splinters under the impact of deregulated multi-channel video services'. These trends are associated with the redefinition of broadcasting 'as a private commodity rather than a public good', which the Peacock report endorsed. The fundamental problem with this is that 'consumers are not all equal in their purchasing power' (ibid.: 26). Therefore, a broadcasting system based upon consumerism is likely to increase cultural inequalities and add them to the social and economic inequalities which prevail. Subsequent developments in popular television have tended to confirm these arguments.

Murdock dates the 'retreat from public service' to 'the policy for broadband cable services developed by the first Thatcher government' (1994: 159). He traces the general conflict between citizenship and consumerism to the respective emergence of mass democracy and mass consumption in the early part of the twentieth century (ibid.: 156). However, the threat to public service broadcasting has clearly become more severe in the modern era. The Thatcher government's policy towards cable led to legislation and covered other related areas such as satellite and multi-channel television. The real potential of cable emerged when technical improvements made a far greater number of channels available and introduced the possibility of interactive services. The installation of such a system would initially be very expensive, but the government was prepared to allow companies to provide a multi-channel service for which consumers would pay (ibid.: 160–1). The introduction of cable thus meant placing the potential to make money before public service requirements. Cable was not regulated by the IBA. The 1984 Cable and Broadcasting Act placed it under a separate Cable Authority which was to be more permissive in awarding and regulating cable franchises. Cable was not 'designed as a public service' and could therefore be shaped by market forces (ibid.: 161). Again, cable does not 'provide shared spaces for exploring "the state of the nation" or negotiating new conceptions of the common good', particularly since most cable channels are 'produced and packaged by companies based outside Britain'. Instead, it tends to 'fragment audiences by offering services tailored to saleable interest groups and ... exclude everyone who cannot afford the entry price' (ibid.: 163).

Similar developments have characterised the introduction of satellite television in the UK. This has entailed the establishment of BSkyB, one arm of Rupert Murdoch's global, corporate, multi-media empire, *News Corporation*. Murdock provides an excellent and concise summary of how this came about. He writes that 'a government initiative, which had begun as a planned extension of the BBC's operations, had ended up accepting a commercial monopoly relaying transnational programming from an "off-shore" satellite under the strategic direction of an American citizen' (1994: 164–5). He argues that 'in place of a universal service committed to diverse representation and open debate, satellite TV offers subscription channels tailored to commercially viable interests and limited to those able to pay' (ibid.: 165).

Cable and satellite 'have established a significant third force within British television' alongside the BBC and ITV. They have introduced a 'new source of competition – for audiences, for advertising and for programme rights', ushering in a more directly commercial, competitive, multi-channel media market, in which viewers exercise more 'choice'. According to consumerism, the latter means there is less need for regulatory bodies to protect quality programmes. Rather, consumers, producers and television channel controllers decide what should be on television. The 1990 Broadcasting Act both underwrites and expresses these changes. It has replaced the IBA with the less stringent Independent Television Commission, while removing 'many of the regulatory supports for diversity and minority representation'. It thus allows commercial imperatives to flourish (Murdock 1994: 165–6).

Likewise, the BBC has increasingly become subject to these pressures. Its moves into commercial subscription services, for example, have undermined the public service principle of equal and universal access to broadcasting, which had been met by the channels it provided for the licence payer (Murdock 1994: 167–71). At the moment, the BBC faces, according to Murdock, a 'severe dilemma'. This means it has to become 'more market oriented, selling programmes more vigorously overseas and entering the new markets opened up by the video, cable and merchandising industries', so as 'to compensate for the falling real value of' the 'licence fee revenue' (ibid.: 168). The examples we cited at the beginning of this chapter provide recent illustrations of how this tension is affecting the BBC.

In conclusion, it can be argued that the commercial interest in 'retaining audiences in a harsher competitive environment' is increasingly taking 'precedence over the public interest in sustaining services that guarantee citizens' rights'. This means that 'an increase in the raw number of channels and programmes serves as a pretext for reducing diversity and organizing schedules around material that is safe and saleable' (Murdock 1994: 166). These conclusions suggest that the conflict between citizenship and consumerism over the production and consumption of popular television in the UK has recently begun to be resolved by the growing dominance of consumerism.

Chapter 7

The television audience

A s a topic of inquiry, the audience has always been important, but, as we shall see, that importance has not always been
recognised.[1] Now, the television audience attracts interest because
of the ever-growing predominance of television as the main, mass
medium and the increasing commercial opportunities it thus
offers. Television viewers have become a clear point of both fascination and concern regarding such questions as who is watching
what and what is it doing to them? Recently, for example, a five-
year study by the British Film Institute, based on respondents'
diaries and questionnaires, revealed that viewers still feel guilty
about watching too much television (*Guardian* 30 April 1999: 5).
In particular, watching day-time television was identified as a 'kind
of moral weakness'. Hence, watching too much television was
deemed 'unhealthy'. This viewpoint is consistent with the 'effects'
and comparable approaches to television audiences, which we
shall consider below. It was also found that television helped
people to relax and to 'interact'. In this sense, television could
enable people to cope with emotional stress, as well as being a
controlled leisure activity and a source of information. This is
consistent with the 'uses and gratifications' and comparable approaches to the television audience, which we shall also consider
below.

Interestingly enough, this study also played down gender differences. It found, for example, that 'men enjoy soap operas', ranking
them second after their favourite category or genre, which was
sport, while women were as interested in news as men. 'The idea of
soap operas as a women's genre was a "dated notion"' for most
respondents, male and female. Indeed, they seemed to question the
relevance of such distinctions. This was supported by the finding
that 'in four out of five mixed-sex households, men and women
made decisions jointly about what to watch'. Men tended 'to have
power over the remote control' to the ratio of '46% compared

with 22% of women'. This obviously led to conflicts, but it did not necessarily mean that women or children were being coerced into watching programmes they did not like.

It is likewise intriguing to note that some of these conclusions seem to be at odds with those reached by another recent study of viewing habits conducted by the Independent Television Commission (ITC) (see Chapter 6). This found that 'differences between the viewing habits of men and women were significant' (*Guardian* 7 May 1999: 8). Men tended to prefer sport and women soap operas, as the previously mentioned study found. However, here 'there was no overlap' between the ten favourite genres of women and those of men. For example, the soap opera did not appear in the latter's top ten. Instead, men preferred 'factual programmes and comedies, whereas women were interested in consumer information and drama'. These findings give some sense of the issues involved in audience studies, although the survey covered other areas including advertising, generations, preferences, digital television and standards (these were thought to be 'constant, although a significant minority claimed they had worsened').

Other recently publicised surveys return to topics of continuing concern in audience studies, namely young people and violence, though for once they are not directly linked. One study points out how 'British children are growing up in a "bedroom culture" where books are boring and two thirds of all children under 17 have a television in their rooms' (*Guardian* 19 March 1999: 3). This study of young people and new media, which found that they used different media for at least five hours a day, also brought out some class and gender differences. Middle-class families were 'much more likely' than working-class families 'to have access' to a personal computer in the home. On the other hand, working-class children were more likely than middle-class children to 'have a television in their room'. Regarding gender it was found that 'boys were twice as likely to have a PC in their bedroom as girls' and even more likely than that to have 'a TV-linked games machine'. Another research study carried out on violence in films found that viewers considered its representation most disturbing and horrifying when it was serious and realistic, accompanied by strong language and unfairly meted out to its victims. However, if even very graphic acts of violence were represented in a humorous and light-hearted way then they could be entertaining and not seem violent. This was because such acts were not meant to be taken seriously (*Guardian* 11 May 1999: 6).

This level of interest and these examples provide an indication of some of the things we shall look at in this chapter and some of the problems they raise. We have not dealt with the audience in a direct and extended way before. However, it has cropped up at a number of key points and is obviously a crucial aspect of any study of popular culture. It seems to have become even more important with the arrival and consolidation of television as a mass medium and the related development of television studies. The academic study of television has been centrally concerned with the audience and with the presumed influence television has on its viewers. This is one reason why an assessment of the television audience must inevitably become an assessment of the stages entailed in the study of this audience.

The cinema audience has been of obvious importance not least to Hollywood itself. This is evident in its many attempts through such things as market research and preview screenings to sell films to the cinema-going public. Also, there seems to have been a re-newed interest in the cinema audience recently and we shall have occasion to refer to this below. But these points should not obscure the differences between the evaluation of cinema and television audiences. Television is available around the clock in the home and the average viewer now watches it for about 25 hours a week. This has fuelled anxieties about its harmful effects upon viewers, for example, in making them more violent and in manipulating them through advertising. Theories which argue that popular culture produces these effects can easily regard television as the most effective medium for influencing and shaping the attitudes and behaviour of viewers, leading to audience exploitation and control. In its time, television has been accused of 'brain washing' the public. However, its potential to educate and inform, through the scope and variety of the programming it can provide, has been used in its defence. Equally, it can be thought to be harmless, as opposed to harmful, entertainment and to give people what they want, or what they are prepared to choose or take. These are the types of arguments we shall look at in this chapter. This will allow us to pick up some of the themes of the previous chapter. There we saw how and why consumerism and citizenship define the audience in distinct ways and have different ideas about the effects of television upon audiences and the benefits they can derive from television.

The study of the television audience has been marked by a number of distinct stages, which have consisted of different theoretical and empirical approaches. In this chapter we shall present a critical outline of these stages. Some of these developments have already been hinted at in our introduction, which has tried to show how the audience continues to be a major problem for academic, political and popular assessments of television. Before we do this, however, there are some general points which need to be made to guide the subsequent discussion.

The first point to be noted concerns the definition of the audience. This might seem a straightforward task. The audience is that group of people who watch television or a particular television programme. However, things are rarely as simple as this. As we saw in the previous chapter, for example, the positions taken on how and why popular television should be provided entail less obvious definitions of audiences. The idea that television should be a public service defines viewers as citizens, while the idea that it should be a consumer good defines viewers as consumers. More commonly, television itself, most usually commercial television, defines the audience as a means of attracting advertising. Beyond this, different theories, including those to be discussed below, will conceive of the audience in different ways as a result of their ideas about how television affects viewers. If television is thought to be a powerful institution which can influence and shape, directly or indirectly, the attitudes and behaviour of those who watch it, then viewers will be understood to be passive, vulnerable and exploitable victims. If, however, television is thought to be a medium which merely provides another store of images for those who wish to undermine the dominant culture and construct and celebrate their own, then viewers will be understood to be active, powerful and manipulative subversives. Yet again, post-structuralism might insist that the audience can only be understood as something created by certain discourses, outside which it does not really exist. These qualifications need to be noted in what follows.

Another point worth mentioning concerns the composition and variety of the audience. This does not just concern the question of how the audience is defined but what its composition is like. Is it, for example, homogeneous and average, or segmented and diverse? Is it a mass or fragmented audience? Is it to be understood primarily by one specific social or psychological characteristic, such as class and gender, or gullibility, passivity and cynicism? Or is it composed of a whole range of different social groups which cannot be reduced to a few, simplified social or psychological traits? For example, the mass culture theory mentioned earlier tends to see exploited viewers as composed of a mass, homogeneous audience, while populists and market researchers alike might see viewers as making up a varied and segmented audience. It has to be remembered that this is a prominent issue for the approaches to be looked at in this chapter.

It is linked to another major concern which focuses upon the power of the audience. This is itself linked to the key question of the extent to which mass media such as television can influence audiences. The question of the power of the audience as against the power of television which can subjugate its audience will be an obvious and frequent point of reference in the following discussion. Are audiences merely open and vulnerable to the influences exerted by television, its programmes and its advertising and thereby prone to manipulation and control? Or are they capable of exercising power in their own right by ignoring or resisting these influences, even turning them to their advantage? It can be seen that these qualifications are brought together by their focus on the question of influence and the relationship between television and the audience. Taking account of what has been argued so far, this will now be considered in more detail.

Debates over the general issues raised so far and the theoretical interpretations associated with them have a very long history which need not be repeated here. Our more immediate concern is with the tradition of audience studies and its related theories of the audience. This provides a convenient and relevant focus for our discussion. The intention is to provide an outline of developments and changes in this area. This should indicate how this aspect of popular television has been studied and some of the conclusions that have been reached.

The 'effects' of popular television upon audiences

The first major stage to be looked at is what is usually called the effects approach, which started in the 1940s and developed during the 1950s and 1960s. This takes a particular explanatory view of the relationship between television and the audience and is often associated with a mass culture theory of popular television. As its name suggests, this approach argues that television has a definite and powerful influence over the thoughts and actions of people, either individually or in groups. Television determines what people think and what they do and thus controls them psychologically and socially. It can make people think things they would not otherwise think and do things they would not otherwise do. Moreover, it has the potential to achieve these changes without its subjects being aware of how, and to what extent, their thoughts and deeds are being controlled and manipulated in these ways. Various metaphors drawn from imagery associated with drugs are sometimes used to define and clarify this approach by calling it the hypodermic model or referring to television as the opiate of the masses. This is a convenient way of trying to understand the argument more concisely, but it can imply that the approach lacks a more precise view of how television is supposed to exercise its influence.

This approach may not derive directly from mass culture theory, nor be intended to feed back into its arguments. Yet it is at least consistent with some of this theory's points, as well as those of other theories such as the Frankfurt School (Lewis 1991: 6). In particular, this theory tends to argue that television can influence audiences in clear and systematic ways, a power it associates with the rise of mass culture. This culture is deemed to be trivial, homogeneous, meretricious, undemanding, intellectually impoverished, standardised and commercially exploitative. Purveyed by mass media such as television, it can take over people's consciousness and encourage them to be passive and compliant consumers of advertising, fantasies, goods and propaganda.

Mass culture may be a culture that people initially desire; it need not be forced upon unwilling recipients. Also, it has a more obvious and accessible appeal than the intellectually difficult and uncommercial, if stimulating and priceless, works of high culture and modernist art. However, once it gains a foothold people become used to the easy pleasures and mindless enticements it offers and it becomes embedded in their routines. Eventually, people become habituated to the types of thinking and acting it introduces.

This brief outline is possibly over-generalised but it hopefully conveys the basic points about how the relationship between popular television and the audience is described and explained. The effects approach, as it has developed, has not necessarily always seen television pacifying the audience; after all, its effect may be, for example, to make people more violent, so that consumption may be passive but not its consequences. The effects approach is associated with more specific claims, including those about the effects on audiences of televisual representations of advertising, politics and violence. As Lewis notes, 'this approach attempted to address a fundamental and very general question: what effect does television have on people?' This meant 'the scope for investigation opened up by such a question is clearly enormous, so it was not surprising that researchers limited themselves to specific kinds of "effect" and used a specific set of investigative tools' (1990: 153). This approach is thus important for asking this question and for setting some of the initial terms of the debates that subsequently emerged. Its failure to sustain this inquiry can bring out some of its theoretical and empirical weaknesses, even though its claims are still very much with us.

Lewis (1991: 12) argues that the overall results of this research are inconclusive and that this has led to a range of criticisms being

levelled at the approach as a whole. He identifies at least six difficulties with the approach, although he concedes that television
may have some influence on its viewers, while a more hostile
survey lists 'ten things wrong' with it (Gauntlett 1998). What can
we make of these critiques? To begin, let us look at Lewis (1991:
8–11). He points out, first, that television viewing may influence
the way viewers think, but not the way they act, which means its
effect is difficult to determine. Second, the effects of television may
be more complex and varied than the approach envisages, which,
ironically, suggests that it may miss seeing effects which do occur.
Third, the viewing of television can be varied and complicated,
pursued along with other activities, and attract widely different
degrees of concentration and attention. Surprisingly enough, the
studies of television viewing which have been done (Lewis 1991: 9)
tend to lend some support to Adorno's idea that people consume
the products of the cultural industries in a 'distracted and inattentive' manner (Strinati 1995: 67–8).

The next problem Lewis identifies is 'the most frequently made
criticism of the "effects" approach'. This refers to 'its tendency to
treat TV viewers as empty vessels, passively absorbing the precon-
structed meanings in television messages' (1991: 9; cf. Gauntlett
1998: 121–2, 126). Instead, viewers 'engage' with television
actively, not taking what they are presented with for granted, often
ignoring and sometimes rejecting the messages broadcast. This
raises the issue of meaning which the effects approach is seen to
neglect (Gauntlett 1998: 126–7). Television produces messages but
it is only the engagement of viewers with them which produces
meaning. Television does not, and cannot, construct and impose its
meanings; they can only result from the related interventions of
viewers. The effects approach does not recognise meaning and thus
has no idea of how it is constructed. However, as we shall see
below, this is precisely the problem semiology was supposed to
resolve for audience studies.

The penultimate criticism we need to consider is strongly
insisted upon by both Lewis and Gauntlett. The former terms it
'the intervening variable', while the latter suggests the effects
approach works 'backwards'. What they both seem to be arguing

is that the approach neglects the social context because it sees the relationship between television and viewers in purely abstract terms. Both take the example of violence and suggest that people who are violent and who watch a lot of violent television programmes may not be violent because of their television viewing. The social backgrounds of such viewers, for example family and education, and their social conditions, for example income and occupation, need to be studied before any definite conclusions can be reached. This is what Lewis means by the intervening variables the effects approach neglects. It also indicates what Gauntlett means when he criticises this approach for working backwards from television violence to violence in society. Instead, he suggests that 'to explain' the latter 'problem', 'researchers should begin with that social violence and seek to explain it with reference, quite obviously, to those who engage in it: their identity, background, character and so on' (1998: 120).

This point is also related to Lewis's last criticism when he notes that audience research cannot experimentally control the context of television viewing. It cannot isolate different aspects of the social context, which makes it difficult to assess their varying effects. Also, viewers start watching television from an early age and they cannot be abstracted from this relationship for its effects on them to be studied. Similarly, the effects of television, such as they are, may be long term, which again makes them difficult to determine. There are, as indicated, other criticisms which can be levelled at the effects approach. For example, Gauntlett (1998) makes a number of other claims, some of which are methodological and theoretical. He argues that this approach is not grounded in theory, which is true, but this does not mean, as we have tried to suggest above, that it is theoretically neutral. Interestingly enough, he argues its assumptions rest on a 'barely concealed conservative ideology' (ibid.: 122–3), while Lewis sets it in the context of the Frankfurt School's theory of mass culture (1991: 5–6). Assuming this theory is not a conservative ideology, we could suggest that any theory which sees television as an all-powerful medium is consistent with an effects approach to its viewers. Also worth noting is that Gauntlett's way forward for 'research on media influences' is not a capitulation to audience populism, though he does stress the importance of 'actually' listening 'to media audiences'. Rather, his suggestion is to think of the relationship between television and its viewers as one of 'influences' and 'perceptions', not as one of 'effects' and 'behaviour' (1998: 127–8).

The 'uses and gratifications' approach to popular television and the audience

Wherever the balance of these arguments may ultimately lie, the problems identified have fostered the emergence of alternative approaches. The first we need to consider is the uses and gratifications or functional approach, which flourished between the 1950s and 1970s. This has obviously had a contribution of its own to make and shares certain similarities with the more recent populist approach to audience studies. However, its initial inspiration at least arose from the way it served as a critical contrast to, if not a complete reversal of, the effects tradition. It seems almost to have been designed to be the opposite of this tradition and the line of research it pursued. As it is by now customary to point out, 'the "uses and gratifications" approach … asks the question not "what do the media do to people?" [a question the effects approach asks] but, "what do people do with the media"' (Katz 1959: 2, quoted in Lewis 1991: 13). As Lewis notes, this 'shifted power away from the television screen toward the viewer, who was understood as using television in order to gratify certain needs' (ibid.). People's social lives mean that they have needs, some of which, such as those for entertainment, leisure and information, can be satisfied by television.

As has happened with the recent audience populism, this approach has been marked by both extreme and moderate versions of its arguments. Some of its proponents began to deny that television had any power over viewers. Others were prepared to accept the potential influence of television but to weigh it against the experiences, needs, aspirations and desires of viewers. For the former, audiences could do what they wanted with the television message, managing it almost 'at will', because they controlled it.

For the latter, the important point was that 'the television message was not negated but *mediated* by active, socially constructed viewers' (Lewis 1991: 14). This moderate variant also had a more social view of the determination of viewers' needs and their chosen gratifications, suggesting that individuals' beliefs, interests and actions were shaped by their roles in society (ibid.: 14–15).

This idea of mediation should alert us to some of the theoretical implications of this approach. Like the effects tradition, uses and gratifications research is not obviously and explicitly theoretical but has some plausible theoretical connections. In particular, it can be made consistent with the liberal-pluralist theory of society which emerged in areas of social and political science in the 1940s and 1950s (Bennett 1982). Among its many claims, this theory sees institutions such as the family, community and voluntary organisations mediating the relationship between the individual and central institutions, such as television and national politics. The idea here is that society is democratic because it is pluralistic and it is pluralistic because individuals can be involved in a range of organised and competing groups. This prevents any one group from dominating them for any length of time. Society is thought to be composed of more or less equally powerful groups and institutions, a set-up which ensures a state of democratic equality and individual freedom. This means that television is prevented from dominating individuals because of the competition between groups and institutions for their attention and commitment. The plural structure of society gives individuals the freedom to use television to gratify their needs.

There are number of criticisms of this theory, some of which can be outlined here. It is said to ignore evident and extreme inequalities in income, wealth and power, to neglect the strategic and dominant power of private capital and the state, and to exaggerate the extent to which individuals become involved with voluntary organisations (Bennett 1982). However, its affinity with the uses and gratifications approach can be seen. Furthermore, this approach is open to the same criticisms in so far as it shares liberal-pluralist assumptions. What is also of interest is how it allows for individuals to be influenced by television. Presumably television can have 'effects' on individuals if there is insufficient mediation of their relationship with television. For example, a restricted range of political information may make voters more dependent on television at election times. In this instance, competing group membership may not provide the information individuals need. Therefore, inadequate mediation can mean that voters may be influenced in their choice by television.

This argument brings us to the problems associated with this approach. The first one which needs to be noted concerns social determination. The approach accepts that what characterises the individual is socially determined, for example social roles, but then seems to lose sight of this determination when this individual sits down to watch television. Then the viewer is able to select and interpret almost at will. This carries the implication that television, unlike almost any other institution, has little or no social influence (Lewis 1991: 15–16).

The more general relevance of this should be noted. The adoption of a populist stance towards the influence of television often seems to rest on the assumption of an a-social and a-historical individual who is capable of exercising free will. This individual is then seen as being able to manipulate television and construct her or his own interpretations of its messages, rather then being manipulated by it and constrained to accept the messages broadcast. There is nothing wrong with simply arguing against the idea that individuals are mere products of their social conditions. However, what is wrong is assuming that anyone is free from social and historical constraints and influences. There is no such thing as an a-social individual who is capable of transcending her or his historical circumstances. This may seem painfully obvious. However, unless a populist-inclined interpretation specifies the particular social and historical factors that enable viewers to think and act towards television in the way it suggests, it will be confronted by this problem. Here, as we have seen, the uses and gratifications approach is forced to vacillate between social determination in some areas, for example social roles, and a lack of social determination in others, for example television viewing. Other populist approaches sometimes seem to sidestep this question completely and endow individuals with the power to do as they chose. The idea of the active audience needs to show how this activity is socially possible.

The uses and gratifications approach also falls into the functionalist trap of assuming that needs can be clearly identified by viewers and researchers alike and readily fulfilled. There is no problem about satisfying needs in principle, but there is often a problem in practice for needs may not be gratified. Also, television programmes become intelligible only as vehicles for gratification and nothing more. This type of explanation thus simplifies the relationship between viewers and television and television's messages, missing out things such as control over scheduling and the role of ideologies. Equally it simplifies the question of power, merely reversing the effects approach's idea of the structure of power, rather than assessing the relative power of viewers and producers over television's messages. In failing to do this, it also seems to lose sight of the wider social context in which television viewing takes place.

The other major difficulty with the uses and gratifications approach, according to Lewis, is its failure to deal with the problem of meaning. Television functions to provide gratification for viewers' needs. However, this does not mean that viewers will all come to the same interpretation of television, or give it similar meanings. So even if we accept this approach's premise that viewers use programmes in this way, it does not follow that they will 'see the same things' or attribute to them 'the same meanings' (Lewis 1991: 16). With this approach, 'the viewer is reduced to a set of needs, the message to a set of gratifications' (ibid.: 18). The inability of uses and gratifications research to deal with the problem of meaning provided an opportunity for introducing semiology into audience studies.

Semiology, theory and audience studies

Put very simply, semiology is 'the study of meaning' (Lewis 1991: 25), though this could be said about other theories such as Weber's interpretative sociology, and Phenomenology. More significantly, semiology is seen as the scientific study of sign systems. As one useful definition puts it, semiology is 'the general (if tentative) science of signs'. These signs are 'systems of signification', or 'means by which human beings – individually or in groups – communicate, or attempt to communicate by signal'. These signals include 'gestures, advertisements, language itself, food, objects, clothes, music and the many other things that qualify' (Bullock and Stallybrass 1977: 607). This definition comes close to that provided by Saussure, the theorist who first coined the term. For him, signs within society could be studied scientifically to show what they are composed of and to discover the laws which govern them. In principle, any sign system could be studied semiologically (Strinati 1995: chapter 3).

The academic interest shown in semiology was part of the more general turn to abstract and rarefied theory which gathered pace in the 1960s. Semiology thus began to make its mark at a time when the limitations of both effects and uses and gratifications research were becoming more apparent. It was not so much the case that semiology offered a new research agenda, though it could have done so. Rather it provided a novel and theoretically informed way of studying the relationship between television and the viewer. The problem that semiology posed for the future of empirical research derived from its study of meaning. In focusing upon the messages of television to clarify their codes and signs, it took little notice of their producers and consumers. Therefore, in its search for the meanings of television, semiology seemed to neglect the audience. Initially at least, the only contribution theories such as semiology appeared capable of making to audience studies was to insist they were no longer necessary. All that needed to be known about viewers could be gleaned from the decoding of television messages to discover their underlying meanings. Some semiologists indeed thought that the position of interpretation accorded to audiences by the analysis of this hidden structure of meaning contained all that needed to be known about them. From this point of view, audiences had no existence outside the meanings of television (Strinati 1995: chapter 3).

It is not possible to discuss semiology in any detail here. Instead, relevant ideas will be outlined when they are applied by particular studies. In the end, semiology did acquire some relevance to the empirical study of audiences and some famous studies did rely on some of its ideas. Perhaps the most famous of these is Morley's study, *The Nationwide Audience* (1980), though it is not just an example of semiological research. We need to look at what led up to this study, recalling what has been said about the initial impact of semiology.

As we have noted, the introduction of semiology appeared to provide new ways of studying television which promised to overcome problems with the effects and uses and gratifications traditions of research. In particular, it was seen as succeeding where these approaches had failed, in finding a solution to the problem of meaning. Also, as noted, it tended to focus most of its attention on television's messages and thereby ignored the audience. This failing seemed to be implicit in the semiological approach. One of the pioneers of this approach was Barthes, whose work probably had most influence on its use in the development of cultural and media studies in the UK (Strinati 1995: chapter 3; Masterman 1984). The problem at issue can be seen in his elaboration of the semiological method and its applications. He argues that people generally take the signs they come across for granted as natural and unremarkable and do not normally analyse them for their meanings. This is the task of the semiologist, who recognises signs as systems which signify meaning. There is therefore no reason to study audiences empirically because it is assumed they take signs and their apparent meanings for granted and do not see beyond them unless enlightened by the semiologist. Instead, semiology is a way of unearthing the deeper meanings of signs and messages that audiences habitually miss because they take them for granted. This inevitably leads to the conclusion that signs should be studied for the meanings they contain, the implication being there is no need to study audiences for the meanings they may confer or derive from signs (Strinati 1995: 115–16).

The development of audience studies has shown, however, that this negative conclusion is not all that semiology has to offer. The introduction of semiology and the interest in theory eventually led to the emergence of the encoding-decoding model, the EDM (Hall

1980: especially 130). This tried to retain the covert and mysti-fying character of signs and codes, while including the producers and consumers of television in an account of television's messages. The EDM is sometimes explained by comparing it with what goes on in spying because it seems to use a similar terminology. This comparison may be of some use but it is, on the whole, misleading. Therefore, saying why the EDM is not like spying may make it a bit clearer. For a start, the message a spy has to decode, be it from a controller, source, informant, or whatever, is intended for her, or his, eyes only. Unlike the television message, it is meaningless without knowledge of the code-breaking system. The television message, unlike the spy's message, is potentially broadcast to everyone. The spy's message and code are deliberately esoteric; those of television are not. Second, in spying there should be no disparity between encoding and decoding. The message decoded by the spy should read the same as the message originally encoded. This is not supposed to be the case with the television message. It is precisely the disparity between encoding and decoding that the EDM is designed to emphasise. With television, the message decoded by the audience for itself may not be the same as the one encoded by the producers for themselves. Equally it may be open to a number of different interpretations. Unlike the spy, the audi-ence is usually not aware of the decoding it does: 'extracting the meaning from a programme is an everyday, taken-for-granted process' (Abercrombie 1996: 143). Also, spying depends upon agreed and consistent but secret codes, whereas television depends upon opaque, sometimes conflicting but public codes. Such differ-ences between television and spying help to bring out the salient features of the EDM.

As Lewis points out, the EDM sees 'the production (encoding) and consumption (decoding) of television as two distinct semiolog-ical processes'. It regards television programmes as 'highly coded' and 'powerful but ambiguous' sign systems, produced by 'specific aesthetic, political, technical and professional ideologies'. The encoding of programmes by producers is meant to 'encourage' viewers 'to "prefer" certain meanings'. However, 'decoding is an active process', not one imposed upon audiences unopposed.

There is no 'guarantee' that the 'preferred' meaning will be the one audiences decode. However, audiences cannot decode television programmes in any way they like. They may be 'active' but they are 'limited both by the message and by their own ideological world' (1991: 58–9). To this we could add the different and unequal positions occupied by audiences in social structures such as class, ethnicity and gender. This draws attention to the social contexts and constraints within which television messages are communicated and received, a point central to the development of the 'cultural studies' perspective (ibid.: 36–41, 60).

Morley's study, *The Nationwide Audience* (1980), assesses both the decoding and social characteristics of audiences because the former is seen as arising out of the latter. Morley's concern was to show how different social groups differed in how they decoded the then current affairs programme *Nationwide*. Representatives of different social groups, distinguished by factors such as class, were shown the programme and their reactions were then identified by subsequent group discussions. The various groups included trade union officials, shop stewards, bank managers, black students in further education and apprentices. The reactions of these groups to the programme were identified and interpreted by three related but distinct sets of meaning. These defined their ideological preferences. We can outline what these preferences are. First, there is the dominant mode where the response to the programme is in keeping with and supports the dominant ideas in society. This is the preferred meaning, the one encoded by producers. The second mode is the oppositional or radical one which overtly rejects the dominant ideas encoded in the programme. Here what is decoded is in direct opposition to the meanings encoded. Lastly there is the negotiated mode where decoding draws on the other two modes to arrive at a compromise position. Here dominant ideas are accommodated rather than emphatically endorsed. This means that oppositional ideas are the subordinate partners in this negotiated compromise (Morley 1980: 19–21, 136; cf. Hall 1980: 136–8; Parkin 1972: chapter 3).

The results, however, were not as consistent as expected. The types of decoding did not correspond neatly or obviously with the social groups. Some responses were as predicted. The bank managers' decoding was conservative and thus consistent with the dominant or preferred meaning. The shop stewards' stance was oppositional and radical; they openly criticised the programme and saw it as being opposed to working-class interests. As might also have been expected, the trade union officials' reaction was primarily a negotiated one.

However, as indeed Morley appeared to recognise at the time (1980: 21, 161–2), the relationship between social groups and the decoding of meaning is more complex and varied and less direct than these findings suggest. This study has been singled out for other criticisms (Lewis 1991: 59), but it has been the relationship between social groups and decoding which seems to have attracted most critical attention. The study itself suggests that this relationship is more complex than originally conceived. For example, both the black students in further education and the shop stewards shared an oppositional response to the programme, though the latter were actively critical of its bias, while the former were quietist and indifferent. On the other hand, the dominant response was not confined to 'dominant groups', such as the bank managers, but was shared by the apprentices.

As Morley has himself recognised, the cultural meanings held by individuals and groups are not automatically and unambiguously determined by their structural locations in society. There seems to be no direct link between social position and decoding practice. Instead, Morley suggests a perspective 'from which we can see the person actively producing meanings from the restricted range of cultural resources which his or her structural position has allowed them access to' (1986: 43). While things are more complex than originally envisaged, this is no reason to dispense with social determination. However, this does raise an interesting question. For if we retain social determination as we should and if we cannot conceive of a-social or a-historical groups or individuals, then the 'actively produced meanings' must still be socially determined. The conclusion this leads us to is that the problem does not lie as such in the activities of audiences, or the messages or meanings of television. Rather it lies in the need for more informed and

sophisticated theories and empirical accounts of the social composition and characteristics of audiences.

This point is backed up by another question which is not usually
asked of the EDM, the *Nationwide* study and others like it: is the
relationship between the producers and consumers of television
messages primarily a meaningful one, or might it be understood
in other ways? Are producers principally interested in encoding
meanings when they produce programmes? Or are their principal
motives things such as profits, marketability, filling the schedules,
justifying the licence fee, attracting advertisers, building careers,
and so on? It could be that encoding occurs unconsciously, but we
would still need evidence that producers were aware in some way
of this process. Our specific concern here is not to develop an alternative account but to raise some critical questions about the
usefulness of the semiological model. However, it does seem that
the construction of meaning may not be the most useful way of
understanding television. It would be the most useful if its role was
to devise and reinforce a dominant ideology, but this argument has
been increasingly called into question (even by the *Nationwide*
study itself) and no longer seems a tenable one (Abercrombie *et al.*
1980; Barker 1989; cf. Strinati 1995: chapter 4).

Similar concerns apply to the audience. Is what they do when
they watch television best understood as the decoding of meaning?
Indeed, to what extent is the activity of viewing necessarily a meaningful and interpretative one? The *Nationwide* study points to
some responses which are not obviously meaningful in the semiological sense. For example, the initial response of the 'black further
education students' to the programme was 'a critique of silence',
which was not clearly oppositional but a reflection of their alienation from the programme (Morley 1980: 142–4). Equally alienated were the apprentices, despite their general endorsement of
dominant ideas. This was evident in their 'overall tone of rejection
and cynicism' (ibid.: 138–41). Although it may be possible to rein-
terpret such reactions semiologically, it is still difficult to see how
they could count as being meaningful in the study's terms, or those
of semiology and decoding more generally. To what extent can alienation, silence and cynicism be understood as constructions of

meaning, or as decodings of already encoded meanings? After all, one of the accepted definitions of alienation is 'meaninglessness', or the lack or absence of meaning either for specific social groups, or in society at large (Ollman 1976: chapter 18). Also, cynicism does imply the rejection of meaning in the sense it carries of beliefs and values.

It has also been found that popular television viewing does not only or always amount to watching what is on the screen. When they are watching television, audiences can carry out all sorts of other activities; they can also do nothing in particular and not pay any attention to what is being shown. This is not to say that they do not watch, but studies have shown they may also do other things while watching. They may talk, eat, sleep or read and they may not necessarily be concentrating even when supposedly watching (Lewis 1991: 9). How can these types of viewing be understood as meaningful activities? They do not seem to amount to decoding or to the active construction of meaning, nor do they inevitably amount to the adoption of specific ideologies. Rather, as noted earlier, they may best suggest what they are – attitudes of distraction and inattention.

This point is linked to recent research on cinema audiences carried out by Barker and Brooks (1998). One of the things they have found is that 'many people who see films' have what they call 'no significant investment at all' in film or cinema. These viewers went to see films, for example, 'by accident', at the insistence of 'someone else, or because they had nothing better to do'. As a result, 'they had almost nothing to say at interviews', thereby posing 'real problems for research' (ibid.: 225). One of the implications they note is the question of why 'so few audience researchers acknowledge the existence of these groups', which leads them to 'doubt the "representativeness" of many pieces of research' (ibid.: 231).[2] This again suggests how difficult it is to see at least some sections of the audience as being engaged in meaningful activity when they go to the cinema or watch television.

As noted, some of the problems indicated led Morley and other writers to question whether social structures directly influence decoding practices. The general supposition seems now to be that there is a looser relationship between the two, but not that there is no relationship. There is little sense in which decoding could not be socially determined, even if some of the more extreme populist statements about audience creativity come close to making this claim. It could be argued that the real need is to develop a more precise and informative account of the relationship between the producers and consumers of television messages. However, more recent debates and research have tended to involve local studies and audience populism.

Conclusions: audiences and power

As a conclusion to this chapter we shall consider these developments in the study of the audience. After the relative neglect which resulted from some excessively abstract and theoretical approaches, the audience is now receiving the attention it deserves. The developments we have just briefly outlined seem to be moving in the right direction. The audience is now recognised as being important but not at either extreme of being all-powerful or powerless. Indeed, how much power it has now seems to be as much an empirical as it is a theoretical question. It is also understood that the audience has social characteristics which need to be studied. These may affect how people think and act when they are viewers, though, presumably, this may not give us the whole picture as other, psychological factors will also play their part. The main point is that we treat audiences neither as completely free agents nor as passive products of their social environment. Whatever qualities of the audience are revealed by research, they will be formed by social conditions (and psychological factors) which should be central to such research and its attendant theorising.

These lines of inquiry have led to research which has focused upon the domestic sphere, as well as to audience populism. These developments are perhaps not that surprising since they arose out of a situation in which the audience was simply not studied and dismissed because it lacked power and significance. Along with the *Nationwide* study, the focus upon the domestic sphere can thus be interpreted as a response to the lack of attention paid to 'actual' audiences. Similarly, audience populism can be seen as a critical backlash to the argument that the audience is made powerless by modern mass media and mass culture. We can conclude this chapter by assessing these developments.

Barker and Brooks have noted a recent turn away from 'textual issues' towards 'more contextualised, perhaps ethnographic methods', which they trace to Morley's own critical postscript to the *Nationwide* study (1998: 221; cf. Morley 1992: chapters 4 and 5). This has led to empirical research on television viewing in the home and the domestic power relations which govern such viewing. In one important respect, it has focused upon gender relations, thereby rectifying to some extent the relative absence of these relations in the original study. This ethnographic research is concerned with what goes on when viewers watch television. It is not intended to uncover the hidden codes by which they interpret what they watch, but to discover the social factors which determine viewing habits and practices in the home. The question here, as Morley puts it, is 'what does it mean to "watch television"', which is related to 'investigating how television is used' (1998: 234). The objectives of this research also raise important questions about the levels of interest attracted by specific genres of programmes and the links between family life and watching television (ibid.: 235).

One of the areas of Morley's research that has attracted much comment has been the power relations between men and women over television viewing in the home (1986, 1998). Here Morley has found, somewhat unsurprisingly, that men tend to determine the use of the remote control and the programme choices made within the home. Women may not give in quietly, but it is the male who tends to have direct physical control over the remote control and its use. Also, men and women appear to differ in the types of programmes they prefer to watch, or at least in the types or programmes they are prepared to admit they watch. For example, men claim to prefer factual programmes and realist fiction, while women claim to prefer fictional programmes and romance. There must obviously be a great deal of overlap between men and women in the programmes they like. Yet these findings suggest that male control and preferences will tend to dominate television viewing in the home (1998: 241). As Morley concludes, 'there is more to watching TV than what's on the screen – and that "more" is, centrally, the domestic context in which viewing is conducted' (ibid.: 244). This approach has not been confined to these studies but has been developed and extended to other topics (cf. Lewis 1991: 49–54; Moores 1993: chapters 3 and 4; see also the introduction to this chapter). Morley's work, however, is again useful in characterising some of the main aspects of this new approach to the study of the audience. This is one which stresses the importance of the social context of television viewing, the domestic influence of the family, class and gender relations, the uses to which television can be put and the power struggles which attend its viewing (Morley 1992: parts 3 and 6; Dahlgren 1998: 304). Criticisms have been levelled at this research, some of them quite scathing. It would, however, be best to look at these once we have considered audience populism since they are relevant to both approaches.

Although the theoretical and political contexts and the questions asked may have changed, we seem to have a similar backlash to that which greeted the failings of the effects approach. The new ethnography of television audiences may not be comparable with the uses and gratifications approach in significant respects. Nevertheless, it is similar in its attempt to accord more power and discrimination to the audience than semiology, structuralism or dominant ideology theories could ever have envisaged. This is even clearer in the case of audience populism, which is more or less synonymous with cultural populism (McGuigan 1992).[3]

The populist approach shares some of the heritage and focus of the new ethnography, but the themes and research of the latter are not necessarily or commonly consistent with those of the former. The new ethnography seems keen to correct some of the previous misconceptions about the audience and to establish a tradition of research. It is not inevitably committed to a particular idea of the audience and what it does. It is certainly not party to the more extreme claims of some supporters of audience populism. A leading exponent of this approach is Fiske, who claims, for example, that 'MTV is orgasm ... No ideology, no social control can organise an orgasm. Only freedom can. All orgasms are democratic: all ideology is autocratic. This is the politics of pleasure' (cited in Buxton 1990: 141). This comes close to suggesting that the audience is free from social determinations and that it has the power to construct what meanings it wants from popular culture. It also, as Buxton argues, represents a 'neo-populist revamping of uses and gratifications theory', 'mysteriously promoting the act of viewing into a form of "resistance" ' (ibid.: 19; cf. 163).[4]

This is a neat and suitably critical summary of audience populism. The populist approach rejects the idea that television and its messages, or ideology, are imposed upon the thoughts of – and thereby also determine the actions of – its viewers. This is so whatever the source and nature of this imposition. Instead, it stresses the 'active audience'. Viewers act in creative and subversive ways to extricate meanings from television which give them pleasure and which successfully resist any other meanings and ideologies which television may contain, including dominant ones. For a very simplified version of populism, what is on television genuinely reflects what people want to watch. This is obviously what the controllers of television would want us to believe anyway. But even if this is not the case, as Fiske would concede, there is nothing to stop viewers from turning what is on television into what they want. The populist case is that television programmes permit a range of interpretations, some of which may conflict with each other. Television programmes are therefore open to a number of constructions which viewers may wish to place upon them. Viewers are understood as 'subcultures' that gather their required meanings from television. They then use these creative interpretations to resist and subvert televisual messages. Thus audience populism not only celebrates a 'politics of pleasure' but also a 'politics of resistance'.

This is, of course, a very limited and superficial vision of politics. It amounts to little more than people watching television programmes to draw meanings contrary to those which they may have been encouraged to draw by their producers. Whether this is what people do when they watch television is debatable anyway considering the evidence mentioned above on how viewing can be a distracted and inattentive activity. It is equally a type of politics which fails to provide any challenge to the power relations that govern television. After all, if the populist argument is correct, people are getting the programmes they want, ones which allow them to be happily subversive. They are thus sufficiently distracted not to attempt anything that would be politically serious.[5] So, ironically, audience populism comes round to the idea that television serves as a type of social control, not because it dupes people, but because it provides them with a surrogate resistance. Also, as Buxton usefully notes, 'promoting' television viewing as 'a form of "resistance" ... is downright incongruous given that no one is actually forced to watch a particular television programme' (1990: 19).

Interestingly enough, audience populism often relies on 'textual' interpretations to make its points (Fiske 1987, 1989b). Indeed, it is reliant on the idea that 'texts', such as television programmes, are sufficiently open to allow audiences to draw a range of meanings from them. Yet as we have noted a number of times, trying to understand audiences by interpreting the 'texts' they encounter is a misguided exercise. One reason for this, as Lewis indicates, is that it does not tell us how such 'texts' are understood by 'real' audiences (1991: 47). Lewis goes on to note that even if there is scope for subversion within television programmes it is usually very limited. He also argues that populism often confuses resistance with opposition (ibid.: 69–70). Resistance is something offered by the television programme itself and it is on this which populism tends to concentrate. Opposition, which it often neglects, requires ideas (and politics?) which are not provided by the programme and which can only be developed outside television.

One of the most important criticisms made of populism is that it neglects the contexts in which television viewing takes place and how these contexts are determined by economic and political forces. This criticism is equally relevant to the new ethnography. As McGuigan argues, populism's neglect of the 'macro-processes of political economy' leads to its consequent failure to 'account for *both* ordinary people's everyday culture *and* its material construction by powerful forces beyond the immediate comprehension and control of ordinary people' (1992: 172, 175). This again raises doubts about the political credibility of populism. 'Economic exploitation, racism, gender and sexual oppression' all 'exist'. Yet 'the exploited, estranged and oppressed cope ... very well ... making valid sense of the world and obtaining grateful pleasure from what they receive' (ibid.: 171). This clearly relates to 'questions of power'. As Murdock argues, populism's inadequate assessment of power means it neglects 'the issue of the audience's relation to control within the media system' and 'the unequal distribution of material and symbolic resources' (1989: 228–9).

This type of criticism has also been made of the new ethnography (Murdock 1989: 228–9). Taking his cue from Adorno's analysis of capitalism, commodities and the culture industries, Willemen develops a highly critical account of Morley's research into domestic relations and television viewing (1990: 107–10; cf. Strinati 1995: 56–64). He argues that concentrating upon the viewing context, the viewers and what they watch, as Morley does, ignores how they are determined 'and constrained by the general logic of capitalist production within which and by which they are located' (Willemen 1990: 107). This logic 'is the process of commodification: the relentless pressure to replace use value by exchange value'; and the more successful it is, the more that commodities become things simply to enjoy. However, these pleasures are always 'created and defined' by the capitalist logic of commodification (ibid.: 108; see Strinati 1995: 56–8).

To focus only on how commodities such as television can be enjoyed is to ignore how they become increasingly dominated by exchange value. To do this when researching the domestic context of television viewing, as Morley does, is to reduce power relations and resistance to the family and the peer group. This ignores how these relations operate 'within the boundaries of capitalism's need to perpetuate itself and its need for profit' (Willemen 1990: 109). Morley's research thus focuses upon the role of television 'in interpersonal relations', rather than seeing how it is shaped and determined by the wider and more basic 'commodity aspect of the use of television'. Even if viewers do not 'adhere to the meanings proffered by television', they 'remain the only material most audiences have to work with' (ibid.: 109). The new ethnography and audience populism thus appear to neglect the social factors which determine the situations they wish to either research or celebrate.

However, this criticism is more damaging for the latter than it is for the former. The arguments of populism make it difficult to accommodate such a problem since it sees power as lying with the audience. The new ethnography, on the other hand, can try to relate the domestic sphere to wider economic and social conditions and determinants. For a start, Morley has argued that his research has connected the domestic context and active audiences with the unequal distribution of economic and cultural resources and conflicts between the powerful and the weak. Equally, he contends, for example, that his research on gender relations and their effect on family viewing does not confine their importance to the home. Rather, he shows that domestic gender relations are necessarily bound up with and organised by their wider dominance within society; in part, they retain this dominance because of how they work domestically (1992: 274–5).

Willemen's argument outlines some of the key determinants of the domestic contexts in which television viewing usually takes place. These include the commodity status of television and the audience's lack of control over what is screened. However, as Morley points out, his view of this relationship is too deterministic, tending to see such viewing as the almost automatic and direct outcome of the commodity status of television. This means he has little to say about the audience and its activities other than that they are the product of commodification. This is an extreme reductionism which dissolves the audience into the logic of capitalism. Again, the audience has become a residual category, not a subject worthy of attention.

By contrast, Morley's concern is to link the 'macro' and the 'micro'. It is only by doing this that their relevance can be established. He wants to produce theory and research which incorporates 'the detail of domestic consumption' with 'the "broader questions" of ideology, power and politics' and the commodity status of television (1992: 275–6). Associating this with the type of research identified by such authors as Barker and Brooks (1998) and Lewis (1991) seems to provide a useful way of studying the television audience.

Chapter 8

Popular television genres

A general introduction

This chapter will consider the issue of popular television genres. Drawing upon the discussion of film genres earlier in the book, it will be concerned with how the idea of television genres can be understood. It will look at the production of television genres, how they are organised as television programmes, and their audiences. It will, for the sake of brevity, focus upon the example of the television soap opera, although some other examples will be referred to where appropriate. It will also assess some of the interpretations offered of this genre along the way.

The case for the importance of genre in the study of popular culture has already been made. There are some evident problems with using the idea of genre, such as maintaining a consistent distinction between specific genres and trying to provide firm evidence that they influence audiences. Despite these qualifications, however, genre is a useful way to study popular culture. It can identify patterns within popular culture, alert us to the collective and individual aspects of these patterns and link them specifically to the production and consumption of popular culture. These points provide a guide to the social determinants and choices which organise popular culture. They also mean that the study of popular culture need not be confined to specific examples such as individual films or television programmes. Rather, the idea of genre means that such examples can be identified as parts of a pattern and then related to their wider social contexts in a more theoretical and precise manner. It also means that analysis need not be confined so much to the text, though this is always a potential problem with the idea of genre. Instead, defined as we have suggested above, genre can focus attention upon the production and consumption of popular culture, the ways popular culture is formed socially and historically. This argument is underpinned by

202

the fact that, historically, the idea of genres has been used by producers and consumers to organise and rationalise their activities. A number of the problems usually associated with genre can be overcome if it is viewed not as an abstract, rule-bound, textual category with universal properties, but as a concrete and specific, historically variable, social construction.

These general arguments about genre, which informed our discussion of film, can also be applied to television. We have, of course, to recognise that there are crucial differences between film and television and that the idea of genre cannot be translated directly from one to the other. Its relevance has to be linked to features specific to television, as well as to those which are relevant to popular culture as a whole.

It is therefore important to note how television genres emerged out of popular radio.[1] This can tell us something about television in general, as well as saying something specific about television genres. Both cinema and radio provided useful sources of established popular genres which television could exploit. However, while such film genres as the western and the murder mystery made the transition to television fairly easily and successfully, the example of cinema was not as relevant as radio for the needs of the new medium. What television did, in scheduling and broadcasting programmes, was far more consistent with the practices of radio than cinema. Rose points out that for early American television, 'radio was the principal raiding ground, as highly rated programs were moved over, or ... broadcast on both media simultaneously' (1985: 3). This was just as clear in Britain, as the BBC moved from broadcasting radio to broadcasting both media (see Chapter 6). Likewise, the scheduling and length of television programmes were more clearly influenced by radio than cinema. Radio had also created certain genres, such as the soap opera and the quiz show, and these proved to be even more popular on television. Also, television could not compete with the visual quality of cinema. This tended to favour the production of genres which suited it as a mass medium and was another reason for radio to be used as a source of programmes (ibid.: 4). Of course, as well as sharing the domestic and familiar qualities of radio, television combined sound and pictures which made it more like cinema.

Television did not borrow genres from radio without changing them. Popular radio genres were adapted to the defining features of television and not simply to the introduction of vision. A good example of this in Britain was the situation comedy *Hancock's Half Hour*. This was originally produced for radio and its novel development of the comedy show proved popular with listeners. The idea behind it was that humour should develop from the characters and the situations they found themselves in, rather than from the straightforward telling of jokes, or from a series of short sketches. Important aspects of character and situation were developed while the programme was on radio, where it ran from 1954 to 1959 (Goddard 1991: 77). One such aspect was the believable or 'realistic' situations characters found themselves in and with which audiences could identify. On radio, these realistic situations and locations had to be left largely to the listeners' imaginations. However, when it made the move to television, where it ran from 1956 to 1961, these generic points could be developed. Television presents the visual details of situations and locations and can thereby enhance the appeal to realism. As Goddard notes, '*Hancock's Half Hour*'s apparent reality of language, characterisation and location ... was ideally suited to and reinforced by the nature of television as a visual medium' (ibid.: 78). As such, television's 'addition of a visible consistency of location and character acted as a further indicator of "reality"' (ibid.: 79). The result was that 'the believability and consistency of *Hancock's Half Hour* – its "reality" – became a model for many of its successors'. This had 'led by the early 1960s to this kind of "sitcom naturalism" becoming almost a defining characteristic of the situation comedy form'. Goddard concludes that 'it has remained so' (ibid.: 79).

This provides a good example of the adaptation of popular genres from radio to television and shows how television has influenced their expansion and development as facets of popular culture. None the less, we must not forget, despite the apparent anomaly of the BBC (see Chapter 6), the primary determinant of popular genres. Television, like radio but unlike cinema, does not require its viewers to buy its products at the point of consumption. However, like any other medium, it does have to produce a marketable commodity. As Rose aptly puts it, television genres 'are essentially commodities, manufactured for and utterly dependent on, public consumption and support'. This may be slightly exaggerated in that some programmes may be given the chance to survive, for a while at least, without such support. This is often the case when they have just started, or when their popularity starts to decline. Also, television sometimes may not be funded in this manner and some programmes may be relatively protected because they are critical rather than popular successes. However, these qualifications should not detract from the argument that genres are 'formulas that have endured' because they 'manage to yield a regular profit for their producers'. They do this by ensuring such programming reaches 'as many people as possible' to meet the demands of advertisers (Rose 1985: 5, 7). Genres need to have a relatively wide popularity to provide audiences for advertisers. This means that those which prove popular will be the ones consistently supported and developed by television producers.

These points are very important for understanding television. As Abercrombie notes, 'it makes sound economic sense ... to work to a formula'. Here the comparison with Hollywood is clear. As Abercrombie continues to suggest, 'sets, properties and costumes can be used over and over again. Teams of stars, writers, directors and technicians can be built up, giving economies of scale.' This equally shapes consumption since 'genres permit the creation and maintenance of a loyal audience which becomes used to seeing programmes within a genre', for 'the audience knows what it is getting' (1996: 43). Abercrombie does go on to argue that television is not as reliant on genre as is sometimes claimed. His reasons for saying this relate to the flexible and unstable nature of the idea. He refers to differences within genres, the ambiguity of some genres such as 'the audience participation talk show', changes in genre 'conventions over time' and the shifting and blurring of the boundaries between genres (ibid.: 44–5). However, these points are consistent with a historical view of genres since they do not dispute the relevance of genre as a specific way of organising production and consumption. These concerns become critical only if it is assumed that genres are relatively fixed and rule-bound.

This argument has a number of implications. Obviously, genres with mass audience appeal will be favoured and nurtured in the production of television programmes. Equally, the organisation of television programmes themselves is affected. For example, it has been noted how the need for a commercial break every fifteen minutes or so has influenced television writing. Scripts lead into these breaks by posing a question or point of excitement to entice viewers to stay with the programme, which is then resolved when the break finishes. In turn, these secondary puzzles and resolutions can build up to the conclusion of the overall story. Also, the fifteen-minute blocks encourage 'broad action and vivid characters at the expense of narrative and emotional complexity' (Rose 1985: 6). Likewise, the need of advertising for programmes to have a wide appeal means that, on the whole, genres develop which are generally conservative in character and which tend not to question the status quo. If genres prove popular then this tendency will only be accentuated.

These implications illustrate a process of standardisation comparable to that we observed occurring with Hollywood cinema as it was being established. Something similar has happened with popular television as can be seen from our discussion of this subject. It is a simple and obvious point that once genres have established their popularity, they tend to be the ones which are sustained over time. Their continuing appeal to audiences supports this continuity. It also relies upon the standardisation of production afforded by making what are roughly the same types of generic programmes, rather than attempting something new and unpredictable.

According to Rose, television genres have become standardised into three general types, 'comedy, drama and variety' (1985: 6). These categories are probably too broad, even if they do capture something about developments in television programming in so far as standardisation is mainly geared towards fictional entertainment. However, although it will not be pursued here, the ordering of television schedules has also been dependent upon the role of factual programmes, such as news, current affairs, discussion forums and the 'docu-soap'. While such programming has often been subordinate to fictional entertainment, its importance for an understanding of television has to be recognised. Also, there are key generic differences between dramas such as the soap opera and the police series which make it difficult to treat them under the same broad category. Indeed, important changes, some of which have been noted, would be missed if they were to be thought of in this way. By contrast, comedy and variety would appear to overlap to some extent. This suggests that it may be best to recognise the range of genres which characterise popular television. Doing this allows historical changes to be recognised more easily, understands genre in a way that is relevant to producers and consumers and is in keeping with television's ever-growing schedules. Abercrombie notes that television does show a 'range of genres – documentaries, news, game shows, soap opera, police series, thrillers, situation comedy, talk shows' which is 'wider' than that of cinema (1996: 41; cf. Rose 1985: 3).

None the less, once these genres become established, they provide 'narrow limits of familiarity' (Rose 1985: 6), within which very little that is new or experimental can be attempted and beyond which it is very difficult to stray. To do either of these things is to risk losing audiences and revenues, while introducing uncertainty into the production process.

The emergence of such considerations into the production of television is related by Caughie to technical changes and competition between channels, in an important article on the development of television. While his specific focus is on television drama, Caughie's argument has a general relevance for the analysis of television. His concern is to show how the emergent 'practices' of early television became 'routines', in much the same way that Bordwell *et al.* and Burch have shown how the framework of Hollywood cinema was established. Caughie's point is that it is in the state of flux, which marks the earliest phase in the history of these media, that routines and frameworks are initially formed. Bearing in mind the differences between these media, understanding this phase can explain crucial features of their subsequent development (1991b: 24, 40).

According to Caughie, one of the most characteristic features of early television in Britain was its immediacy. Programmes could not be recorded, which meant television was dependent on the 'live relay' of outside events, 'the direct transmission of live action' (1991b: 23). In turn, this meant that early television was essentially ephemeral in character. The possibility of recording television programmes onto film was not realised until 1947, while recording onto tape first became possible in America in 1953. It 'was probably not readily available in Britain till around 1958' and 'not in routine use till the 60s' (ibid.: 24–5; cf. Goddard 1991: 83–5). Also, it was then that commercial television began to compete with the BBC, Independent Television (ITV) having been introduced in 1955. This phase is central to Caughie's overall case. He argues that it is 'at that technological moment when television ceases to be *necessarily* ephemeral that its commodity form and with it its aesthetics and its function, begins to be decided' (1991a: 25).

Examples of how early television was live and immediate are provided by the way drama was first televised. Dramas drawn from the theatre or literary classics, including those such as *Jane Eyre* which are now defined as costume dramas, were transmitted live. And repeats, which were common, were also live, the 'cast and crew' being called 'back for a second performance' (Caughie 1991a: 27–8). This situation began to change with the arrival of commercial television, the competition for viewers between ITV and the BBC and the emergence of marketability and profitability in the production of television programmes. Programmes had to become marketable goods which attracted and retained audiences.

Equally significant 'was the arrival of new technology' (Caughie 1991a: 36). As noted, this permitted the recording of television programmes onto film and tape; for example, a 'television picture-on-tape recorder' became available in 1953. Though 'the change was slow to take effect' in Britain, due to trade union concerns about jobs and repeat fees and commitment to the aesthetic of 'immediacy', it did mean television did not have to be live and immediate anymore (ibid.: 37). Television programmes could now be recorded. This made them tradable items which could be bought and sold. However, recording was expensive. The most economic way of off-setting the cost was to find the most profitable market, which was America. Thus, the recording of programmes and the arrival of commercial television 'marked a new interest in international trade' (ibid.: 38–9). For example, *The Adventures of Robin Hood* was 'sold to the US as a series before ITV began transmission' in 1955, and by 1961 the BBC was recording *Maigret* on tape and film 'for an international market' (ibid.: 39).

This indicates that 'what recording did was to lift television out of ephemerality and give it a commodity form. The shift from direct transmission to recording turned television from use value to exchange value, re-forming even public service television as not only a cultural but also a tradeable good.' Hence, 'cultural production entered the market place as a commodity'. For example, 'much of the subsequent development of British television drama' – 'the drift ... towards an International style drama' and 'the rise of the classic serial' – can be traced to 'the moment at which drama becomes expensive, marketable and recordable' (Caughie 1991a: 39). In putting forward this case, Caughie does not argue that the commodity form completely eliminates immediacy; rather he sees the two existing in 'contradiction' with each other, even if the former becomes dominant (ibid.: 40).[2]

All of this does not mean that genres or programmes do not change, but that any changes which occur do so within the limits set by the commodity status of television. Changes in genres occur within a context organised by the demands of production and consumption. The need for popularity is crucial in shaping the nature of such changes. There should therefore be little surprise that the conventions of genres change over time. For example, the popularity of the soap opera has meant that some of its conventions have been borrowed by other popular genres such as the police series. Good examples of this would be *The Bill* and *Hill Street Blues* (Rose 1985: 9; Abercrombie 1996: 45). Similarly, the need for soap operas occasionally to ring the changes, within limits, has led to their adoption of story-lines more usually characteristic of the police and crime series. Major soap operas in the UK, such as *EastEnders* and *Brookside* have adopted this strategy.

Again, this may not mean that the idea of genre has become less relevant because the boundaries between them are shifting. As Abercrombie, who puts forward this very argument, notes, 'there may be sound economic reasons' for this to occur. For example, 'new audiences are won by inventing new genres or mixing up old ones; the need for innovation produces a tendency to tamper with genre conventions' (ibid.; cf. 43).

To some extent, there is almost a 'predictable cycle' whereby 'a new format' or, more commonly, 'an innovative variation on an old format emerges' (Rose 1985: 6–7). This happens as a result of changes in production and consumption, such as in 'programming practices and production techniques', or the 'intense competition' between television channels (ibid.: 8). The 'new' genre programme attracts large audiences, introduces a new cycle and leads to imitations which try to cash in on its initial success. The crossovers between the soap opera and the police series could be seen as one example of this, though, presumably, this argument could also be applied to the development of specific genres. Equally, the recent upsurge in competition for viewers between the increasing numbers of channels may mean genres are continually relied upon as easily identifiable attractions. At the same time, the mixing of genres may be encouraged. But this need not make the idea of genre redundant. Rather, it brings out the significance of the changes in production and consumption which are occurring.

So far we have set down some guidelines for assessing popular television genres. Now we need to consider some of these points in more detail. First, we shall look at production.

The production of popular television genres

We can focus upon the soap opera to illustrate some of the introductory points that need to be made about the study of popular television genres. The soap opera has probably been the most popular genre on British television. For a long time now it has dominated the audience ratings for British television programmes. Indeed, since the introduction of *Coronation Street* in 1960, it is the genre which has consistently attracted most viewers according to the weekly listings of the most watched programmes. The prominence of the soap opera on popular television suggests it is a good example to assess. Our introductory discussion above has tried to show how important production is to the study of popular television genres and we shall begin with this, after trying to define our subject matter.

A soap opera is usually thought of as a fictional drama serial, broadcast at least two or three times weekly and continuously from one year to the next until it is taken off the air. Some soap operas, such as *Coronation Street* on television and *The Archers* (1950) on radio, started a long time ago and are still going strong. By contrast, once highly popular television soap operas, such as *Crossroads* (1964–88), have been discontinued. Yet others, such as *Eldorado* (1992–3), never acquired a large enough audience and therefore did not last very long. Of course, this way of thinking of soap operas does raise certain minor definitional problems. For example, some programmes usually thought of as soap operas, such as *Dallas* and *Dynasty*, glamorous and glossy American sagas of the rich and powerful, do not conform to the common definition because they are broadcast in 'seasonal runs' and not all the time. However, they are still thought of as soap operas.

The term 'soap opera' derives from the serials sponsored by major detergent manufacturers and broadcast on American radio in the 1930s and 1940s. According to Kilborn, 'soap' refers to the role of these manufacturers 'in exploiting daytime serials as a vehicle for advertising and promotion'; and 'opera' refers to the way 'most soap dramas' were 'larger than life and often prone to indulge in melodramatic excess' (1992: 26). This is therefore another genre which has its roots in radio, but which was successfully adapted for television. In America, this often involved drawing upon the appeal of Hollywood glamour, while in Britain it was usually shaped by some version of social realism. We shall not present a history of soap operas here (see ibid.: 24–35), though some points will be returned to where relevant. In any event, a history informed by the theoretical points raised above is beyond the scope of this book.

The first key point to note about the production of soap operas is in keeping with the arguments of Caughie and Rose above and concerns the emergence of production routines and norms. One of the most important factors in limiting the cost of making television soap operas is how 'the whole production process has become relatively routinized'. In this process, 'groups of highly trained workers' operate 'according to a set of working practices developed to ensure the best use of the available facilities'. As such, 'only ... the strictest discipline and routine' can achieve 'the level of through-put ... necessary to ensure the constant flow of programmes' (Kilborn 1992: 21). The use of time and resources has to be maximised to a greater extent than with less continuous types of drama. Not all television production is necessarily organised and constrained to such a degree, but the need to produce such a popular and enduring genre favours the development of 'a broadly industrial mode of production'. This 'production process is ... broken down into a chain of separate operations and individuals or groups are given responsibility for carrying out specific tasks'. Examples of these include executive production, scriptwriting, story editing and continuity, directing, acting, rehearsal and recording. This process 'can be likened to other manufacturing processes where each phase of production is routinized to the greatest possible degree' (ibid.: 58).

The development of such an industrial mode of production for making television soap operas is related to minimising costs and to making the most of the genre's popular appeal. Soap operas can be produced at a relatively low cost after initial expenditures have been met (Kilborn 1992: 21). There is therefore a strategic advantage in using a routinised production process since it keeps costs low while still tapping into the high audience viewing figures the soap opera can achieve. The popular soap opera is a programme which 'can be easily and regularly accounted for' because 'expensive equipment and studio resources' are being used on a 'regular and intensive basis'. This minimises costs and encourages the continued and routine production of such a programme (ibid.: 57). Also, soap operas are normally confined to a small number of characteristically 'standard' and 'domestic' 'locations or settings'.

The costs incurred in building these sets may be high initially, though they need not be; but their continued use, possibly over a number of years, means they represent an efficient investment of finance and resources (ibid.: 21). This applies notwithstanding the possibility that producers of soap operas may even decide occasionally to burn down a set for the sake of a story-line.

One interesting illustration of the importance of these considerations is contained in a letter sent by Lew Grade to prospective writers about a projected new soap opera, which eventually reached television screens as *Crossroads*. What he was looking for was

> a soap opera, five days a week across the board, to go out at 4.30 for 25 minutes. A programme that would appeal in the main to the housewife – a kind of Mrs. Dale's diary – but one that would reflect the midland life and could at the same time be acceptable in the rest of the country ... The sets could not be large, nor moved around too much. The cast would be small.
>
> (quoted in Hobson 1982: 36)

These points show how the soap opera, as a popular television genre, involves the balancing of running costs and potential audiences in the organisation of its production. It is possible to see the soap opera as a relatively low-cost programme with a very high yield in viewing figures.[3] However, it can also entail relatively high starting costs. The major American soaps clearly have fairly large budgets to pursue their representation of the affluent and glamorous life-style of the corporate rich (Kilborn 1992: 52). Some of the newer soap operas in the UK have also involved high initial production costs. For example, the houses which form the small estate upon which *Brookside* is based were purpose built for the programme. Soap operas can normally rely upon their ability to attract large numbers of viewers, more than any other television genre. So whether the initial production costs are relatively high or low, they can usually be set off against the ratings successes of the genre (ibid.: 52–6). As Kilborn notes, 'soaps always have the advantage of being much less costly than other forms of TV drama, especially if the very large audiences which a soap can usually be relied upon to generate are included in the calculations' (ibid.: 54).

These features are linked to the way the soap opera becomes a commodity, since it can be traded and used to generate advertising revenues. The soap opera becomes a commodity because it can be bought and sold. For example, soap operas have proved popular on the international market. A number of soap operas have generated large international sales. This is partly due to the number of English-speaking countries world-wide, but sales are not necessarily limited to such customers. We have to recall here the relevance of Caughie's argument (see above). Kilborn notes that *EastEnders* has been sold to one-time members of the British Empire such as Canada, New Zealand and Australia; to European countries such as Norway, Denmark, Holland, Belgium and Catalonia in Spain; and to television stations across America (1992: 106–7). Other soap operas, such as *Coronation Street*, have also sold well, particularly in English-speaking countries apart from America (ibid.). Kilborn argues that 'the international popularity of the soap opera format and the voracious appetite of television stations all over the world for scheduling material' has led to 'soaps becoming part of a multi-million pound export trade' (ibid.: 107). Also, the potential for international sales is playing an ever more important part 'in the economic calculations of would-be producers' setting up new programmes, as happened with *EastEnders* (ibid.: 107–8).

However, the story does not end here. For example, 'commercial exploitation' can be extended to 'direct spin-offs from the programme itself' such as books, videos, theme music, clothes, T-shirts, mugs, duvet covers and jewellery (Kilborn 1992: 51). The video has been especially significant in making the soap opera a commodity. This is because it provides the programme in a material and accessible form and allows it to be profitably extended and repeated. More violent or sexually explicit story-lines can be featured in special episodes made for sale on video. Programmes can be repeated by being redefined for special videos concentrating, for example, on particular characters or specific story-lines. There are also indirect spin-offs, such as how the stars and story-lines of popular soap operas provide tabloid newspapers with items to fill their pages and exacerbate celebrity journalism. This may involve the sort of merchandising mentioned above. Equally, it can enlist stories about the stars to sell the paper and the programme; and this can work even if the celebrity of some stars is not a consistently saleable item.

It might be objected that a soap opera such as *EastEnders* is not a good example to use since it is produced by the BBC and not by commercial television. If it is not produced by the latter, how can it be interpreted as a commercial product? We have noted, both above and in Chapter 6, that the BBC is subject to constraints similar to those experienced by private enterprises operating in media and popular cultural markets. As such, *EastEnders* indicates how the BBC has to compete with commercial television for audiences. The ratings success of *EastEnders* means that the BBC is able to defend the licence fee and even petition for increased funding because it has produced a highly popular soap opera. *EastEnders* has managed to dominate the weekly ratings, along with *Coronation Street*, since its introduction in 1985. The BBC can thus claim to be competing effectively with commercial television. In its turn, as indicated above, *EastEnders* has extended the 'opportunities for commercial exploitation' open to the BBC through international sales and other merchandising (Kilborn 1992: 51). Also, it is said that *EastEnders* provided the BBC with the kind of 'big ratings success' it needed at a time when it was subject to severe criticism (ibid.). Therefore, there are good reasons for regarding this example in the way we have suggested. It also provides another indication of the important part played by channel competition in forming and developing popular television genres.

Another major aspect of the commodity status of the soap opera lies in its popularity with audiences and the relation of this to advertising revenues. The simple point here is that the large audiences soap operas attract make them attractive for advertisers and profitable for producers and television network companies. The more conceptual point is that the capacity to attract advertising is important in making the soap opera a commodity. Public service broadcasting may have its specific reasons for producing particular programmes, but this does not mean it is not interested in ratings and competition. We have already considered the BBC's rationale for having a successful and popular soap opera in its schedules. For companies in commercial television, 'a premium rate can be charged for advertising in the slots before, during and immediately after the screening of a popular soap'. This ensures 'that the flow of advertising revenue – the economic life-blood of the independent/commercial operation – is maximised' (Kilborn 1992: 17). Commercial television delivers audiences to advertisers; the immense popularity of the soap opera genre facilitates this process. Therefore, 'it is not difficult to see why such reliable audience-producing programmes as soaps should always have featured prominently in commercial schedules' (ibid.: 50).

The placing of the most popular soap operas in the early evening schedules is further evidence of this. Such scheduling does not only maximise the popularity of the soap opera itself. It tries to make the most of the high ratings achieved for subsequent programmes, thus extending the potential to make money from advertising. The thinking here is that if viewers turn to a specific channel to watch one of their favourite soap operas, then perhaps they will stay with that channel for the following programmes. Since the BBC has to compete with commercial television to the extent we have suggested, its own popular soap opera needs to generate large enough audiences to retain viewers in sufficient numbers for subsequent programmes. Obviously, the scheduling issues involved are more complicated than this suggests. Hopefully, however, it has been made clear that the popularity of the soap opera is crucial to the overall organisation of the schedules of popular television. This derives from its competitiveness and its capacity to attract audiences and advertising revenues which are bound up with its production conditions. It is worth singling out the soap opera for special attention precisely because of its strategic importance for popular television.

The structure of popular television genres

The attempt to arrive at an understanding of popular television genres, such as the soap opera, clearly relies upon assessing the audience as much as it does upon analysing industrial conditions and the production process. It is these features, after all, which define the television programme as a commodity. Before we consider the audience, however, we need to say a few words about the structure of the soap opera itself. This does not necessarily determine how audiences will view the programme any more than it will shape production. If anything is a 'dependent variable' here it is the programme. None the less, this structure may suggest links between production and the audience.

The first thing to say about our chosen example, the soap opera, is that it relies upon an 'open' rather than a 'closed' narrative. A 'closed' narrative is exemplified by the narrative structure of the typical Hollywood film. With this, the initial cause or enigma which sets the film in motion is resolved or answered by its conclusion. The progression of the narrative restores the order originally disturbed by the cause or enigma. Few if any questions are left unanswered at the film's end, when everything seems to reach its appropriate conclusion. An important part of this, as we have seen, is how frequently the solution of the problem entails the coming together of the male and female leads in a romantic happy ending. This is a 'closed' narrative.

The 'open' narrative of the soap opera, by contrast, it is argued, does not provide such conclusions. It presents a seemingly continuous set of stories, not all of which are resolved quickly or at any one time; some may not be resolved at all, though this is unlikely; and some may reach a conclusion only to be re-opened sometime later. Most commonly, a soap opera will not provide a rapid solution to a particularly dramatic problem, but will delay its introduction for as long as possible. The soap opera often seems to defer, sometimes almost interminably, answering the questions it asks or resolving the problems it poses. Think generally of how soap operas deal with personal and family relationships. A good example is how the coming together of the romantic couple, which characteristically provides the happy ending of the Hollywood film, is merely a pretext in the soap opera for further problems to beset the couple, such as arguments over money, illness, adultery and even murder. This potential openness means that story-lines are by definition subject to a number of different interpretations as to how they can possibly be resolved, even if only on a temporary basis.

This is related to other key features of the soap opera: how they rely upon a number of different and disparate story-lines; and how this means they have to represent a relatively wide range of characters. Drawing comparisons with other popular genres such as the police series or the situation comedy is useful here. The typical, fictional, police drama tends to confine itself, over its one- or two-hour schedule slot, to one main story-line, the investigation of a crime such as murder (Sparks 1993).[4] This will involve a few main characters, the investigator, the 'superior' officer, the 'side-kick' and possibly a main suspect, though a cast of usual suspects may make their entrances and exits. Another story-line may intrude, particularly the now common one about an aspect of the main investigator's personal life. However, this will usually remain sub-ordinate to the investigation, even if it is eventually found to be relevant to solving the crime. The situation comedy tends to be about a small number of characters, not infrequently a family, and its common half-hour duration concerns supposedly funny attempts to resolve an initially humorous problem (Woollacott 1986). Changes have clearly occurred over time in these narratives with, for example, the introduction of soap-operatic elements into both and 'serious' content into the latter. Notwithstanding these developments, both genres still tend to be marked by closed narratives, a few, inter-related story-lines and a small number of identifiable characters.

The contrast between these genres and the soap opera should be clear. The latter, in its pursuit of open narratives, tends to set up and follow a relatively large number of story-lines. It is not unusual for a typical half-hour episode to cover at least three stories, while perhaps referring to ones that have passed, or hinting at new ones to be introduced. In turn, this necessarily raises the number of characters who need to be represented simply because of the number of story-lines and their deferred resolution. The range of characters covered by the soap opera is one of the reasons why it has been seen to be a feminine, if not feminist, genre. The wide representation it affords means that women need not be marginalised, nor confined to stereotypical roles. Instead, they can be represented outside as well as inside the family, in different occupations and at different ages. As Hobson notes, for example, the soap opera deals with 'problems which are experienced by women whatever their age or class' and 'incorporates a deep commitment to women's cultural values' (1982: 34 and 32). Of course, for other writers, the representation of women in the soap opera is not necessarily as simple as this argument suggests (see Geraghty 1991, 1992).

The last feature that needs to be noted here is the 'realism' of the soap opera. The typical British soap opera is often prized for its realism (Glaessner 1990: 124). This is commonly seen as being one of its defining features and an explanation of its popularity, because realism entails focusing upon gossip, local communities and the family (Kilborn 1992: 85–7, 91–2; Abercrombie 1996: 50–4; Geraghty 1992; Glaessner 1990: 122). The soap opera's concern with realism is seen in the way it concentrates upon the domestic, the everyday and the mundane (Kilborn 1992: 85–7). As Hobson puts it, 'soap operas are about people and the problems of their everyday lives', 'the problems of everyday personal life and personal relationships' (1982: 33–4). Or, as Glaessner argues, 'social realism demands the suggestion of unmediated access to the real world, the real world being understood as the terrain of the ordinary and the everyday' (1990: 121, cf. 120–5; Abercrombie 1996: 26–30, 194–5; Buckingham 1987: 180–6; Geraghty 1992; Kilborn 1992: chapter 5).

These 'dramas of everyday life', as Kilborn calls them (1992: 91), rely upon certain features, besides those already mentioned, such as the focus upon gossip and personal relationships, for their realistic appeal. Kilborn, for example, notes how, unlike other types of fictional genres, soap operas try to approximate real time by relating time in the programme to time as it is in real life. The soap opera can be visited at regular times during the week as if it is always there and as if time was passing by in the soap opera at the same pace as in real life. The weekend repeats might appear to cause some confusion on this count, but presumably repetition is also a defining feature of everyday life. Similarly, the problems dealt with by particular stories might take the same time to be resolved in real life as they do in the soap opera (ibid.: 92–3). Equally, Kilborn notes that the soap opera relies upon a 'strong sense of real place' to secure its realistic appeal. The way soap operas are identified with particular regions or areas is a good illustration of this effect (ibid.: 94–5, cf. 85–8). The sense in which realism is used here is not a documentary or a scientific one. The type of realism it conforms to is similar to Todorov's idea of cultural realism (see Chapter 2). The intention of the soap opera is to convey the impression that it represents, in a dramatised form, some of the real features of the world around us. This is why so many commentators mention its concern with the everyday when they refer to its realism. But the soap opera is primarily occupied with entertainment and its realism is shaped by its aim to become and remain popular.

Production, audiences and genres

There are clearly important differences in the way different types of television programmes are produced. Not all programmes will be produced by the process which has been argued to typify the soap opera. However, differences are said to exist even within the genre itself, for example, between British and American soap operas, or between newer and older British soap operas. The production of some programmes, such as the situation comedy, may be similar in that they may be relatively cheap to make and rely on only a few settings, perhaps a sitting room, kitchen and garden. Other programmes, however, such as prestige period dramas or peak-time police series, may be produced quite differently. They may use a wider range of more expensive locations and more lavish costumes and interiors; they may also employ established film and stage actors, include expensive action sequences and devote more time to the making of each episode. This does not mean that costs or profits do not matter for this type of production. On the contrary, higher initial costs may be necessary to make them profitable, particularly given the popularity of such productions on the international market.

Despite this, we can none the less suggest there are apparent continuities between the production process and the structure of the soap opera. The relatively routine, disciplined and specialised production of soap operas seems consistent with a continuously scheduled, regularly screened programme with fairly predictable story-lines, which is reliant upon a small number of constantly used sets and a reasonably stable cast of characters and actors. Similarly, the use of realistic settings would appear to be well suited to the attempt to keep costs down. This contrasts with the American soap opera serials, such as *Dallas* and *ER*, which are only screened in seasonal runs and depend upon higher budgets. However, their glossy lack of realism should not be taken as a sign of an undisciplined or unprofitable production.

There is an emerging awareness that an adequate understanding of popular culture needs to take account of production, the audience and the 'text'.[5] Our argument here does not dispute this. However, it is also concerned with how popular culture, such as films and television programmes, may be organised and determined by its wider social and historical conditions, such as its processes of production. It is therefore necessary to take account of all three. Yet this need not mean they are all equally important. Nor need it endorse any analysis of popular culture which merely adds them together to achieve the desired result. More attention could be devoted to what each of these terms actually covers. Also, useful questions could be raised about their relative importance and whether some factors have a more determining influence than others. After all, it might be argued that one of the tasks of theory should be to develop empirically plausible explanations of popular culture. To do this it may be necessary to argue that some factors are more important than others. One way of beginning to do this might be to try to show how a form of popular culture, such as a television genre, is shaped by its production routines which, in turn, relate to its commodity status. At the very least, it might be possible to show how, as implied above, they complement each other. This type of explanation need not be mechanical and will obviously involve looking at how such a relationship has evolved historically. The point to be stressed here is that it may be usefully clarified and assessed in the fashion suggested. Rather than dealing with production, the audience and the 'text' separately, or treating them as having equal importance, it may be helpful to consider their relative causal importance and how this may determine the emergence and development of types of popular culture. An introduction such as this may not be the best place to pursue such an argument, but it does have the potential to make some sense of the material discussed in this book.

Audiences and the soap opera

Along with production, the audience provides another key to understanding popular television genres. Much of the debate about the audience for soap operas has tended to follow the debate about the audience more generally, which we outlined in the previous chapter. Many of the points and arguments covered there are equally applicable here. For example, a number of the most recent commentators on the soap opera audience favour a version of the 'active audience' approach. We can therefore assume some familiarity with the previous chapter and conclude with a relatively brief discussion of this topic.

The 'active audience' approach to the soap opera audience is, for example, argued for by Kilborn. He values this approach since it provides a compelling critique of the 'effects' approach and tends to be supported by empirical research (1992: 68–72). Its development from the 'uses and gratifications' approach is likewise emphasised. He also refers to the research on family television viewing to show how such viewing is particularly conducive to watching soap operas. Accordingly, people usually watch television at home with other people who may, not uncommonly, be other members of their family; and they tend to do this along with other activities, such as reading and talking. Gossip, as such, is a widespread feature of everyday life and the soap opera thus tends to concentrate upon it. Consequently, discussion among viewers about the soap opera provides another level of gossip, this time about what is going on in the soap opera itself. Similarly, the emphasis placed by the soap opera upon the domestic and everyday life complements and reflects the contexts in which it is watched. It is not always possible to 'presuppose a high level of sustained concentration' because of the pursuit of other activities. Viewers often watch in a distracted and inattentive state. However, 'this form of distracted viewing' can be catered for by the familiarity, the gradual development of plots and the switching between story-lines of the typical soap opera (ibid.: 73).

It is equally possible to contest the idea that there are typical ways for viewers to watch soap operas. Audiences can become emotionally involved in watching the soap opera, wallowing in the escapism offered and identifying with the characters and their lives. Involvement here may arise, for example, from the escapism and fantasy offered by the American soap opera. However, it may also arise from the realism often associated with the British soap opera. These soap operas provide 'a fairly close parallel between the fictional world' of the soap opera and 'the everyday world' of the audience. 'The resemblance between the two' encourages in viewers 'a strong sense of identification with soap characters and the places they inhabit' (Kilborn 1992: 75). Alternatively, some sections of the audience can become cynically detached, making ironic fun of the melodramatic excesses and mind-numbing banality of the typical soap opera (ibid.: 73–4; Ang 1985). Presumably, the 'distracted and inattentive' and 'emotionally involved' viewers must be placed alongside these 'cynically detached' viewers to indicate different ways of watching – and not watching? – the soap opera.

Studies show that viewers give a number of reasons for watching soap operas. In his summary of this research on the 'pleasures which are most commonly associated with soap watching', Kilborn defines them as 'needs' that the soap opera seems 'to be fulfilling or gratifying' (1992: 75). A number of these 'needs' indicate points of compatibility between the soap opera and its audience. The first of these is the provision of a 'regular source of entertainment'. For various reasons, such as the need to relax or reward themselves, people need to be entertained. The soap opera, like many television genres, is a way of achieving this. This shows how important the soap opera is for the television schedules, since large numbers of viewers will organise their lives so they can return repeatedly to the regular slot allocated to the programme. As Kilborn notes, 'one of the special appeals of soaps is the ease with which they can be integrated into the rhythms and patterns of domestic or workaday life' (ibid.: 76).

The second pleasure offered by the soap opera is the opportunity it provides for 'social and personal interaction'. People need to interact and share their tastes and pleasures with other people. One of the principal types of interaction is conversation. Thus the soap opera serves as an 'aid to social interaction' because it is something people can talk about. The soap opera does not isolate people or undermine communities and community sentiment. Rather, it achieves the opposite. Indeed, encouraging this 'sense of cohesion and togetherness' becomes especially relevant 'in an age when individuals are suffering increasingly from feelings of alienation' (Kilborn 1992: 77).

Third, not only can the soap opera can fulfil social needs, it can also fulfil individual ones. For example, they can provide 'compensation' for socially isolated individuals. By providing the comforts of contact and 'companionship' for these people, the soap opera helps them to cope with their 'loneliness' (Kilborn 1992: 77–8). The soap opera, in this instance, serves as a type of 'surrogate' or 'substitute' community: some individuals may no longer have any meaningful contact with a real community, so they make do with the artificial one represented by the soap opera. Fourth, and related to this, the soap opera provides 'identification and involvement' (ibid.: 78–9). It has been shown that viewers do identify with characters in soap operas and become involved with their lives and problems. While these pleasures will vary among viewers, most 'make some reference to the relationships they are able to form with soap characters'. This means that identification and involvement are more likely to develop with the soap opera, because 'no other genre allows the same sustained contact with characters' and, we might add, their lives and problems (ibid.: 78). Perhaps these viewers, as well as those referred to in the previous point, conform to the 'involved' type of television viewing identified above (cf. ibid.: 12). For example, the identification and involvement offered by 'this harmless form of emotional indulgence' can become so intense it can meet the need to release viewers' 'pent-up emotions' (ibid.: 79).

Fifth, the soap opera is said to provide 'escapist fantasy' in that it meets people's need to escape from the real world, with its ever-present troubles, to an alternative reality, a fantasy world. Some soap operas will provide more fantasy than others. As we have seen, many British soap operas are thought to be realistic by their producers and audiences, while some American examples are seen as offering viewers the glamorous, fantasy world of the super-rich. However, whatever the world retreated to, the idea 'is that viewers use soaps to detach themselves from the worries and concerns of everyday life and immerse themselves in a fictional world'. This is, for 'some viewers', 'a major part of the genre's continuing appeal' (Kilborn 1992: 79–80).

Lastly, the soap opera is instructive in that it meets people's need for 'learning'. Many soap operas are 'realistic', which means that viewers can learn from them how to deal with problems they confront in real life. As dramatised fictions, soap operas can enable viewers to learn things about the world. Some soap operas may provide direct information about such things as social problems; the soap opera is often mentioned as a television genre in which contemporary social problems can be broadcast and discussed, both on and off screen. More generally, however, soap operas help viewers to learn by educating them about such things as relationships and emotions. However, these 'educative functions' are usually subordinated to the soap opera's need to provide dramatised fiction as a type of popular entertainment (Kilborn 1992: 80–2).

One consequence of this is that the social problems raised by the soap opera are usually confined to the private and domestic sphere and resolved within the prevailing political and cultural consensus (Kilborn 1992: 81–2, 96–7). This should come as no surprise given the often mentioned focus of this genre. What it does mean, however, is that social problems are frequently defined as individual and personal problems and not problems deriving from, and related to, the wider economic and political organisation of society.

For Kilborn this may not be that significant because audiences bring their own frames of reference to bear in interpreting the soap opera (1992: 81–2). However, we might want to ask where these frames of reference come from. Are they made up by soap opera audiences? And what role does regular soap opera viewing play in their formation? To provide evidence of the active and independent audience, Kilborn notes how viewers can be critical of soap operas as a result of the competence they acquire in watching them. They may, for example, criticise what they see as implausible storylines, or inappropriate behaviour by a particular character (1992: 14–16, 71–2, 83, 88–91). Yet is this really evidence of an active audience applying its own frames of reference, or of an audience which has already accepted the frame of reference provided by the soap opera? After all, it is a criticism which is confined to and does not stray beyond the conventions of the soap opera. Kilborn appears to be referring to involved viewers, but even cynically detached viewers do not seem to go that far in criticising the soap opera itself when they make fun of its conventions. For example, not only do they not stop watching, they do not even seem to fall into the posture adopted by distracted and inattentive viewers.

Like other writers on the soap opera, Kilborn adopts what is termed an 'active audience approach' (1992; see also Chapter 7). Yet a number of the findings he describes could equally show the alienation and lack of power of the audience. The socially isolated viewers deal with their social estrangement and individual loneliness by tuning in to the surrogate community presented by the soap opera. Other viewers watch the genre in a cynical, detached and ironic manner. Still others, who cannot be attributed with a 'high level of sustained concentration' (Kilborn 1992: 73), appear too distracted and inattentive to bother with being ironic – though they may also be pragmatic in how they watch television. Even viewers who use the soap opera as a basis for social interaction, as something to talk about, discover in the community it offers a sense of belonging that helps them cope with their 'feelings of alienation' (ibid.: 77). In their turn, other viewers appear to invest high levels of involvement and identification in the life and characters of the soap opera (cf. Barker and Brooks 1998). Still other viewers look to it for 'escapist fantasy', sometimes into a supposedly realistic world. Whatever the level of competence, interest and commitment expressed by a particular section of the audience, few seem to entertain any idea of directly determining what is on television and, despite some experiments, what should happen in the soap opera (Kilborn 1992: 14–15). The audience may not be passive in the way the effects approach and other theories have assumed (though presumably most viewers must be passive sometimes). Yet this does not mean that it has any real power nor that it – or at least sections of it – may not be alienated. We need, of course, to work out precisely what we mean by alienation and to gather empirical evidence of its existence in people's consciousness apart from their thinking about the popular soap opera. But it is none the less interesting to consider how such an idea can provide another way of understanding the television audience.

The preceding discussion has clearly shown that the soap opera has been a significant genre in the development of popular television. It has also proved to be a good example to use when discussing the production of, the audience for and the programme structure of a popular television genre. The soap opera has tended to dominate British television as the most popular type of tele-vision programme and the weekly ratings figures show that this is still the case. However, what these figures also show is that the numbers of viewers soap operas attract are declining. At the moment (1999), the top soap operas such as *Coronation Street* and *EastEnders* attract between approximately 14 and 17 million viewers per episode according to the BARB figures provided each week by tele-text. By contrast, both soap operas have previously proved capable of attracting audiences of over 20 million per episode. For example, the highest number of viewers attracted by an episode of *Coronation Street* in 1989 was nearly 24.5 million, while the most-watched episode of *EastEnders* in the same year attracted 21.6 million viewers (Gambaccini and Taylor 1993: 105, 146).

The reasons for this decline are perhaps not yet clear. However, it is possible to speculate that the increasing competition for television audiences is producing a relative increase in the number of satellite and cable (not to mention video) viewers and a relative decline in the number of viewers watching BBC1 and ITV, the major terrestrial channels. The television audience is thus being spread across – or fragmented between – these viewing options. One possible consequence is that the mass audience for the main soap operas is beginning to decline. The soap opera remains the most popular television genre. Soap operas are the most watched programmes and their repertoire has been drawn upon by other genres such as the docu-soap. Nevertheless, their singular importance may be tied up with the fate of terrestrial television. The status of the soap opera as a focus of national, popular television may begin to be undermined if the competition for television audiences increases. Note also that *EastEnders*, which was first broadcast in 1985, was the last successful soap opera to be launched on British television. One result could potentially be the fragmentation of the soap opera audience. Much of this is speculative, though it does again raise questions about understanding the importance of the soap opera. The ideas of fragmented audiences and media-produced realities, such as the surrogate communities represented by the soap opera, have been associated with the theory of postmodernism. The next chapter will consider the relevance of this theory to the study of popular television.

Chapter 9

Popular television and postmodernism

THE THEORY OF postmodernism would appear to have become increasingly relevant to the study of the contemporary mass media and popular culture. Indeed, it sometimes seems as if we should take it for granted that such media and culture can now only be understood as examples of postmodernism. There is little doubt that postmodern theory does raise significant issues such as the power of the media, the seemingly increasing prominence of consumerism and the nature of identity. Whether these issues have been posed and analysed more adequately by other theories and whether they are that novel are questions that need not detain us for the moment. The point is that postmodernism has become a prevalent interpretation of popular culture and raises issues which have been discussed at various points in this book. In this chapter, we shall assess it as a way of understanding popular television. A critical examination of postmodern theory should allow us to bring our introduction to the study of popular culture reasonably up to date and provide a basis for the arguments outlined in the conclusions.

Postmodernism is now a term common to the social sciences.[1] It has become the focus of continuing debates in such obvious areas as cultural and media studies and social theory, but also in such areas as gender, race and ethnicity, and crime and the media (Boyne and Rattansi 1990; Osborne and Kidd-Hewitt 1996; Richardson 1996: 72–6). It has raised the prospect of 'post-industrialism' and 'post-capitalism' and has figured significantly in arguments over the continuing relevance of social class and the future of work (Featherstone 1991; Lash and Urry 1994; Rose 1991). Equally, there have been a number of different levels to which postmodern theory has been applied, from wholesale, global changes in the structure and direction of modern societies to the local sphere (Featherstone 1991: chapter 1; Lash and Urry 1994; Morley 1991; Rose 1991).

230

Arguments take place not only over the precise meaning of the idea of postmodernism, but over whether to define it is either to betray its spirit and intention, or to engage in a hopeless cause. None the less, the points raised by these arguments suggest there are definite meanings which can be given to such an idea.[2] In particular, from our point of view in this book, it can be regarded as a specific theory of the mass media and popular culture. It has been significantly concerned with culture, the media and communication. Indeed, for some theorists, changes in these areas are crucial for the development of postmodernism and all it entails (Baudrillard 1983). We shall thus try to say what postmodernism is by seeing what its theory has to say about developments in the mass media and popular culture.[3] In particular, we shall look at the areas of the media, consumption and identity in relation to popular culture and popular television. We shall also suggest there are problems with postmodernism and limitations to what it has to say. This raises the possibility of alternative explanations of popular television and popular culture.

The mass media, culture and society

As we have said, postmodern theory is especially relevant to popular culture and the media. Its first main claim, therefore, is that the distinction between culture and society is being eroded.[4] According to this view, a postmodern society is one in which it becomes increasingly difficult to distinguish between the sense of reality produced by the mass media and the reality which exists outside media culture. The implication of this is that the latter gradually disappears as postmodernism emerges. This happens because the defining sense of social reality that people have is increasingly provided by the popular culture produced and distributed by the mass media. It therefore determines how they conceive of and respond to reality. This claim shows how important culture is as an idea for postmodern theory. For example, it asks the question: did something really happen if the television cameras were not there to record it happening?

This point can be seen as an attempt to understand the emergence of a media-saturated society. To use a common metaphor, the mass media were once thought of as holding a mirror to reflect reality. Now, it is argued, reality can only be glimpsed in the surface reflections of this mirror. Society is being incorporated – or 'imploded' – within the mass media. It is not even a question of distortion. This implies there is a reality outside the media which can be distorted, but the possibility of thinking about such a reality is what is questioned by postmodern theory.

Postmodernism is thus an attempt to account for the seemingly increasing importance and dominance of the mass media in modern society. The rise of various types of mass communication and the associated spread of popular media culture, such as popular television, is a significant development for postmodern theory. It argues that the mass media have become so important for communication, the broadcasting of culture and the flow (and control) of information, that they begin to blur the distinction between media and social reality. Their prominence provides one base from which postmodern culture emerges and proliferates.

The consequence is a postmodern world dominated by media screens (based on the television screen) and popular cultural images. Examples include televisions, VDUs, videos, computers, computer games, the internet, adverts, theme parks, shopping 'malls', 'fictitious capital' or credit, 'hole in the wall' banking, personal stereos, etc. This is also visible in the sheer amount of television people can now watch due to the introduction of round-the-clock programming and cable, satellite and digital delivery systems. These developments have made multi-channel, twenty-four-hour television a reality. Accordingly, as Fiske notes, for example, 'in one hour's television viewing, one of us is likely to experience more images than a member of a non-industrial society would in a lifetime ... we live in a postmodern period when there is no difference between the image and other orders of experience' (1991: 58). This claim, of course, depends upon what you watch and fails to distinguish between images and experiences and between important and unimportant images and experiences.

There are a number of ways to relate this argument to popular television. One useful way is Eco's (1984) distinction between paleo-television and neo-television. Paleo-television refers to the world outside itself, to the reality outside television. It prides itself on its ability to represent the outside world, or the real world, and can be taken to define the earlier stages of popular television. By contrast, neo-television predominantly refers to itself. It is television which is about television. Its concern is with the world of television, its conventions, programmes and personalities, rather than with its capacity to open a window onto the real world outside television. Neo-television can be taken to define more recent stages in the development of popular television; it is, more or less, another term for postmodernism.

The history of popular television in Britain can be used to provide one way of illustrating this point. Early television almost virtually provided a window on the world. This was the original subtitle of *Panorama*, 'the oldest established current affairs programme on television', which started broadcasting in 1953 (Vahimagi 1996: 41). Also, early television broadcast events such as concerts, sporting occasions and plays directly from the world outside. It served to transmit outside events to viewers. Television was there to reflect the world but not to define what it broadcast. Corner refers to the 'early emphasis on television as a relay device' and how this eventually gave way to 'television as a separate *cultural form*' (Corner 1991a: 13; cf. Caughie 1991a).

Now television abounds with a regard for itself, whether it is its conventions, programmes or personalities. Programmes such as quiz shows, situation comedies, police series and serial dramas have emerged which rely upon a recognised knowledge of the conventions television has developed for these genres. Knowledge of these conventions becomes consciously shared between the producers and the audiences. Examples include such programmes as *French and Saunders*, *Knowing Me, Knowing You with Alan Partridge*, *Miami Vice*, *Never Mind the Buzzcocks*, *Shooting Stars*, *The Singing Detective*, *Twin Peaks* and *The Young Ones*. Programmes and advertising have become more dependent on referring self-consciously to themselves and to other examples of popular culture, and thus dependent, to some extent, on audiences sharing this knowledge. The point of reference here is television and

233

popular culture and not a real world outside these phenomena. Equally, there are the substitute communities created by the television soap opera which were referred to in the last chapter. Together with this, there is the way actors in television soap operas can become confused with the characters they play, something which the tabloid press plays upon. This further suggests how news itself has become more focused upon the media and popular culture and upon the 'personalities' and 'celebrities' thereby created.

Consumption, style and meaning

One implication of the point we have just considered is that in a postmodern world, surfaces and style become the most important defining features of the mass media and popular culture. They evoke what can be called a type of 'designer ideology'; or, as Harvey succinctly puts it, 'images dominate narrative' (1989: 347–8). The argument is that images are increasingly consumed for their own sake rather than for their utility, or for any deeper meanings or values they may possess. They are consumed precisely because they are images and allow questions of meaning, utility and value to be disregarded. People increasingly consume goods and images not for their usefulness, as might once have been the case with consumer goods, nor for any profound value they may possess, as might once have been the case with cultural objects such as works of art. In this process, it is the style not the substance of consumption which matters.

It is argued that this is apparent in popular culture, where surfaces and style, jokes and playfulness, and referencing and irreverence take precedence over such qualities as content, substance, narrative and meaning. The result is that qualities such as artistic merit, integrity, seriousness, authenticity, realism, intellectual depth, plausible stories and politics tend to be undermined. Reference is frequently made to the playful, surreal and superficial quality of much contemporary popular culture. Also, this culture is argued to be increasingly self-conscious and self-referential (if not self-reverential) in tone and emphasis. At the same time, virtual reality computer graphics mean that people can experience various types of reality second-hand or vicariously. The surface simulations produced by this technology have the potential to replace their real-life counterparts. These features are what Grossberg summarises in his idea of the 'indifference of television' (1987; cf. Collins 1992; Fiske 1991).

This change is seen as a result of the increasing importance of consumption in modern, capitalist societies.[5] This arises from dramatic changes in how their economies work. Putting it very simply, the transition from substance to style is linked to a transition from production to consumption. Postmodern theory thus draws on some fairly long-standing ideas about the scale and effects of consumerism on these societies. The argument is that, during the twentieth century, the economic needs of capitalism shifted from production to consumption and that this has led to the emergence of postmodernism. In their earlier stages, capitalist societies needed to establish their conditions of production. The machines and factories for the manufacturing of goods had to be built and continually updated. Heavy industries concerned with basic materials, such as iron and steel and energy, had to be fostered. The infrastructure of a capitalist economy – roads, rail, communications, education, a welfare state, etc. – had to be laid down. The workforce, in turn, had to be taught the 'work ethic', the discipline for industrial labour.

Once capitalist production had been established the need for consumption began to grow. It thus became more important for people to acquire a leisure or consumer ethic as well as a work ethic. Consumption is not confined to the recent history of capitalism, nor are the problems of capitalist production necessarily resolved. However, what is suggested is that in an advanced capitalist society such as Britain, the need for people to consume has become at least as important as the need to produce. Developments such as increased affluence and leisure time and the growth of working-class consumption have served to accentuate this process. Television itself has become a major item of leisure-time consumption or viewing. In addition, the rise of consumer credit and the expansion of advertising, marketing, design and public relations have also encouraged people to consume and assist the progress of consumerism. Television obviously plays an important part in this process. In turn, all these factors favour the emergence of a popular culture dominated by consumption and style.

This trend towards consumerism has been associated with changes in occupations and markets.[6] The increasing importance of consumption and the media has given rise to new and related occupations (or converted more traditional ones) concerned with encouraging the consumption of greater and greater numbers and varieties of commodities. These occupations, in their turn, construct and manage new consumer markets, or try to serve already established markets more effectively. Examples include areas such as advertising, marketing, sales, design, accountancy, finance and the media, which are, in one way or another, involved with consumption. A number of these occupations entail the use of cultural symbols and media images to encourage and extend the consumption of goods and services. This type of work, it is argued, leads to the development of a postmodern popular culture, the manipulation of popular culture in the cause of consumption.

The most obvious example is advertising. This is not merely because of its growing physical presence in the media and the wider environment; nor simply because it does not just service existing markets but creates new ones. It is also because of its increasing reliance upon imagery rather than content, or style rather than substance, and upon references drawn from popular culture. This reliance is evident from even the most cursory glance at an evening's television viewing (Strinati 1993: 364–5, 373–4). It is also evident in the number of television programmes given over, however indirectly, to shaping viewers' life-styles and consumption. Relevant examples of these programmes include those which cover such topics as consumer affairs, cooking, shopping, clothes, 'looking good', holidays, motoring, gardening, home improvements, house decoration and recently released films and records. Equally relevant are the channels now available through satellite and cable which are devoted almost entirely to life-style and shopping.

It is thus possible to find whole swaths of programmes across the channels involved with presenting life-style themes of one kind or another. Also, some cable channels specialise in such programmes. One important point about these programmes is that they are relatively cheap to make. Equally, they clearly represent the devotion of large amounts of screen time to the virtues of consumption. They tell us what to buy and where to buy it; why and how we should consume; how it is crucial for our well-being; what we will otherwise miss out on; and what it takes to be the consummate consumer. We cannot assume that viewers – if, indeed, they are watching – necessarily buy these virtues of consumerism. But it does at least show how the nature of television programmes can be determined by the importance of consumption.

Popular culture, fragmentation and identity

So far we have looked at the mass media and consumption. These are two main areas in which it is possible to identify and assess the arguments advanced by postmodern theory about the patterns and directions of contemporary popular culture and popular television. The other important area we can look at here is the postmodern argument about the relationship between fragmentation and identity. This still involves the areas we have covered and the points we have made since they are linked with each other. It is merely convenient to organise our discussion in this way. The interpretation of identity, both personal and collective, has become a key issue in the debates initiated by postmodern theory. It provides another reason why postmodernism may be emerging in modern societies as well as identifying yet more trends in contemporary popular culture. The theme that links the two is fragmentation since it affects social relationships and identity and thus influences popular culture and the mass media.[7]

The specific claim made by postmodern theory does not refer to a simple process of decline. Rather it suggests that a limited and dependable set of coherent identities has begun to fragment into a diverse and unstable series of competing identities. The increasing fragmentation of personal identities has resulted from the decline of what were once well-established identities, which gave people a secure sense of their position in the world. It is argued that the traditional and valued frames of reference by which people defined themselves and their place in society, and which furnished relatively secure collective and personal identities, have begun, gradually, to disappear. These traditional sources of identity include social class, the extended and nuclear family, local communities, the 'neighbourhood', religion, trade unions and the nation state. They might also be seen as coinciding with the so-called 'golden age' of television when many of its popular genres reached fruition and watching major dramas or key sporting events became a national pastime. Their decline is traced to certain tendencies in modern capitalism such as rapid and global rates of social change. For example, the tendency for investment, production, marketing and distribution to be internationally rather than nationally or locally based is seen as an important reason for the erosion of traditional sources of identity. This economic globalisation undermines the significance of local and national industries and their supporting institutions. It thereby undermines the occupational, communal and familial identities they once sustained. Similarly, an increasingly bland, global, fragmented and disjointed television culture undermines its role as a focal point for national and collective identities.

The other side to this argument is that no comparable and workable sources of identity emerge to replace the traditional and once viable ones. This means that the problem of identity is exacerbated. Postmodern theory argues that no new institutions or beliefs emerge to give people a secure and coherent sense of themselves, the times in which they live and their place in society. Indeed, the major features we have identified with postmodernism merely make matters worse. Consumption by its very nature bolsters a self-centred individualism which is no basis for stable and secure identities. Television has a similar effect because it is both individualistic and universal. Television encourages people to watch it as isolated, individual viewers and yet television has access to these viewers as a universal whole. As Ewen puts this regarding contemporary television, 'those who speak have access to a mass of people, while those within the mass watch in relative isolation from each other' (1988: 202). In most industrial societies, television is viewed by individuals or families, rather than by wider collectivities, except on relatively rare occasions. Television is a universal medium which defines its viewers, for the most part, as anonymous, individual members of an abstract and universal audience, cut off from any wider and more genuine social ties. With either consumption or television, the wider collectivities to which people might belong and the legitimate ideas in which they might believe, tend not to exist, fail to be established, or emerge as mere fragments. Neither consumerism, nor popular culture and the mass media, such as television culture, can provide viable and acceptable sources of belief, community and identity. However, since there are no alternatives, they come to serve as the only bases from which collective and personal identities can be formed. The result is the fragmentation of identity.

There are a number of ways in which this can be illustrated. One way, integral to postmodern theory, is what has been called the decline of the metanarratives. To put it very simply, metanarratives are the big stories, or over-arching belief systems, which allow people to organise and interpret their lives and which provide a universal and integrated frame of reference for society. Examples which have been mentioned include religion, science, art, modernism, Marxism and historical progress. These are criticised by postmodernism because they claim either to possess absolute and universal knowledge, or to know how it can be achieved. According to postmodern theory, these narratives assert they know, for example, the singular pattern of human history, the decisive fate of human society, or the methods by which ultimate knowledge can be reached. They make absolute, universal and all-embracing claims to knowledge and truth.

For postmodern theory, these claims are questionable and dubious and the systems which have sustained them are in decline and will eventually disintegrate. Metanarratives such as science or religion can no longer confer meaning on people's lives or offer progress, nor uphold distinctions such as those between good and evil, truth and falsity, or art and mass culture. They are in the process of losing their validity and legitimacy. Postmodern theory argues that belief systems which are absolute, universal, uniform and unified will become a thing of the past as a result of the rise of the postmodern society. Even the linear, coherent and integrated narrative which has characterised many popular cultural stories, such as the typical Hollywood film, or television's fictional dramas, will no longer be sustained. The supposed fall in the significance of the narrative occurs because postmodern popular culture is preoccupied with style to the detriment of the story. Television series, such as *Twin Peaks*, are argued to have initiated this process. *Twin Peaks*, for example, is seen to rely upon the style or mood it tries to convey, rather than observing the traditional conventions of the detective story narrative (Collins 1992; Strinati 1998). Therefore, this general decline provides another condition which can lead to the fragmentation of identity.

The blurring of the distinction between art and mass culture associated with postmodern popular culture is another good example of this. If postmodern culture consists mainly of surface simulations, then the values which could once have supported such a distinction are no longer available. In postmodern culture, anything can supposedly become a joke, a quotation or a pastiche in an eclectic play of style, simulations and surfaces. The definition of reality by the media and the predominance of style which make this culture possible cannot generate any more profound values and meanings. The television programmes mentioned above as examples of neo-television also illustrate this point. The postmodern world cannot thus provide the meanings which could defend the hierarchical division between art and mass culture.

However, this does not mean that art totally disappears. Rather it becomes submerged and mixed in with mass culture, in the composition of postmodern popular culture, as well as providing another convenient store of images for advertisers. Popular cinema provides some examples of this tendency. The films of writer-director Quentin Tarantino – *Reservoir Dogs* (1991) and *Pulp Fiction* (1994) – combine the 'B' film crime genre with the art film style introduced by the French new wave. The television plays of Dennis Potter, with their frequent quotations from popular culture and their concern with serious themes, may be cited as another example of this trend. A number of other types of film have also been cited as examples of postmodern popular culture due to their excessive concern with style and their conscious retrieval of cinema's past (Hill 1998). Examples here include films ranging from the retrieval of the Saturday morning suspense serials represented by the *Indiana Jones* trilogy (1981, 1984, 1989), to such aspirant art films as *Blue Velvet* (1986) (Corrigan 1991: 71–7; Denzin 1991: chapter 5). However, *Blade Runner* (1982) has often been taken, in these respects, to be the typical postmodern film (Harvey 1989: chapter 18; Strinati 1995: 229–31, 242–4; cf. Hill 1998; Instrell 1992). According to the literature, one of the most typical television shows in this regard was *Miami Vice* (Grossberg 1987: 28; Fiske 1987: 255–62; Butler 1985). It was based, it is argued, on the surface pleasures it provided, such as its glossy and stylish look, its music soundtrack and the designer clothes of the protagonists, rather than the more conventional appeal of the police show narrative.

Some of these examples also indicate another feature of postmodern popular culture, which can be called 'generic confusion'. Not surprisingly, postmodern theory suggests that with this culture, popular genres can no longer possess the relatively fixed meanings and conventions they once enjoyed. Therefore, they will become less important for the production and consumption of popular culture. Conventional genres become less identifiable and coherent in a popular culture dominated by postmodernism. They cease to be distinct and instead are eclectically mixed together. This leads to generic confusion.

We have already mentioned the way films and television programmes can mix art and popular culture together. There are equally a number of television programmes and films which can be argued to exhibit generic mixing or confusion. The television programme, *The X Files*, for example, brings together the detective story with the science fiction and horror genres, while also borrowing some of the conventions of the romantic comedy. The series *Millennium* is similar, though it is even more clearly identified with horror and science fiction. Another comparable series, *Ultraviolet*, uses the narrative of the police series to tell a story about vampires which depends upon the conventions of this strand of the horror genre. One of the earlier examples of this tendency, *Twin Peaks*, is seen to combine a wide range of genres, including the soap opera, the detective story, the murder mystery, horror, science fiction, comedy and *film noir* (Lavery 1995; cf. Collins 1992; Strinati 1998).

Examples can also be drawn from popular cinema. *Titanic* (1997) is a love story as well as a disaster film. *Armageddon* (1997) is both a science fiction film and a disaster film. *Godzilla* (1997) is a science fiction film, a monster film and a disaster film. *Men in Black* (1996) combines comedy with science fiction and, like many of its contemporaries, provides plenty of merchandising opportunities. One of the most archetypal films in this context, *The Rocky Horror Picture Show* (1976), managed to be a comedy, a musical and a horror film as well as a parody of these genres. It is suggested that this generic confusion will become a more prevalent feature of popular culture in the foreseeable future. It is also another example of fragmentation.

The implication of what we have outlined so far is that post-modernism cannot provide the basis for coherent and stable identities. It has been argued that this also applies because of the increasing incoherence of time and space associated with post-modernism. Postmodernity is said to introduce profound and qualitative changes in time and space. The growing immediacy of global space and time, which results from the increasing dominance of the modern mass media, make the previously unified senses of time and space distorted and confused. The postmodern compression and focusing of time and space mean that people's sense of these things becomes less coherent and more uncertain. The maps that people have of where they live and the ideas of time they have that organise their lives are being continually subverted and moved and thus become less stable and more fluid. The rapid international flows of capital, money, information and culture disrupt the linear unity of time and reduce the expanse of geographical space. Time and space thereby become less stable and comprehensible and more confused and incoherent. This is due to the speed and scope of modern mass communications and the relative ease and rapidity with which people and information can travel the globe (Harvey 1989: part 3).

The title and narrative of the three *Back to the Future* films capture this point fairly well. Postmodern popular culture is seen to exemplify this process. Its products lack identifiable locations, or draw upon different periods in time, without regard to geographical or historical accuracy. Again, some of the television series we have referred to can be used to illustrate this point. A number of television programmes, such as *Twin Peaks* for example, refer to different television series and films, from different points in time and accordingly drift from more to less realistic spatial locations. Think also of the sometimes indistinct locations in television adverts. The films *Blade Runner* and *Blue Velvet* are also often seen as good illustrations of this point. More generally, postmodern popular culture is said to have few identifiable locations, apart from the imaginary postmodern city itself and little overall appreciation of historical time. In other words, time and space become culturally fragmented and this leads to the fragmentation of identity.

One last point, linked to this argument, is about the fragmentation of the television audience, which has already been mentioned a number of times above. The emergence of multi-channel television and the remote control can be argued to lead to the fragmentation of the viewing experience. These developments suggest that viewers have an increasingly large number of channels to watch and the technical possibility afforded by the remote control to skip from one to another in rapid and random succession. If this is the case, then smaller sections of any particular programme will be watched. Also, programmes may not be watched from start to finish. In turn, the potential for higher numbers of programmes to attract lower numbers of viewers, even if some may achieve reasonable audience ratings, means that greater numbers of viewers will have fewer programmes in common. What is watched and how it is watched, will change, leading to increasing fragmentation of the television audience and the viewing experience. The result could be said to be a further fragmentation of identity.

Conclusion

To consider how postmodern theory may be relevant to the study of popular television, we have looked at some of the arguments it has made regarding the mass media, consumption and identity. It would be useful to conclude by raising a few questions about the validity of these arguments. Postmodernism would appear to be an increasingly acceptable way of talking about contemporary society. It therefore seems appropriate to point to some of its limitations.

There are a number of criticisms which can be made of postmodernism. First, it clearly exaggerates the influence of mass media such as television. The question of the effects of the media remains a contentious and unresolved one in media sociology. The view that the media exercise a decisive influence over people's attitudes and behaviour does not yet command a general academic consensus; the debate over the media and violence comes to mind here (Dickinson *et al.* 1998: chapters 8, 9, 10). As we have seen, postmodern theory depends upon the idea that the mass media, in some way, influence people's beliefs and actions. For example, it is thought that the mass media play an important role in defining reality for their consumers. However, in view of the evidence, it is difficult to see why postmodern theory should so readily assume its case has been proven beyond doubt.

The extent to which popular culture has become postmodern has equally been exaggerated. For example, much of television's output is not postmodern. It is not easy to see how such a popular genre as the soap opera could be defined as an instance of postmodernism.[8] Narratives would appear to remain as important to the popularity of this genre as they do to police series such as *Inspector Morse* (Vahimagi 1996: 310; Sparks 1993). Also, the idea of social realism still seems integral to the soap opera, as well as to police series such as *Between The Lines* (Vahimagi 1996: 336) which also uses complex narratives. Indeed, postmodern programmes seem most notable for their relative absence from the schedules. It may be possible to find a few, more telling, examples in television advertising, but this is hardly evidence of a widespread or novel phenomenon.

244

Similarly, interpreting items of popular culture, such as television programmes, in terms of their postmodernism may be a very limited and shallow exercise. As we have noted, *Miami Vice* is often referred to as a prime example of postmodernism. However, Buxton, for example, has argued that this postmodern interpretation is 'unhelpful' and superficial because it neglects the ideologies the series constructed about conspicuous consumption and the difficulties of maintaining law and order. Buxton shows there is nothing particularly unique about *Miami Vice*. He points out that 'for all its stylistic force, *Miami Vice*, is no more or no less "ideological" than any other series; for all its stylishness, it is no more or no less "styled" than any other series' (1990: 141–2; cf. Fiske 1987: 255–62).[9]

Moreover, even a cursory glance at the history of television shows it has always been about itself, while also representing the outside world. For example, the situation comedy, *Hancock's Half Hour* (Vahimagi 1996: 58; Goddard 1991), focused on an actor (and his purported agent) who did television work and directed some of its humour at television advertising and other television programmes. Likewise, popular film and television genres have not always been clear-cut or readily distinguished from each other and have often been combined or confused throughout the history of these media (Neale 1990). An early example of the television police series, *Z Cars* (Vahimagi 1996: 113; Laing 1991), incorporated social realism and elements of everyday life into the fictional world of a police force often working on fairly routine cases. Similarly, the cult of the celebrity has been a long-standing feature of twentieth-century popular culture. There is, for example, the emergence of the media's obsession with Hollywood film stars in the 1920s and 1930s and, from the 1950s, the promotion within television of a different kind of star, the television personality.

People's general awareness also poses problems for the relevance of postmodern popular culture. In one respect, interesting points about the audience are made by postmodern theory. For example, the emergence of multi-channel television can fragment audiences and the viewing experience in a way that would not have been conceivable before. At the same time, audiences can compound this effect by using their remote controls to switch constantly between the increasing number of channels on offer. However, some research suggests this picture may again be exaggerated. A recent study found that, 'despite a big increase in satellite and cable television – from about 8% in 1991 to 26% in 1996 of those surveyed – there was "little evidence" this led to a "fragmented audience". New channels found families "as more or less united as they ever had been around the TV set"' (Gauntlett and Hill 1999, cited in *Guardian* 30 April 1999: 5).

Equally, questions can be raised about how people interpret the postmodern stress on popular culture. For example, what do they make of popular cultural references? It may be that audiences are not aware of the references being made by a particular item of popular culture, which suggests they are unimportant; or they may be aware but not that interested, which suggests they are insignificant. To some extent, the postmodern argument depends upon the idea that the television audience watches programmes avidly and attentively, constantly on the lookout for hidden meanings, cultural references, puns, jokes and the opportunity to be ironic. There is some evidence that this occurs with so-called cult shows, such as *Twin Peaks* and *The X Files* (Jenkins 1995; Clerc 1996). However, this seems to apply to only a small, self-selected, highly educated, middle-class audience, which prides itself on its cultural capital. It appears to communicate with its members about its favourite programmes through the internet; and prizes its education and taste, its difference from the mass audience and the superiority of the programmes it prefers to those characteristic of mainstream television. As we have seen above, many viewers just do not watch television in this manner and with these attitudes. They may also watch television in an emotionally involved, or a distracted and inattentive, or indifferent manner, or criticise what they see using realist rather than postmodern criteria.

Comparable questions can be raised about the incoherent representations of time and space said to be provided by some television programmes. Even if we accept that the latter is a plausible conclusion to draw, we can still ask if temporal and spatial confusions really bother television audiences. Presumably, the references made and representations provided have to register at some level with audiences generally to become interesting and significant for postmodern theory. However, the problem of supplying arguments and evidence to answer these questions does not really appear to have been addressed.

The related ideas that society has collapsed into the media and that style is what is now consumed can equally be questioned. It could be argued that postmodern theory usefully stresses the importance of consumption and the consumer society. However, other theories, such as Frankfurt School Marxism (and not forgetting Marx himself), have also put forward powerful and sophisticated analyses of these phenomena (Strinati 1995: chapter 2). Nevertheless, looking at postmodern theory, we can suggest that, among the problems which confront people in capitalist societies, the most relevant may not be how dominant the mass media have become. Other factors, such as the family and work, may contribute as much, if not more, as the media to their sense of reality. Also, people's thoughts and actions may well be more constrained and shaped by work and income than by television and culture.

In turn, the capacity of popular media culture to regulate consumption may have been exaggerated, though the question of the extent to which this can occur obviously remains an important one. There is little reason to suppose that, whatever else they do, many people do not consume goods for their utility. Some groups may consume in the way postmodern theory suggests, but this raises another problem because the ability to consume is determined, in one respect, by the unequal distribution of wealth and income. Some people may consume more than they need and others consume less, while others remain excluded almost completely from the consumer society. Thus, the extent to which the mass media and popular culture are available to consumers regardless of inequalities is questionable. Even in more affluent societies such as Britain, there appear to be marked inequalities in the ownership of video recorders and computers and in access to the internet. It has recently been reported, for example, that '68 per cent of ABC1 households own a PC', but 'only 40 per cent of

C2DE homes do so' and that '72 per cent of working class families have a TV linked games machine' (*Guardian* 19 March 1999: 3). Apart from the class inequalities these figures illustrate, it is noticeable that in both cases 60 per cent and 28 per cent respectively of working-class families are excluded from such ownership. Also, consumers may not make full use of the media technology they buy. There are similarly significant international inequalities. For example, the distribution of television 'receivers per 1000 population actually ranges from a high of 783 per thousand in North America to a low of 13 per thousand in the non-Arab states of Africa' (Sreberny-Mohammadi 1991: 122–3).

There are also problems with the postmodern argument about the breakdown of the divide between art and mass culture. If art and mass culture can still be distinguished, then how far has the breakdown of the distinction between the two gone? If postmodern culture can be distinguished from other types of culture, such as modernism, then the possibility of using criteria to achieve this cannot be disappearing. If this is so, what are the general criteria which allow postmodern theory to discriminate between types of culture?

We might also ask if there are many television programmes, for example, which clearly illustrate the breakdown of the distinction between art and popular culture? Just as there may not be that many programmes on television which can be classified as postmodern, so there are even fewer which seem to illustrate this breakdown. It may again be possible to refer to *Twin Peaks* as an example. This series acquired the status of a serious drama which referred to popular culture, involved the art-house film maker David Lynch as a producer, writer and director, and bore a strong similarity to his film *Blue Velvet*. It quickly became defined as a quality programme which clearly placed it on the 'art' side of the divide with popular culture. There appeared to be little confusion about where to place it according to certain critics and some sections of the audience. That such a judgement could be made suggests that the divide between art and popular culture may not have become significantly blurred, or confused (Strinati 1998).

We have referred to *Twin Peaks* at a number of points to illustrate and challenge postmodern theory's claims about popular television. This series is also useful in that it provides another way of looking at what are sometimes seen as postmodern programmes. *Twin Peaks* has been defined by critics, fans and the television network as a quality programme, set apart from mainstream television. They have also identified it with a producer who has a cult and art-house reputation. It was an artful, playful and self-conscious series, littered with popular cultural references and dependent upon making apparent – if not making fun of – the conventions of the many genres it included. These qualities seem to be the most important ones, as it appeared to value the surface images and moody atmosphere it created, rather than the pursuit of an obviously clear-cut narrative. It failed to hold on to a large, mass audience for very long, but instead, attracted a fairly small but devoted and committed set of viewers. While not that much academic work has been done on the subject, it could be argued that these features define the idea of cult films and television programmes. Therefore, *Twin Peaks* and programmes like it may be better understood as cult rather than postmodern television (Strinati 1998).[10] The analysis of cult television might therefore prove useful in making sense of an idea which has often been mentioned but rarely studied.

This brings us finally to what is perhaps the major difficulty with postmodern theory: its assumption that metanarratives are in decline. For what is postmodernism, if it is not another metanarrative? It presents a general account of what it sees as the significant changes occurring in modern societies. It presumes to tell us something new about the world and knows why it is able to do this. It has a particular idea of knowledge and how it can, and cannot, be acquired. It therefore appears to be a metanarrative. But how can it be if they are in decline? Perhaps postmodernism is the last of the metanarratives. However, this can only be argued on the basis of some type of metanarrative since a claim is being made that something is known.

The above discussion has tried to indicate some of the limitations of postmodernism and the difficulties it confronts when it is used to study popular television. It is hoped that the nature of the criticisms raised and the arguments developed in various parts of this book suggest the beginnings of a different, though not original, approach to the study of popular culture. The concluding chapter will attempt to provide a brief outline of some of the relevant points this approach raises.

Conclusion

IN THIS BOOK we have looked at how various areas of popular culture have been studied. In particular, we have been concerned with how the production and consumption of popular cinema and television have been and can be studied. It has not always been possible to develop some of the arguments as fully as we could have, for the scope of the book has been selective and introductory. However, it is hoped that some important and promising areas of study have been indicated. Although each chapter should be able to stand or fall on its own, it is perhaps by now evident that certain more general themes and guidelines have also emerged during the preceding discussion. These can now be identified in this conclusion.

The first point which can be made is that popular culture usually becomes available, or is produced, because it is a commodity (cf. Mosco 1996: chapter 4). We have noted, for example, how the economic power of Hollywood cinema has rested upon the development of and changes in the Hollywood studio system. This, in turn, has been associated with varying degrees of control over production, distribution and exhibition. The attendant growth of popular narrative and genres has consolidated the dominance of this type of popular cinema (see Chapters 1 and 2; cf. Chapters 3, 4 and 5). We have made a similar point about popular television and noted the argument that technical changes permitting the pre-recording of programmes also formed them as commodities (see Chapters 6 and 8).

This point also involves taking note of the importance of production in studying popular culture. We have tried to show how, with Hollywood and popular television genres, the production process has a crucial role to play in forming and establishing aspects of popular cinema and television. For example, we have tried to suggest how production conditions have influenced film narrative and film genres and how television genres, such as soap operas, can be related to their production. Similarly, it has been suggested that the typical film narrative and popular television genres were importantly influenced by the relatively early standardisation of production practices and routines. In their turn, this narrative and these genres have stabilised and favoured such production (see Chapters 1, 2 and 8).

To be a commodity, popular culture not only has to be produced, it also has to be consumed. It needs to be profitable, or has to have the potential to be profitable. To achieve this, it has succeeded, or will succeed, for its producers in finding profitable outlets or markets. Popular culture is therefore a marketable commodity. This is shaped, in part, by some of the powerful institutions referred to above. As we saw with the development of Hollywood cinema and the outcome of the studio system's decline, the production, distribution, exhibition and marketing of popular cinema and popular culture more generally has tended to be dominated by large corporations. The studio system, for example, was controlled by an oligopoly. Nowadays, as we also noted, domination is exercised by massive global conglomerates that control or influence many media outlets and types of popular culture. Such examples include News Corporation, Time-Warner and Viacom, which are managing to reintegrate production, distribution and exhibition (see Chapter 1).

It need not be assumed that everything can, or will, become a commodity, or that commodification is inevitable. There may be forces, such as audiences or governments, which oppose specific instances of it, or areas where it may not work, that is, which are not profitable. However, it is arguably a highly significant process which has a determinant influence on popular culture and the mass media. The importance of the commodity, which involves both its production and consumption, is not confined to the context it provides for popular culture. It can directly shape popular culture as well. One example is the growth of subscription-based, multi-channel digital and cable television, which has some channels devoted to direct selling and others to facilitating the consumption of products. This involves the further expansion of advertising and sponsorship and has meant that an increasing number of television programmes have become consumer guides in all but name. They are about organising an appropriate consumer life-style for viewers, be it in the areas of clothes, cooking, travel, motoring, entertainment, etc., or, more generally, about how to be a good consumer (see Chapters 6 and 9).

A consequence of what has been argued so far is that audiences have to be regarded, at least initially, as consumers. This is the way popular culture, which is produced as a commodity, treats them. They are evaluated by producers as potential buyers, not only, say, of a film, but of the products associated with it, such as CDs, books, posters, T-shirts, toys, computer games, fast food specials, sunglasses, watches, etc. This may be the first word on audiences but it is obviously not the last. The reservations we had about the extent to which popular culture need be turned into a commodity also apply here about the extent to which audiences will be forced to become consumers. Many studies show how audiences can react in a variety of ways to popular culture (Moores 1993; Morley 1992; cf. Ang 1991). They can be passive, active, critical, indifferent, distracted, or even alienated, regarding what they consume. They can interpret it from a range of perspectives, or resist, or not care about interpretation. They can, for example, accept the ideas or meanings presented, reject them, turn them into something new, or ignore them. All of these reactions are not the result of free choice exercised by individuals; they are socially (and psychologically) determined in ways we have yet perhaps to fully understand.

However, it is rare for audiences not to be addressed by popular culture as consumers, or potential consumers. This is again the context in which popular culture becomes available to us, although it does not mean that audiences can be thought of only as consumers. This book has placed great emphasis upon the audience. Hopefully, these points suggest we need to define this importance more precisely, rather than merely taking it for granted, or confusing it with populism (see especially Chapters 6, 7 and 8; see also Chapters 3, 4 and 5).

Audiences may not be thought of only as consumers, but popular culture can be directly shaped by the need to treat audiences as consumers, a point we have already noted above. As Murdock (1990, 1994) has shown, treating audiences as consumers, as people who are there to be sold things to, increasingly clashes with and threatens their citizenship rights. In particular, it threatens to undermine their right to free and equal access to the information, knowledge and culture they need to enable them to participate as citizens in a democratic society. His case is that, in the end, consumerism and citizenship are probably incompatible, but that the forces behind the former are much more powerful and therefore more likely to succeed. Popular culture will therefore be shaped by this process and become a culture which focuses more and more upon audiences as consumers (see Chapter 6; cf. Chapters 7 and 9).

Another example of how production and market considerations can shape popular culture is provided by the making and promotion of films which acquire prestige and cult status, such as *Blade Runner* (1982) (Instrell 1992). This film initially received poor receptions at preview screenings. The production company therefore tried to increase its appeal to potential audiences and thereby improve its chances of making money. It introduced a 'tough guy', voice-over narration 'to clarify the story-line', and cut certain scenes and changed the original ending to make it less 'despairing' and more 'upbeat'. The voice-over has added to what some have seen as the postmodern quality of the film, because it introduces the *film noir* into the science fiction film. Similarly, the cuts and other changes made have been talking points for the film's cult audience ever since. This example shows that the film itself is shaped by its commodity status and suggests that 'pure textual analysis which ignores the institutional context can never lead to full understanding' (ibid.: 166, 164 and *passim*; cf. Hugo 1992; see also Chapters 2, 3, 4, 5 and 8).

This book has indeed tried to argue that there are a number of problems with a purely textual analysis of popular culture. This assumes that popular culture reflects wider beliefs and values, acts as a mirror for history and society, or gives collective expression to the general culture of a society. We can now summarise the criticisms that have been made of this theory (see Chapters 3, 4, 5 and 8; cf. Maltby 1984: 49–51; Neale 1990: 54). First, there is no reason why what are decisions made by audiences about consumption should add up to a type of collective, cultural expression. It is difficult to reduce the former to the latter. Second, there is no reason why producers should or could, consciously or unconsciously, have the required knowledge of the wider culture which would enable them to express it in the popular culture they produce. Any such expression is, in any event, likely to be incidental to the drive for profitability. Third, popular culture can remain remarkably consistent in form and content over time, despite evident historical and social changes. For example, the *film noir* has been attributed to the 1940s and early 1950s, the 1970s, the 1980s and the 1990s (see Chapter 5). Also, if producers choose to tackle a current issue or problem, it does not mean they will treat it competently or seriously, or confer any significance upon it merely because it features in a film or television programme. The use of such a theme may simply be contingent, or sheer opportunism.

Fourth, there are problems with assuming that a direct relationship exists between the 'texts' of popular culture and the wider society. This is because popular culture is produced by commercial industries for markets of consumers and these always come between the wider society and popular culture. As we have seen, production and consumption can themselves directly shape the texts of popular culture. Moreover, the wider society is not composed of one uniform audience. It consists of different audiences, in different situations, with different values and attitudes towards popular culture. This is not to say they do not have things in common, but it is difficult to see how these values and attitudes can be confined to a set of limited but available meanings which inevitably end up in films and television programmes. Also, this theory rarely provides evidence of the beliefs or collective expression being reflected other than that supposedly inferred from the films or television programmes themselves.

Fifth, the texts of popular culture need not reflect the wider culture or society at all, but may be inaccurate, misleading, deceptive or illusory. They may also exclude, or fail to express, some ideas and values altogether. This is one of the areas where a theory of ideology becomes relevant. We have noted above that there are major difficulties with this theory (see Chapter 2). While we cannot assume that popular culture is necessarily ideological, there is equally no reason to suppose it is always capable of revealing some deeper meanings to us. A theory of ideology may suggest that some deeper meanings can be obscured within popular culture, but it does at least argue that certain ideas may not be expressed in popular culture and that therefore we should not always trust it.

The sixth and last point in this critique also concerns the theory of ideology as well as inequalities in power. It suggests that not all individuals and groups in society have equal access (most do not have any access) to the production and circulation of culture and ideas, except perhaps as consumers. And even here there are large inequalities. This means that the prevailing character of popular culture may not reflect the ideas and values of the society as a whole, nor those of most of the groups within it. Rather it may be more directly related to the interests and ideas of those groups with access to and control over the production and circulation of culture, ideas and knowledge.

These criticisms, which, among other things, relate to our discussion of narrative, genre and audiences, suggest that a reworking of the theory of ideology may be useful for studying popular culture. The proposal here is that the ideas and values to be found in popular culture could usefully be related to the interests and ideas of the groups involved in its production and distribution, as well as its consumption. They also have to be related to the inequalities between these groups and those excluded from production and distribution. However, they still have to be related to these excluded groups since popular culture regards them, too, as consumers and their interests therefore have to be accommodated. Observers have clearly differed over how powerful and effective a force ideology is in society and some have even questioned its usefulness. It is also an idea with a long history (Abercrombie *et al.* 1980; Barker 1989; McLelland 1995; Strinati 1995: chapters 4 and 7). However, the points we have made suggest it could prove a fertile area for the study of popular culture (see Chapter 2 above).

This book has also tried to indicate how a particular version of the idea of genre is useful for studying popular culture (see Chapters 3, 4, 5, 8 and 9 above). This is partly because it can identify patterns in popular culture which are related to production and consumption. Genre is a way of distinguishing particular types of popular culture and showing how they differ from each other. It is likewise a way of standardising such differences. The popular genres of film and television have been defined, used and promoted by producers and consumers of popular culture. For example, producers use them to sell their products as commodities and audiences use them to organise their consumption. Genre as an idea can therefore be used to interpret the production and consumption of popular culture, remembering that this is an unequal and changing relationship and that definitions vary. It describes one aspect of the production of popular culture as a commodity and one way in which its consumption occurs. Genres also embody ideas and values, which means they can be assessed for their ideological content. Genre is an idea which can capture a general pattern of popular culture as we have noted. However, it can equally focus on the social formation of tastes and preferences, since choices are made by individuals and groups about which genres to produce and consume. It can therefore provide a way of understanding some aspects of the collective and individual features of popular culture. However, its usage may consequently be more loosely defined and more historically varied than some critics would like.

Studying popular culture clearly involves a lot more that just reading texts. It also cannot be related simply to production, nor reduced to its disruptive audiences. The arguments we have developed in this book equally indicate that studying popular culture involves more than merely putting production, text and audience together (Abercrombie 1996; Barker 1989; Ryall 1979). As our discussions above have tried to show, it also involves weighing up the relative influence of these things, assessing what they are thought to entail and imply, and being more specific about the precise ways they come together. The suggestions that have been made about commodities, production, consumption, audiences, genre and ideology have had these objectives in mind. For, in the end, studying popular culture comes down to explaining popular culture. If there is one last way to make the purpose of this book clear, it is to say that it offers a contribution to the sociology of popular culture.

Notes

I Popular cinema: the Hollywood system

1   There is clearly a very large literature on Hollywood cinema, so it will only be possible, in such a brief note, to indicate the sources which have been used for this book, including this opening chapter. Probably the best book on Hollywood cinema is Bordwell *et al.* (1985). As will be evident, its impressive argument, scope and detail have made it an invaluable source for this book. However, it is not necessarily a book for someone completely new to this area. Thus, both Balio (1985) and Maltby (1995), which provide very helpful, informed and detailed accounts of Hollywood, have also been used extensively in what follows. Gomery (1986) is an equally useful source, particularly on the economic and industrial aspects of the studio system, while Neale (1985) is an effective source on the major technical changes associated with the development of cinema. As will become evident, Burch (1978) has also proved particularly useful. A good, introductory summary is provided by Kuhn (1985: 2–31).

2   Although its relevance here clearly has to be recognised, the issue of narrative is considered at greater length in Chapter 2.

3   This is one of E.S. Porter's films and Burch's argument is based, in part, on an analysis of these films, a subject we cannot pursue here.

4   In view of the importance attached to the already mentioned argument that early practices, once established, continue to be important factors shaping the development of popular culture, it is worth

quoting Bordwell *et al.* further on this point. They argue that these 'types of product – fictional narratives, variety entertainment, scenics, topicals and tricks – had appealed to customers before film companies introduced moving pictures commercially'; and that 'they still constitute the fare of television and other entertainment sources' (1985: 115).

5 Gomery's highly valuable and impressive study (1986) examines the studios mentioned and concentrates upon the period between 1930 and 1949.

2 Popular cinema: Hollywood narrative and film genres

1 There have been attempts to link Hollywood cinema to the American dream and to dreaming and to relate cinema to the analysis of dreams. Some aspects of the former will become evident as the book proceeds, but see, for example, Adorno and Horkheimer (1979); Carroll (1988: chapter 1); May (1983); Powdermaker (1950); and Sklar (1975). The source which has proved to be most useful on narrative is Bordwell *et al.* (1985). Along with Neale (1990) it has also been a useful source on genre. Other sources which have proved useful on both these topics are mentioned in the main text. But see also Maltby (1995).

2 The argument put forward by Bordwell *et al.* in this section is based upon the contrast between Hollywood and art cinema, as well as a detailed analysis of the form and development of the Hollywood narrative (1985: 372–7 and chapter 31).

3 Carroll (1988) outlines and criticises a number of film theories derived from structuralism, Lacanian psychoanalysis and Althusserian Marxism which argue that Hollywood films are inevitably ideological.

4 The difficulties involved in using any notion of ideology suggest we need to avoid any glib and facile applications of the idea and that it clearly needs to be re-examined. However, this is not something which can be pursued in this book.

3 The gangster film

1 A number of sources have proved to be very useful in the writing of this chapter. See, in particular, Cook (1990); Gledhill (1985); Raeburn (1988); Ryall (1979); Tudor (1974); Whitehall (1964); and Winokur (1991). Also useful are Clarens (1980); McArthur (1972); and Pearce (1978).

2 All the films mentioned here, have, at one time or another, also been defined as *noir* films.

3   This type of approach is criticised more fully in the conclusions.

4   See Raeburn (1998: 57) for further discussion of the decline and death of the gangster in the classic films and in *The Godfather*.

4 The horror film

1   A number of sources have proved to be very useful in the writing of this chapter. See, in particular, Cook (1990); Doherty (1988: especially chapter 6); Gledhill (1985); Huss and Ross (1972); Jancovich (1992, 1994, 1996); Pirie (1973); Tudor (1974); and Wood (1988).

2   Examples of this include teen horror, parodic horror and postmodern horror, which are discussed below in the main text.

3   Discussions of rationalisation, rationalisation and social change, mass society, power elites and post-industrialism abound in the sociological literature. They focus upon the work of theorists such as Adorno, Bell and Weber. See, for example, Adorno (1991); Bell (1962, 1973); Giddens (1973); Harvey (1989); Mills (1956); Rose (1991); and Strinati (1995: chapters 1 and 2). Bell (1962: chapter 3) contains a critique of Mills (1956). Giddens (1971: chapter 12) provides an extensive account of Weber's theory.

4   Pirie (1973: 18) does, however, recognise how this appeal can slide into sensationalism and morbidity.

5   Jancovich's attempt to interpret the modern horror film by relating it to 'Fordist' rationality is not confined to the 1950s, but is intended to cover the subsequent history of the genre. The reservations about this argument, which are laid out here in the main text, also apply to this extension of the argument and therefore need not be repeated. See Jancovich (1992: chapters 6 and 7, 1994: 10–11 and 1996: *passim*).

5 Film noir

1   Bordwell *et al.* (1985: 74–7), Kaplan (1980), Kerr (1986) and Maltby (1984) have proved very useful sources in the writing of this chapter. Other very useful sources have been Cameron (1992); Copjec (1993); Gledhill (1985); Hirsch (1981); Kemp (1986); Krutnick (1991); Nachbar (1988); Palmer (1996); Quart and Auster (1984: 22–9); Reid and Walker (1993); Schrader (1972); Silver and Ward (1980); Tuska (1984); and Vernet (1993). The discussion which follows in the main text does not explicitly focus upon the style of *film noir*. On this subject see Place and Peterson (1974) and Schrader (1972).

2   Analyses of the representation of women in contemporary popular culture can be found in a number of sources. See, for example, Baehr

(1981); Franklin *et al.* (1991); Mulvey (1975, 1981); Tuchman (1981); Tuchmann *et al.* (1988); Van Zoonen (1994); and Williamson (1978).

3   An excellent historical account of how the idea of *film noir* emerged in relation to some of the social and political forces of the time is provided by Maltby (1984; cf. Vernet 1993). It is possibly worth reading this article before tackling the other reading suggested. It also provides an effective critique of the 'film as a reflection of society' argument. It is also perhaps worth noting here that the standardisation of relatively novel variations, which has marked developments and changes in film genres, has also been a feature of *film noir*. See Bordwell *et al.* (1985: 111).

6   Popular television: citizenship, consumerism and television in the UK

1   As will be evident from the main text, the most useful sources for this chapter have been Murdock (1994, see also 1990), Scannell (1990) and Seaton (1997). Other very useful historical sources are Corner (1991) and Crisell (1997). A very useful general reference book is Vahimagi (1996).

2   The topics covered in this chapter have obviously been governed by the themes we have chosen to consider. This means that important issues, such as political censorship and government intervention, have not received the attention they deserve. However, the sources already mentioned, such as Crisell (1997) and Seaton (1997), can be referred to for more general background on these and other issues.

7   The television audience

1   A number of sources have proved very useful in the writing of this chapter. See, in particular, Barker and Brooks (1998); Buxton (1990); Dickinson *et al.* (1998); Lewis (1991, see also 1990); McGuigan (1992); Morley (especially 1980, 1991 and 1992); and Willemen (1990).

2   Barker and Brooks cite Bordwell (1989) in their critique of psychoanalytic theories about films and audiences and suggest it is an 'under-examined' study (1998: 230). This is undoubtedly true and it is also relevant to the issue of meaning, for Bordwell (1989, especially chapter 11) develops a compelling critique of the attempt by film criticism (including that influenced by semiology) to 'read' films primarily for their meaning.

3   McGuigan (1992) provides a clear and effective critique of the general drift towards populism, which covers audience populism.

4   See, for example, Fiske (1987, 1989b). However, Fiske (1989a, 1991) indicate there is more to his approach than these examples suggest. Note that a number of sources refer to Fiske's work as one of the main examples of the populist approach to the audience. See, for example, Barker and Brooks (1998: 221–2); Buxton (1990: 19, 141); Dahlgren (1998: 299–300); Lewis (1991: 68); and Morley (1992: 273). Note also that Dahlgren (1998) takes a more favourable attitude towards Fiske's contribution than the other commentators.

5   This conclusion would appear to support Adorno's argument that popular culture makes its audience distracted and inattentive and thus less likely to confront politically the society which produces such a popular culture. See Adorno (1991: chapters 1 and 3); cf. Strinati (1995: chapter 2).

8 Popular television genres

1   Television genres can also, of course, derive from other media, such as cinema and literature. But there appears to be a close relationship between television and radio, especially given that both were initially developed in the UK by the BBC. The most useful sources for this chapter have been Abercrombie (1996); Caughie (1991b); Corner (1991); Geraghty (1992); Goddard (1991); Kilborn (1992); and Rose (1985). Other useful sources include Alvarado and Buscombe (1978); Alvarado and Stewart (1985); Buckingham (1987); Geraghty (1991); Glaessner (1990); Laing (1991); Sparks (1992, 1993); and Woollacott (1986). A very useful general reference book is Vahimagi (1996).

2   Caughie's argument is an important one and future research can perhaps show how it can be applied to other genres. However, the problem with it is that it appears to confine its scope to discourses. Caughie says that his interest 'is in identifying some of the discourses and practices which were in circulation at that moment' – the 'technological moment when television ceases to be necessarily ephemeral' and 'its commodity form … begins to be decided' (1991b: 25). The value of this argument would also seem to lie in a number of related issues: how this moment becomes translated into programme production; how it may be relevant to the general patterns of popular television; and how, in view of the relatively slow increase in the availability of television, this 'moment' may have been extended beyond the period Caughie is concerned with. For example, could the early organisation of other television genres be traced to and influenced by this moment? Caughie does suggest some answers in his analysis of television drama. None the less, it is possible to give too much weight to discourses, since they can be more about what people think and how they idealise and rationalise developments and

situations, rather than about their actions. Therefore, they may not tell us that much about the actual production of popular television genres. Perhaps more weight needs to be given to practices in developing the argument.

3 *Crossroads* appears to be an example of a fairly cheap production. See Hobson (1982: *passim*); cf. Kilborn (1992).

4 For some idea of what is involved in the development and production of the police series, see Alvarado and Stewart (1985). For a study of an example of the private eye genre in British television, see Alvarado and Buscombe (1978).

5 For some examples of this, see Abercrombie (1996); Barker (1989); Morley (1992); and Ryall (1979). It can also be noted here that the term 'text' is not the best one to use to refer to types of popular culture. This is because it suggests that they can all be 'read' in the same way as literature. However, ways of interpreting the latter are not necessarily appropriate for films and television programmes. Also, as should by now be clear, the study of popular culture involves far more than merely 'reading' 'texts'. Bordwell confines the term 'reading' to interpreting literature, rather than using it to refer to the interpretation of all potentially meaningful works. However, he says there is no useful alternative to the idea of 'text' (1989: 2, 277). But if the idea of 'reading' is misleading, then so is the idea of 'texts'. Therefore, we have tried, as far as possible, to avoid using the term 'text' in this book, preferring instead to refer to the specific type of popular culture in question. And, instead of 'reading', we have used more relevant terms, such as explanation.

9 Popular television and postmodernism

1 For discussions and assessments of postmodernism, either as a whole, or of some of its specific features, see, for example, Baudrillard (1983); Boyne and Rattansi (1990); Collins (1989, 1992); Corrigan (1991); Featherstone (1991); Fiske (1991); Gitlin (1989); Grossberg (1987); Harvey (1989); Hebdige (1988); Lash (1990); Lash and Urry (1987, 1994); Lyon (1994); McRobbie (1994); and Smart (1993).

2 The following sources have proved especially useful in the writing of this chapter: Boyne and Rattansi (1990); Collins (1989, 1992); Connor (1989); Featherstone (1991); Fiske (1991); Gitlin (1989); Grossberg (1987); Harvey (1989); Hebdige (1988); Lash and Urry (1987, 1994); and Lyon (1994). The picture presented is inevitably a composite and partial one, and many authors who might support or concede some of the points made need not necessarily be held respon-

sible for all that passes for postmodernism. The outline presented has, therefore, to be viewed in this light.

3 Particularly useful sources on this point have been Collins (1992); Connor (1989); Featherstone (1991); Fiske (1991); Grossberg (1987); Harvey (1989); Hill (1998); and Lash and Urry (1987, 1994).

4 See the sources cited in note 2 above, in particular Collins (1992); Connor (1989); Fiske (1991); Grossberg (1987); and Harvey (1989).

5 See the sources cited in note 2 above, in particular Featherstone (1991); Harvey (1989); and Lash and Urry (1987, 1994). See also Bourdieu (1984).

6 On this see, for example, Bourdieu (1984); Featherstone (1991); Gitlin (1989); and Lash and Urry (1987, 1994).

7 Particularly useful sources on this point have been Gitlin (1989), Harvey (1989) and Lash and Urry (1987, 1994). The question of identity has become important in the more general theoretical and philosophical concerns of what is called post-structuralism. On this see, for example, Sarup (1988). The argument presented in this section could equally be seen as suggesting that alienation is increasing in modern societies.

8 It could be argued that the way the soap opera provides a surrogate community for some of its viewers is a sign of its postmodernity. However, this could also indicate how alienated such viewers have become and it does not, in any event, undermine the realism which other viewers attribute to this community.

9 It is perhaps worth quoting Buxton at greater length on this point. He argues:

> attempts to discuss a series like *Miami Vice* in terms of an idealist 'condition' like postmodernism are not so much wrong as unhelpful. Once the series has been categorised within the positive or negative features that make up the master discourse, nothing more can be said: as with all forms of culturalism, discussion is reduced to academic posturing. For all its stylistic force, *Miami Vice* is no more or less 'ideological' than any other series; for all its stylishness, it is no more or less 'styled' than any other series. What needs to be analysed is the way form and content come together in the particular ideological strategy of *Miami Vice* ... The two major pillars of Reaganian free market ideology have been condensed into its assemblage: law and order and conspicuous consumption.
>
> (1990: 141–2)

Here, Buxton is clearly criticising the attempts of authors, such as Fiske (1987: 255–62), to understand *Miami Vice* as a postmodern television series.

10 On this see also Collins (1992) and Lavery (1995). There is relatively little in the academic literature on the idea of 'cult' popular culture and what there is tends to focus upon cinema. See, for example, Austin (1989: 83–7), Corrigan (1991: 80–91) and Tellotte (1991).

Bibliography

Abercrombie, N. (1996) *Television and Society*, Oxford: Polity Press.

Abercrombie, N., Hill, S. and Turner, B.S. (1980) *The Dominant Ideology Thesis*, London: Allen & Unwin.

Adorno, T. (1991) *The Culture Industry*, London: Routledge.

Adorno, T. and Horkheimer, M. (1979) 'The culture industry: enlightenment as mass deception', in T. Adorno and M. Horkheimer, *Dialectic of Enlightenment*, London: Verso.

Allen, R. (1990) 'From exhibition to reception: reflections on the audience in film history', *Screen*, vol. 31, no. 4.

Altman, R. (1999) *Film/Genre*, London: British Film Institute.

Alvarado, M. and Buscombe, E. (1978) *Hazell: The making of a TV series*, London: British Film Institute.

Alvarado, M. and Stewart, J. (1985) *Made for Television: Euston Films Ltd.*, London: British Film Institute.

Ang, I. (1989) *Watching Dallas*, London: Routledge.

——(1991) *Desperately Seeking the Audience*, London: Routledge.

Austin, B. (1989) *Immediate Seating: A look at the movie audience*, Belmont, Calif.: Wadsworth.

Baehr, H. (1981) 'The impact of feminism on media studies – just another commercial break?', in D. Spender (ed.), *Men's Studies Modified*, Oxford: Pergammon Press.

267

Balio, T. (ed.) (1985) *The Hollywood Film Industry*, Madison, Wis.: University of Wisconsin Press (rev. edn).

Barker, M. (1989) *Comics: Ideology, power and the critics*, Manchester: Manchester University Press.

Barker, M. and Brooks, K. (1998) 'On looking into Bourdieu's black box', in R. Dickinson, R. Harindranath, and O. Linne (eds), *Approaches to Audiences*, London: Arnold.

Baudrillard, J. (1983) *Simulations*, New York: Semiotext.

Bell, D. (1962) *The End of Ideology*, New York: The Free Press (rev. edn).

——(1973) *The Coming of Post-Industrial Society*, New York: Basic Books.

Bennett, T. (1982) 'Theories of the media, theories of society', in M. Gurevitch, T. Bennett, J. Curran and J. Woollacott (eds), *Culture, Society and the Media*, London: Methuen.

Bordwell, D. (1989) *Making Meaning: Inference and rhetoric in the interpretation of cinema*, Cambridge, Mass.: Harvard University Press.

Bordwell, D., Staiger, J. and Thompson, K. (1985) *The Classical Hollywood Cinema*, London: Routledge.

Bourdieu, P. (1984) *Distinction*, London: Routledge.

Boyne, R. and Rattansi, A. (eds) (1990) *Postmodernism and Society*, Basingstoke: Macmillan.

Buckingham, D. (1987) *Public Secrets: Eastenders and its audience*, London: British Film Institute.

Bullock, A. and Stallybrass, O. (eds) (1977) *The Fontana Dictionary of Modern Thought*, London: Fontana.

Burch, N. (1978) 'Porter, or ambivalence', *Screen*, vol. 19, no. 4.

Buscombe, E. (1986) 'The idea of genre in American cinema', in B. Grant (ed), *Film Genre Reader*, Austin, Tex.: University of Texas Press.

Butler, J. (1985) 'Miami Vice: the legacy of film noir', *Journal of Popular Film and Television*, Fall issue.

Buxton, D. (1990) *From the Avengers to Miami Vice: Form and ideology in television series*, Manchester and New York: Manchester University Press.

Cameron, I. (ed.) (1992) *The Movie Book of Film Noir*, London: Studio Vista.

Carroll, N. (1988) *Mystifying Movies: Fads and fallacies in contemporary film theory*, New York: Columbia University Press.

——(1996a) 'The power of movies', in N. Carroll, *Theorizing the Moving Image*, Cambridge: Cambridge University Press.

——(1996b) 'Film, rhetoric and ideology', in N. Carroll, *Theorizing the Moving Image*, Cambridge: Cambridge University Press.

Caughie, J. (1991a) 'Adorno's reproach: repetition, difference and television genre', *Screen*, vol. 32, no. 2.

——(1991b) 'Before the golden age: early television drama', in J. Corner (ed.), *Popular Television in Britain*, London: British Film Institute.

Ceplair, L. and Englund, S. (1979) *The Inquisition in Hollywood: Politics in the film community*, Berkeley, Calif.: University of California Press.

Chartier, J. (1996) 'The Americans are making dark films too', in R. Barton Palmer (ed.), *Perspectives on Film Noir*, New York: G.K. Hall & Co. (originally published in 1946).

Clarens, C. (1980) *Crime Movies*, London: Secker and Warburg.

Clerc, S. (1996) 'DDEB, GATB, MPPB and Ratboy: the X Files' media fandom, online and off', in D. Lavery, A. Hague and M. Cartwright (eds), *Deny All Knowledge: Reading the X Files*, London: Faber and Faber.

Clover, C. (1992) *Men, Women and Chainsaws: Gender in the modern horror film*, London: British Film Institute.

Collins, J. (1989) *Uncommon Cultures: Popular culture and postmodernism*, London: Routledge.

——(1992) 'Postmodernism and television', in R. Allen (ed.), *Channels of Discourse Reassembled*, London: Routledge (2nd edn).

Connor, S. (1989) *Postmodernist Culture*, Oxford: Basil Blackwell.

Cook, D. (1990) *A History of Narrative Film*, New York and London: W.W. Norton & Co. (2nd edn).

Cook, P. (ed.) (1985) *The Cinema Book*, London: British Film Institute.

Copjec, J. (1993) *Shades of Noir*, London and New York: Verso.

Corner, J. (1991a) 'General introduction: television and British society in the 1950s', in J. Corner (ed.), *Popular Television in Britain*, London: British Film Institute.

Corner, J. (ed.) (1991b) *Popular Television in Britain*, London: British Film Institute.

Corrigan, T. (1991) *A Cinema Without Walls: Movies and culture after Vietnam*, London: Routledge.

Crisell, A. (1997) *An Introductory History of British Broadcasting*, London and New York: Routledge.

Dahlgren, P. (1998) 'Critique: elusive audiences', in R. Dickinson, R. Harindranath and O. Linne (eds), *Approaches to Audiences*, London: Arnold.

Damico, J. (1978) 'Film noir: a modest proposal', *Film Reader*, no. 3, February.

Denne, J. (1972) 'Society and the monster', in R. Huss and T. Ross (eds) *Focus on the Horror Film*, Englewood Cliffs, N.J.: Prentice-Hall.

Denzin, N. (1991) *Images of Postmodern Society*, London: Sage.

Dickinson, R., Harindranath, R. and Linne, O. (eds) (1998) *Approaches to Audiences*, London: Arnold.

Doherty, T. (1988) *Teenagers and Teenpics*, Boston: Unwin Hyman.

Durgnat, R. (1970) 'Paint it black: the family tree of film noir', *Cinema*, nos. 6–7, August.

Eco, U. (1984) 'A guide to the neo-television of the 1980s', *Framework*, 25.

Ewen, S. (1988) *All Consuming Images: The politics of style in contemporary culture*, New York: Basic Books.

Farber, M. (1972) 'Val Lewton and the school of shudders', in R. Huss and T. Ross (eds), *Focus on the Horror Film*, Englewood Cliffs, N.J.: Prentice-Hall.

Featherstone, M. (1991) *Consumer Culture and Postmodernism*, London: Sage.

Fiske, J. (1987) *Television Culture*, London: Methuen.

——(1989a) 'Popular television and commercial culture: beyond political economy', in G. Burns and R. Thompson (eds), *Television Studies: Textual analysis*, New York: Praeger.

——(1989b) *Understanding Popular Culture*, Boston and London: Unwin Hyman.

——(1991) 'Postmodernism and television', in J. Curran and M. Gurevitch (eds), *Mass Media and Society*, London: Edward Arnold.

Flinn, T. (1972) 'Three faces of film noir', *Velvet Light Trap*, Summer.

——(1973) 'Out of the past', *Velvet Light Trap*, Fall.

Franklin, S., Lury, C. and Stacey, J. (eds) (1991) *Off-centre: Feminism and cultural studies*, London: Harper Collins.

Gallafent, E. (1992) 'Echo Park: film noir in the seventies', in I. Cameron (ed.), *The Movie Book of Film Noir*, London: Studio Vista.

Gambaccini, P. and Taylor, R. (1993) *Television's Greatest Hits*, London: Network Books (BBC Books).

Gauntlett, D. (1998) 'Ten things wrong with the "effects" model', in R. Dickinson, R. Harindranath and O. Linne (eds), *Approaches to Audiences*, London: Arnold.

Gauntlett, D. and Hill, A. (1999) *TV Living: Television, culture and everyday life*, London: Routledge.

Gehring, W. (ed.) (1988) *Handbook of American Film Genres*, New York: Greenwood Press.

Geraghty, C. (1991) *Women and Soap Opera*, Oxford: Basil Blackwell.

——(1992) 'British soaps in the 1980s', in D. Strinati and S. Wagg (eds), *Come on Down?: Popular media culture in post-war Britain*, London: Routledge.

——(1998) 'Audiences and ethnography', in C. Geraghty and D. Lusted (eds), *The Television Studies Book*, London: Arnold.

Giddens, A. (1971) *Capitalism and Modern Social Theory*, Cambridge: Cambridge University Press.

——(1973) *The Class Structure of the Advanced Societies*, London: Hutchinson University Library.

Gitlin, T. (1989) 'Postmodernism: roots and politics', in I. Angus and S. Jhally (eds), *Cultural Politics in Contemporary America*, London: Routledge.

Glaessner, V. (1990) 'Gendered fictions', in A. Goodwin and G. Whannel (eds), *Understanding Television*, London: Routledge.

Gledhill, C. (1980) 'Klute 1: a contemporary film noir and feminist criticism', in E. Ann Kaplan (ed.), *Women in Film Noir*, London: British Film Institute.

——(1985) 'Genre', in P. Cook (ed.) *The Cinema Book*, London: British Film Institute.

Goddard, P. (1991) 'Hancock's Half Hour: a watershed in British television comedy', in J. Corner (ed.), *Popular Television in Britain*, London: British Film Institute.

Gomery, D. (1985) 'The coming of the talkies: invention, innovation and diffusion', in T. Balio (ed.), *The American Film Industry*, Madison, Wis.: University of Wisconsin Press.

——(1986) *The Hollywood Studio System*, Basingstoke: Macmillan.

Goodwin, A. and Whannel, G. (eds) (1990) *Understanding Television*, London: Routledge.

Gouldner, A. (1954) *Patterns of Industrial Bureaucracy*, New York: Free Press.

Grant, B. (1991) 'Science fiction double feature: ideology in the cult film', in J. Telotte (ed.), *The Cult Film Experience*, Austin, Tex.: University of Texas Press.

Grist, L. (1992) 'Moving targets and black widows: film noir in modern Hollywood', in I. Cameron (ed.), *The Movie Book of Film Noir*, London: Studio Vista.

Grossberg, L. (1987) 'The in-difference of television', *Journal of Communication Inquiry*, vol. 10, no. 2.

Hall, S. (1980) 'Encoding/decoding', in S. Hall, D. Hobson, A. Lowe and P. Willis (eds), *Culture, Media, Language*, London: Hutchinson.

Harvey, D. (1989) *The Condition of Postmodernity*, Oxford: Basil Blackwell.

Harvey, S. (1980) 'Woman's place: the absent family of film noir', in E. Ann Kaplan (ed.), *Women in Film Noir*, London: British Film Institute.

Hebdige, D. (1988) *Hiding in the Light*, London: Routledge.

Hill, J. (1998) 'Film and postmodernism', in J. Hill and P. Church Gibbon (eds), *The Oxford Guide to Film Studies*, Oxford: Oxford University Press.

Hirsch, F. (1981) *Film Noir: The dark side of the screen*, New York: Da Capo.

Hobson, D. (1982) *Crossroads: The drama of a soap opera*, London: Methuen.

Hodgens, R. (1959) 'A brief, tragical history of the science fiction film', *Film Quarterly*, 13, Winter.

Hugo, C. (1992) 'The Big Combo: production conditions and the film text', in I. Cameron (ed.), *The Movie Book of Film Noir*, London: Studio Vista.

Huss, R. and Ross, T. (eds) (1972) *Focus on the Horror Film*, Englewood Cliffs, N.J.: Prentice-Hall.

Instrell, R. (1992) 'Blade Runner: the economic shaping of a film', in J. Orr and C. Nicholson (eds), *Cinema and Fiction*, Edinburgh: Edinburgh University Press.

Izod, J. (1988) *Hollywood and the Box Office 1895–1986*, London: Macmillan.

Jancovich, M. (1992) *Horror*, London: Batsford.

——(1994) *American Horror from 1951 to the Present*, Keele: Keele University Press.

——(1996) *Rational Fears: American horror in the 1950s*, Manchester and New York: Manchester University Press.

Jenkins, H. (1995) ' "Do you enjoy making the rest of us feel stupid?": alt.tv.twinpeaks, the trickster author and viewer mastery', in D. Lavery (ed.), *Full of Secrets: Critical approaches to 'Twin Peaks'*, Detroit: Wayne State University Press.

Kaplan, E. Ann (1980) *Women in Film Noir*, London: British Film Institute (rev. edn).

Katz, E. (1959) 'Mass communications research and the study of popular culture', *Studies in Public Communication*, vol. 2.

Kemp, P. (1986) 'From the nightmare factory: HUAC and the politics of noir', *Sight and Sound*, vol. 55, no. 4.

Kerr, P. (1986) 'Out of what past?: Notes on the B film noir', in P. Kerr (ed.), *The Hollywood Film Industry*, London and New York: Routledge & Kegan Paul.

Kilborn, R. (1992) *Television Soaps*, London: Batsford.

Krutnik, F. (1991) *In a Lonely Street: Film noir, genre, masculinity*, London and New York: Routledge.

Kuhn, A. (1985) 'History of the cinema', in P. Cook (ed.), *The Cinema Book*, London: British Film Institute.

Laing, S. (1991) 'Banging in some reality: the original "Z Cars" ', in J. Corner (ed.), *Popular Television in Britain*, London: British Film Institute.

Lash, S. (1990) *The Sociology of Postmodernism*, London: Routledge.

Lash, S. and Urry, J. (1987) *The End of Organized Capitalism*, Cambridge: Polity Press.

——(1994) *Economies of Signs and Spaces*, London: Sage.

Lavery, D. (ed.) (1995) *Full of Secrets: Critical approaches to 'Twin Peaks'*, Detroit: Wayne State University Press.

Lavery, D., Hague, A. and Cartwright, M. (eds) (1996) *Deny All Knowledge: Reading the X Files*, London: Faber and Faber.

Lewis, J. (1990) 'Are you receiving me?', in A. Goodwin and G. Whannel (eds), *Understanding Television*, London: Routledge.

——(1991) *The Ideological Octopus: An exploration of television and its audience*, New York and London: Routledge.

Lyon, D. (1994) *Postmodernity*, Buckingham: Open University Press.

McArthur, C. (1972) *Underworld USA*, London: Secker & Warburg and the British Film Institute.

McGuigan, J. (1992) *Cultural Populism*, London: Routledge.

McLelland, D. (1995) *Ideology*, Buckingham: Open University Press (2nd edn).

McQueen, D. (1998) *Television: A media student's guide*, London: Arnold.

McRobbie, A. (1994) *Postmodernism and Popular Culture*, London: Routledge.

Maltby, R. (1984) 'Film noir: the politics of the maladjusted text', *Journal of American Studies*, vol. 18, no. 1.

——(with Craven, I.) (1995) *Hollywood Cinema*, Oxford: Blackwell.

Maltin, L. (1991) *Movie and Video Guide*, London: Penguin Books.

273

Masterman, L. (ed.) (1984) *Television Mythologies*, London: Comedia.

May, L. (1983) *Screening Out the Past: The birth of mass culture and the movies*, Chicago and London: University of Chicago Press.

Messner, S. and Rosenfeld, R. (1994) *Crime and the American Dream*, Belmont, Calif.: Wadsworth.

Mills, C. Wright (1956) *The Power Elite*, New York: Oxford University Press.

Moores, S. (1993) *Interpreting Audiences*, London: Sage.

Morley, D. (1980) *The Nationwide Audience*, London: British Film Institute.

——(1986) *Family Television*, London: Comedia.

——(1991) 'Where the global meets the local: notes from the sitting room', *Screen*, vol. 32, no. 1.

——(1992) *Television, Audiences and Cultural Studies*, London and New York: Routledge.

——(1998) 'Domestic relations: the framework of family viewing in Great Britain', in R. Dickinson, R. Harindranath and O. Linne (eds), *Approaches to Audiences*, London: Arnold.

Mosco, V. (1996) *The Political Economy of Communication*, London: Sage.

Mulvey, L. (1975) 'Visual pleasure and narrative cinema', *Screen*, vol. 16, no. 3.

——(1981) 'Afterthoughts on "visual pleasure and narrative cinema" inspired by "Duel in the Sun"', in L. Mulvey, *Visual and Other Pleasures*, Basingstoke: Macmillan.

Murdock, G. (1989) 'Critical inquiry and audience activity', in B. Dervin, L. Grossberg, B. O'Keefe and E. Wartella (eds), *Rethinking Communication*, vol. 2, Newbury Park and London: Sage.

——(1990) 'Television and citizenship', in A. Tomlinson (ed.), *Consumption, Identity and Style*, London: Comedia.

——(1992) 'Embedded persuasions: the rise and fall of integrated advertising', in D. Strinati and S. Wagg (eds), *Come on Down?: Popular media culture in post-war Britain*, London: Routledge.

——(1994) 'Money talks: broadcasting finance and public culture', in S. Hood (ed.), *Behind the Screens: The structure of British television in the nineties*, London: Lawrence and Wishart.

Murphy, R. (1992) *Sixties British Cinema*, London: British Film Institute.

Nachbar, J. (1988) 'Film noir', in W. Gehring (ed.), *Handbook of American Film Genres*, New York: Greenwood Press.

Neale, S. (1980) *Genre*, London: British Film Institute.

——(1985) *Cinema and Technology*, London: British Film Institute.

——(1990) 'Questions of genre', *Screen*, vol. 31, no. 1.

Newbould, C. (1996) *Narrative Analysis for Moving Image Research*, Discussion Papers in Mass Communications, Leicester: University of Leicester.

Ollman, B. (1976) *Alienation*, Cambridge: Cambridge University Press (2nd edn).

Osborne, R. and Kidd-Hewitt, D. (eds) (1996) *Crime and the Media: The post-modern spectacle*, London: Pluto Press.

Palmer, J. (1991) *Potboilers: Methods, concepts and case studies in popular fiction*, London and New York: Routledge.

Palmer, R. Barton (ed.) (1996) *Perspectives on Film Noir*, New York: G.K. Hall & Co.

Parkin, F. (1972) *Class Inequality and Political Order*, St Albans: Paladin.

Pearce, F. (1978) 'Art and reality: gangsters in film and society', in D. Laurenson (ed.), *The Sociology of Literature*, Sociological Review Monograph, University of Keele.

Pirie, D. (1973) *A Heritage of Horror: The English gothic cinema 1946–1972*, London: Gordon Fraser.

Place, J. and Peterson, L. (1974) 'Some visual motifs of film noir', *Film Comment*, vol. 10, no. 1.

Powdermaker, H. (1950) *Hollywood: The dream factory*, Boston, Little & Brown.

Prawer, S. (1980) *Caligari's Children: The film as tale of terror*, New York: Da Capo.

Pye, M. and Myles, L. (1979) *The Movie Brats: How the film generation took over Hollywood*, New York: Holt, Rinehart and Winston.

Quart, L. and Auster, A. (1984) *American Film and Society since 1945*, London and Basingstoke: Macmillan.

Raeburn, J. (1988) 'The gangster film', in W. Gehring (ed.), *Handbook of American Film Genres*, New York: Greenwood Press.

Reid, D. and Walker, J. (1993) 'Strange pursuit: Cornell Woolrich and the abandoned city of the forties', in J. Copjec (ed.), *Shades of Noir*, London and New York: Verso.

Rey, H.-F. (1996) 'Hollywood makes myths like Ford makes cars (last installment): demonstration by the absurd: films noirs', in R. Barton Palmer (ed.), *Perspectives on Film Noir*, New York: G.K. Hall & Co.

Richardson, J. (1996) 'Race and ethnicity', *Developments in Sociology*, vol. 12.

Robinson, D. (1997) *Das Cabinet Des Dr. Caligari*, London: British Film Institute.

Roddick, N. (1983) *A New Deal in Entertainment: Warner Bros in the 1930s*, London: British Film Institute.

Rose, B. (1985) 'Introduction', in B. Rose, (ed.) *TV Genres: A handbook and reference guide*, Westport, Conn.: Greenwood Press.

Rose, M. (1991) *The Post-modern and the Post-industrial*, Cambridge: Cambridge University Press.

Rowe, A. (1996) 'Film form and narrative', in J. Nelmes (ed.), *An Introduction to Film Studies*, London: Routledge.

Ryall, T. (1979) *The Gangster Film*, London: British Film Institute Education (teachers' study guide).

Sarup, M. (1988) *An Introductory Guide to Post-structuralism and Postmodernism*, New York: Harvester Wheatsheaf.

Scannell, P. (1990) 'Public service broadcasting: the history of a concept', in A. Goodwin and G. Whannel (eds), *Understanding Television*, London and New York: Routledge.

Schrader, P. (1972) 'Notes on film noir', *Film Comment*, vol. 8, no. 1.

Seaton, J. (1997) 'Broadcasting history', in J. Curran and J. Seaton, *Power Without Responsibility: The press and broadcasting in Britain*, London and New York: Routledge (5th edn).

Silver, A. and Ward, E. (1980) *Film Noir: An encyclopedic reference guide*, London: Bloomsbury (rev. and expanded edn).

Sklar, R. (1975) *Movie-made America: A cultural history of American movies*, New York: Random House.

Smart, B. (1993) *Postmodernity*, London: Routledge.

Sparks, R. (1992) *Television and the Drama of Crime*, Buckingham: Open University Press.

——(1993) 'Inspector Morse', in G. Brandt (ed.), *British Television Drama in the 1980s*, Cambridge: Cambridge University Press.

Spencer, S. (1984) *Dark City: The film noir*, Chicago and London: St James Press.

Sreberny-Mohammadi, A. (1991) 'The global and the local in international communications', in J. Curran and M. Gurevitch (eds), *Mass Media and Society*, London: Edward Arnold.

Street, S. (1997) *British National Cinema*, London and New York: Routledge.

Strinati, D. (1993) 'The big nothing? Contemporary culture and the emergence of postmodernism', *Innovation*, vol. 6, no. 3.

——(1995) *An Introduction to Theories of Popular Culture*, London and New York: Routledge.

——(1998) 'Post-modern and cult television: a case study of "Twin Peaks"', unpublished paper, Sociology Department, University of Leicester.

Telotte, J. (ed.) (1991) *The Cult Film Experience*, Austin, Tex.: University of Texas Press.

Thompson, J. (1990) *Ideology and Modern Culture*, Cambridge: Polity Press.

Todorov, T. (1973) *The Fantastic: A structural approach to a literary concept*, Cleveland and London: Case Western Reserve University Press.

Tuchman, G. (1981) 'The symbolic annihilation of women by the mass media', in S. Cohen and J. Young (eds), *The Manufacture of News*, London: Constable (rev. edn).

Tuchman, G., Daniels, A. Kaplan and Benet, J. (eds) (1988) *Hearth and Home: Images of women in the mass media*, New York: Oxford University Press.

Tudor, A. (1974) *Image and Influence: Studies in the sociology of film*, London: Allen & Unwin.

Tuska, J. (1984) *Dark Cinema: American film noir in cultural perspective*, Westport, Conn.: Greenwood Press.

Vahimagi, T. (1996) *British Television: An illustrated guide*, Oxford: Oxford University Press.

Van Zoonen, L. (1994) *Feminist Media Studies*, London: Sage.

Vernet, M. (1993) 'Film noir on the edge of doom', in J. Copjec (ed.), *Shades of Noir*, London and New York: Verso.

Warshow, R. (1964) *The Immediate Experience*, New York: Anchor Books.

Wayne, M. (1998) 'Counter-hegemonic strategies in "Between the Lines"', in M. Wayne (ed.), *Dissident Voices: The politics of television and cultural change*, London: Pluto Press.

Whitehall, R. (1964) 'Crime Inc. A three part dossier on the American gangster film. Part one: the rackets and the mobs', *Films and Filming*, January: 7–12.

——(1964) 'Crime Inc. A three part dossier on the American gangster film. Part two: G-Men and gangsters', *Films and Filming*, February: 17–22.

——(1964) 'Crime Inc. A three part dossier on the American gangster film. Part three: public enemies', *Films and Filming*, March: 39–44.

Willemen, P. (1990) 'Review of John Hill, "Sex, Class and Realism – British Cinema 1956–1963"', in M. Alvarado and J.O. Thompson (eds), *The Media Reader*, London: British Film Institute.

Williamson, J. (1978) *Decoding Advertisements: Ideology and meaning in advertising*, London and Boston: Marion Boyars.

Winokur, M. (1991) 'Eating children is wrong', *Sight and Sound*, vol. 1, issue 7, November.

Wood, G. (1988) 'Horror film', in W. Gehring (ed.), *Handbook of American Film Genres*, New York: Greenwood Press.

Wood, R. (1986) *Hollywood from Vietnam to Reagan*, New York: Columbia University Press.

Woollacott, J. (1986) 'Fictions and ideologies: the case of situation comedy', in T. Bennett, C. Mercer and J. Woollacott (eds), *Popular Culture and Social Relations*, Buckingham: Open University Press.

Index